"*Questions & Answers for Catholics* is a love song to the church which emerged from the Second Vatican Council. Like Msgr. Songy, I was stirred by the call to 'open the windows'; to let the freshness of God's Spirit in, as Pope John XXIII urged when he called the reform into being. Vatican II was a big part of my childhood, from which I learned what it means to be Catholic. I share Msgr. Songy's hope that all will be well with the church so long as we continue to travel the road of faith together. The very warm and personal dialogue in this book may help us find our way. God bless the pilgrim church!"

Alice Camille
Author, *God's Word Is Alive* and *Seven Last Words*

"I love this book! Here is an author unafraid to tackle major questions facing the church and respond with honesty and love! I'd like to give a copy to everyone I know asking questions of the modern church—which is everyone I know!"

Bill Huebsch
Author, *A New Look at Grace: A Spirituality of Wholeness*

"In this book Msgr. Songy has given us a valuable resource for Catholics of all persuasions: practicing post-Vatican II Catholics, recovering Catholics, lapsed Catholics, Catholics-in-training (i.e., catechumens and RCIA candidates), fundamentalist Catholics, returning Catholics, and even non-Catholics. This book is certainly going to have a place on my shelves as a handy reference for those times when I'm faced with some of the same questions addressed by Msgr. Songy."

Sandra DeGidio, OSM
Author, *Sacraments Alive; Prayer Services for the Elderly;*
and *Praying with the Sick*

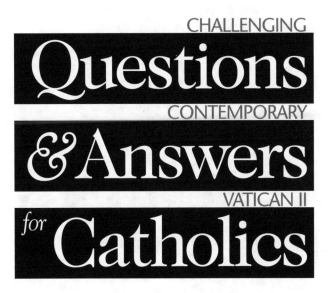

CHALLENGING
Questions
CONTEMPORARY
&Answers
VATICAN II
for Catholics

Msgr. James B. Songy

TWENTY-THIRD PUBLICATIONS
BAYARD ◉ Mystic, CT 06355

Second printing 2000

Twenty-Third Publications/Bayard
185 Willow Street
P.O. Box 180
Mystic, CT 06355
(860) 536-2611
(800) 321-0411

ISBN: 1-58595-110-2
Library of Congress Catalog Card Number: 00-133674
Printed in the U.S.A.

This work is dedicated to

His Holiness
Pope John XXIII

"Open the windows..."

Contents

Jesus Christ

PART TWO

Sacraments and Liturgy

The Mass

Baptism and Original Sin

Confirmation

Reconciliation

Sacramental Celebrations

PART THREE

Priesthood and Ministry

Priesthood and Celibacy

Priesthood Today

Women and Ministry

Lay Ministry

PART FOUR

Church Teachings

Authentic Teaching

Mary, Our Blessed Lady

Vatican II and Change

Heaven, Hell, and Purgatory

Creation and Evolution

The Soul

Angels

Ecumenism

PART FIVE

Marriage, Divorce, Annulments

General Questions

Annulment and Divorce

PART SIX

Sin, Morality, and Church Law

Morality

Suicide

Conscience and Law

Homosexuality

PART SEVEN

Prayer and Spirituality

Prayer in our Lives

Miracles and Apparitions

Acknowledgments

Through the years I owe so much to so many
And that debt will never be repaid
Until "his kingdom comes" for them:

My parents, Fabiola (Chippy) and Claude Songy
For so many obvious reasons

My Five Sisters and Four Brothers
For more of these obvious reasons
With a special word for my sister Cleo (Cody) deGraauw
and her friends in Abbeville
Whose urging and encouragement made this book a "must"

My dear, dear friends Marie and Ronnie Rogers
and their three daughters
Who for years now have graced my life with theirs;
Who inspire and help me ever to grow as human and as priest
And without whom I could not have faced these questions

Bill Huebsch, lay theologian, author, lecturer, teacher,
And most of all: Friend
Who coaxed me toward this book and gave me invaluable
Help in making it a reality
"No words can tell..."

The Editor, Louis Aguirre, and the Staff of The Bayou Catholic
Newspaper of the Diocese of Houma-Thibodaux
For their support and encouragement to continue writing

The People of God, within the church and out
Whose gifts, needs, lives, and questions
presented here inspired me
To never be satisfied with the present or past
But ever to grow into the future

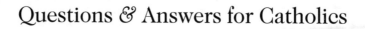

Questions & Answers for Catholics

Introduction

I remember Pope John XXIII. I remember where I was sitting when I heard his opening speech at Vatican II. The whole world was mired in the cold war at the time. The Soviets were moving into Cuba. No one knew what would happen. There was a deep sense of despair around the world. Much of the church itself seemed mired in the sixteenth century, unable to reconcile itself to modern times. So listening to Pope John speaking of unity and peace was remarkable. I remember the chills that went up my spine as I realized how this old man in Rome was filled with optimism and hope! He believed we could reapproach one another with charity, that the gospel could be better understood, and that people could join together in peace.

He was dedicated to the ancient, sacred treasures of the church's doctrine and to the deep well of eternal truth from which the church draws its life. There have always been such leaders in the church. But Pope John went further. "Our duty," he said in that opening speech, "is not only to guard this precious treasure, as if we were concerned only with antiquity, but to dedicate ourselves *with an earnest will and without fear* to that work which our era demands of us..." (emphasis added).

The church, he said, "must ever look to the present, to the new conditions and new forms of life introduced into the modern world which have opened new avenues to the Catholic apostolate."

He filled the church with hope that autumn. He called us all to be our very best. With an optimism and cheerful grace that were contagious, he set afoot in the church a renewal in which we still find ourselves joyfully engaged.

I am an old man myself now. Like Pope John I've always loved the church. For fifty years, maybe sixty, I've been keeping my eye on the pastoral life of the people of God. I've watched and listened carefully, first as a layperson, then as a pastor, and finally as a diocesan official. Somewhat like Pope John XXIII, I've never believed that age-old questions must be answered with age-old solutions. These are modern times that call for modern solutions.

I believe that for too long a time, people have looked to the church—which they believe to be embodied mainly by the pope, bishops, priests, and men and women religious—for the answers to all religious and moral questions. For many reasons, many people had come to believe that some "religious authority" must judge them as sinful or not. These people seemed to feel they weren't competent to judge their own guilt or innocence. And who can blame them? Most Catholics were taught to let someone else do their thinking and make their religious decisions.

There are many questions afoot in the church today. Some of them are rather new; some of them are as old as the texts of the gospels themselves. But, as Pope John taught us, they must all be given contemporary and pastoral answers. We must not be afraid to ask, but we must also not be afraid to look more deeply into our faith. In his own words, we must approach today's issues *with an earnest will and without fear.*

Early in my priesthood, I used to give out copies of a little book called *The Question Box for Catholics.* Looking back, I'm not sure that was always the best pastoral response. But we believed then that all the answers could be neatly arranged in order and bound into book-like permanence. If we didn't know how to respond to a situation in life, we "looked it up." But today, thank goodness, we realize that life is more engaging than that, more complicated and more exciting! Life is filled with possibilities for love—and also the chance for hate. Ours is to negotiate this life, to hold our faith uppermost in our souls as a light for our path, but to head out on the journey and live fully.

This series of questions and answers was collected over the past three decades as eager and sincere people have asked me about the core of our faith. Like the old *Question Box* I've tried to respond to them all. But unlike the old *Question Box*, my answers aren't tidy, certain, and final. Read these with your faith life engaged. Read them, look into your own soul, wrestle with the angels of light and of darkness, find there your own answers to these questions, and grow in your faith—*with an earnest will and without fear.*

NOTE: Throughout this book, I have made every effort to be gender sensitive. In some places, however, I succumbed to using the male pronoun for God, because, in these places, when I tried to eliminate it completely the writing became so awkward and problematical that I feared the reader's attention might be drawn away from the substance of the answer. It is my sincere hope and prayer that you will excuse me for these isolated incidences and for any other gender insensitivities that might have inadvertently slipped by me. Please know, dear readers, that gender sensitivity is of the utmost importance to me, as I think it should be to all of us.

Scripture, Fundamentalism, Jesus

The Bible

How did the Bible get started?

In my religion class, we hear a lot about the Bible and hear it quoted quite a bit. Can you tell me: how did the Bible get started?

■ *Answer*

The Bible "got started" through some ancient stories people wrote about themselves, the world, and God; stories told to them by their parents, grandparents, and other ancestors for hundreds of years.

You see, my dear young friend, we must realize that the Bible is not one book. It is a combination of some 73 books, of which 46 form the Hebrew Scriptures or the Old Testament, and 27 form the Christian Scriptures or New Testament. Furthermore, almost every one of these books (especially the Old Testament ones) is the combination of the writings of many people over many, many years (sometimes hundreds of years). These writings were then collected by someone or by a group of people and written into one series that came to be called a "book" of the Bible.

Take, for instance, the first five books of the Bible. These are a collection made about 500 B.C. from hundreds of ancient writings, some of them perhaps as much as 500 to 1,000 years old in their original form. The "collectors" or "editors" had to use just "bits and pieces" of ancient scrolls. They had to fill in some of the missing words or stories from memory or from other writings. They had to get somebody to actually sit down and write all that by hand, one word at a time, on scrolls made of things like sheepskin or what was known as Egyptian papyrus, a form of ancient paper. (And remember, they didn't even have ink pens or lead pencils in those days! And no word processors, either!)

What they did with these first five books was to write them all together into one big scroll, and it came to be known among the Hebrews as the "Torah" or "The Law." Later it was divided into the five books we have now, and then further divided (much, much later) into chapters and verses as we have them today.

So you see, dear friend, I am really glad you asked "how" the Bible started rather than "when" it started. The "how" is what I said above; the "when" is almost anybody's guess, because the answer to that can only be that it was started whenever human beings began to know themselves, the world around them, and then God; and then to relate these experiences to one another and to their children. Thus did the Bible begin. And under God's loving guidance of this entire process, it became, and is known today, as God's book, God's work, God's loving revelation to all of us who have inherited it through our tradition.

Does the Bible give us factual history or just "stories"?

A question came up at our last Renew small group meeting. Is everything in the Bible factual or recorded history? Did Abraham really live 500 years? Did Moses really part the Red Sea? Did Jesus really change water into wine at Cana? Are some parts of the Bible factual and other parts not?

■ *Answer*

First, let me make it quite clear that the Bible is not a history book, and therefore it is certain that not all of the events or people mentioned in the Bible are historically factual in every detail. The Bible is the revealed Word of God, written by humans in their own style of writing, in their own language. The writers of the Bible used some history, some fables, some tribal customs, some myths, and some mythological characters as a means of conveying to us their own faith about God, about humanity, and about the relationship between God and humans (religion). In doing so they did not bother to distinguish between what category a particular passage or character might fit in; that was simply not their purpose. Only Scripture scholars and historical experts can begin to divide "fact from fiction" in the Bible, and none of us should presume to do so unless we have expertise in both of these fields.

It is the firm doctrine of the church that the Bible contains only truth, and no falsehoods. So while some of the passages or personalities of the Bible might not be historically accurate, the message or Word of God that the author intended to convey is absolutely accurate and true. When we read the Bible, it is this message or Word of God behind or inside the human words of the Bible that we must look for.

In other words, dear friend, we ordinary people should not concern ourselves too deeply about trying to determine what is or is not historically accurate in the Bible. It really isn't of monumental importance to our understanding of the Bible whether Abraham's age is accurately recorded or not, or whether Moses really parted the Red Sea, or whether Jesus really changed water into wine at Cana. What we must be concerned about is what message these passages are trying to convey to us; what God is revealing to us through these passages.

By the way, I think the best Scripture experts today would say that Abraham's age and the "parting of the Red Sea" as given in the Bible would certainly not be historically accurate, and some would consider the "water-to-wine" miracle of doubtful historicity.

Finally, may I caution you and your small group that, while the discussion of various Bible passages by an "untrained" group of Christians can be very helpful and is to be highly recommended, it can also be very dangerous if the group is not careful to find some guidance when difficulties arise (as they will). If you do not have an opportunity to attend special courses on Scripture, you might find one or both of the following brochures somewhat helpful: *Fundamentalism: A Pastoral Concern*, by Fr. Eugene LaVerdiere; or *How to Interpret the Bible*, by Fr. George T. Montague. Both are published by The Liturgical Press, Collegeville, Minnesota 56321.

Is the story in the Bible about Christ's infancy true?

Our pastor said that the infancy narrative in St. Luke's gospel was created by the early Christian community. So is Luke's story of Christ's infancy not true? Doesn't this destroy the doctrine of the immaculate conception, which relies on Luke 1:28 and Genesis 3:15 as the only scriptural references available to us?

■ *Answer*

Let me assure you from the outset that neither the doctrine of the immaculate conception nor any other doctrine of the church depends on the historical accuracy of any part of the Bible. Please notice I use the words *"historical* accuracy." By that I do not mean that I am doubting the validity or the accuracy of the text itself as a true part of the Bible; nor am I doubting that the text accurately depicts the inspired Word of God as intended by the author or authors. All I am saying is that the *intent* of the scriptural writers and of God's inspiration was *not* the writing of historical facts, and therefore we cannot depend on the historical data or events related in the Bible as being accurate history.

Therefore, dear friend, if the infancy narrative of Luke's gospel is not historically accurate, if the events of the conception, birth, and infancy of Jesus Christ did not actually happen as stated there (and they obviously did not), this would have absolutely no effect whatsoever on the doctrine of the immaculate conception. That passage in Luke's infancy narrative is just as supportive of the immaculate conception as it would be if it were historically accurate. Luke 1:28 simply expresses the faith of the early Christian community that Mary was "full of grace." Exactly what that meant to them, I am not entirely sure.

What I am sure of is that the magisterium of the church, in defining the doctrine of the immaculate conception in 1854, used this passage in support of that doctrine. In so doing, our pope and bishops were officially interpreting that passage for us, and saying that the faith of the early church in Mary's "fullness of grace" implies that from the first moment of her existence and throughout her life as a human being, she was totally free from all sin.

The same can be said of the passage you mention from the book of Genesis (3:15), which was also cited in support of the doctrine of the immaculate conception. But the Genesis story of creation and the early days of human existence cannot be considered *historically* accurate. It is simply a story used to depict God's word or revelation to us. This lack of historical accuracy takes nothing away from that text as a valid and accurate part of the Bible. Furthermore, its lack of historical accuracy leaves it as fully supportive of the church's teaching on the immaculate conception as it would be if it were historically accurate.

Can taking the Bible literally be confusing?

I read the Bible daily. I've just begun to gain more insight in reading the Scriptures than I did in the past. Now I'm a little confused. My neighbor says many young people are getting involved in "cults" because of their reading of the Bible. Are young people taking a too-literal interpretation of the Bible, and thus confusing themselves?

■ *Answer*

I have no idea as to whether this is particularly true of young people, but it certainly is true that many people have begun reading the Bible, which is good. And it is also true that many of these also inter-pret what they read in a literal way, which is not so good. A literal or fundamentalist interpretation of the Bible can have disastrous results.

While I would certainly encourage your newfound love for the Bible, I would strongly urge you to enroll in a Scripture course given by an instructor who is well-versed in the Catholic understanding of the Bible, if such a course is available in your area. If no course is available, at least talk to one of your local priests and ask for some reading material that might assist you in your Bible reading.

Please understand, dear friend, that I am not saying that one needs to be a Scripture scholar or even a Scripture student in order to find value in the Bible. On the contrary, I firmly believe that the Bible is a "people's book," and by that I mean it was written for ordinary people like me and you to read as one of the means by which God's revelation comes to us. But when ordinary people like you and me try to interpret the meaning intended by the authors of the Bible for the benefit of others, we can wander into error. Or when we assume that we should apply to ourselves a lit-eral (word-for-word) interpretation of biblical texts, more error is possible.

In order to use the Bible as an inspirational book of prayer in our daily lives, a little study will help. In order to allow the Word of God to unfold for us out of biblical texts written by humans under God's inspiration, it is extremely helpful to know what the authors intend-ed. If we are to use the Bible as another "point of contact" with our loving, creating God, we need to understand the Bible more fully. All of this is to use the Bible as it was intended by the One whose Word it reveals. To use the Bible in this way requires no special formal education, although such education will certainly make the Bible ever more effective in becoming for us what it indeed can be.

Can Catholics use the King James Bible?

What is the church's teaching on Catholics using the King James Version of the Bible?

■ *Answer*

The King James Version of the Bible was the original result of a commission appointed by King James I of England to revise what was then known as "the Bishop's Bible," the official Bible of the Church of England. This original King James Version, completed in 1611, was the effort of the best scholars in England, working in groups at Westminster, Oxford, and Cambridge. Once this new translation was published, it quickly replaced the Bishop's Bible. The language in the King James Version gradually came to be thought of as classically beautiful, and it had considerable influence on English literature for some time.

It was not until 1870 that any effort was made by English Protestant scholars to revise the King James Version, or "Authorized Version" as it was officially called. The Revised Version, which was published between 1881 and 1885, was not favorably received at first, and did not really begin to be accepted until it reappeared in 1901 as the "American Standard Version, " but then it soon came to be preferred by American scholars. Finally, in 1937, the National Council of Churches in America commissioned what has come to be called the "Revised Standard Version," and this American work is readily accepted by all scholars to be the best revision of the original King James Version.

According to the *Jerome Biblical Commentary*, an officially recognized Catholic commentary, the "Revised Standard Version" labors under two difficulties. First, its loyalty to the Authorized Version (King James) prevents its translators from using modern scientific methods to update the wording and arrangement of passages. Second, since it states clearly in the preface that it is not a new translation in the language of today, it retains much "bible English," e.g., "thee," "thou," "behold," etc.

I give this brief history of the King James Version before answering your question so that we might all understand what we are talking about when we mention this translation. The general law of the church permits Catholics to read non-Catholic editions of the Bible, even when they have not been approved by the church, if the Catholic is in some way engaged in the study of Scripture and if the edition is complete and faithful, and without notes that constitute attacks on Catholic dogma. According to the *Jerome Biblical Commentary*, most of the well-known modern non-Catholic bibles meet the latter requirements. However, this would not be true of the original King James Version, or of the original Revised Version. However, the Revised Standard Version has been given approval of the church through an "imprimatur" from Cardinal Cushing of Boston. Therefore, anyone should feel free to read that version.

Getting back to the original King James Version: if you have ever tried to read it, I think you will understand why anyone who really knows the Bible well would discourage you from using it. The English in it is very outdated, and tends to hinder, rather than enhance, our understanding of the real Word of God.

The most highly recommended translations of the Bible for Catholics today would be what are known as *The New American Bible* and *The Jerusalem Bible*. *The New American Bible* is the same as the *New Confraternity Bible*, and was translated between 1952 and 1969, with a revised New Testament published in 1986, and a revision of the Psalms published in 1991. As of this writing the Old Testament of the New American Bible is still being revised and has not yet been published.

The Jerusalem Bible was originally published in French in 1954, under the editorship of the Jerusalem Dominicans. The English translation, published in 1966, despite being "a translation of a translation" is really an excellent work, because of the outstanding and tedious scholarship that went into the original French version. By 1973 the French edition of the Jerusalem Bible had been extensively revised, including its notes and introductions, to take advantage of advances in Scripture scholarship, and *The New Jerusalem Bible* was published in English in 1985, although the original *Jerusalem Bible* is still available.

The New Revised Standard Version of Scripture, translated by an ecumenical committee, including several Roman Catholics, was published in 1989. It has become popular with scholars, was used in the revision of the Catholic lectionary for English-speaking Canada, and has an official Catholic edition.

Finally, then, I would recommend to all English-speaking Catholics today that, rather than reading the King James Version, with all the practical difficulties it presents, they read one of these newer translations that have the support and official endorsement of the church.

How did the Catholic Bible come about?

Would you please explain how the Catholic Bible came about? Do you know why the English church left out some of the books of the Bible when they broke away from the Catholic Church and made their own Bible? Many non-Catholics I know point to the King James Version of the Bible as the original and source of all other Bibles. Would you comment on that?

■*Answer*

It is almost impossible to speak about any one book as *the* Bible, or *the* Catholic Bible, or *the* Protestant Bible, or *the* Jewish Bible. On the other hand, there are any number of books in existence today that can truly be described as "the Bible," although probably none of them are exact reproductions or even exact translations of the original writings of which the Bible is composed, nor can we be absolutely certain that every single piece of inspired writing in the history of humanity is contained in any one of them.

Second, we must always remember that what we are all dealing with in our Bibles today are translations and copies of the original works. No originals of the full text are known to be in existence today. Furthermore, most of our English versions of the Bible were not translated from the original language in which they were written. They were translated from copies of translations from the original language.

Also, even if we had the original manuscripts, we must realize that most of what was written down in the Old Testament were stories remembered and handed down over hundreds of years, from generation to generation. We must assume that each generation added its own twist to meet the demands of that culture and time.

In the New Testament, we also have stories, remembered and retold, about the events that occurred in the lifetime of Jesus and in the early Christian communities, including the teachings of the apostles and disciples of Jesus.

Over the first fifteen hundred years of the existence of Christianity there was much debate as to which books should or should not be included in the Bible. Although the church made a number of official pronouncements concerning this in the course of those fifteen hundred years, for us Roman Catholics it was not until April 8, 1546 (when the Council of Trent issued its decree called in Latin: *De Canonicis Scripturis*) that we had a "final" official definition by the church of which books were to be accepted by Catholics as belonging in the Bible. This document named 45 books of the Old Testament and 27 books of the New Testament as being part of what was called the "canon" (meaning "full contents") of the Bible. The First Vatican Council in the mid-nineteenth century reissued the Trent decree and further declared that being part of the canon of the Bible meant that the church believes a particular book is inspired.

Declaring a book part of the canon of the New Testament, however, does not mean that the translations we have today are absolutely accurate copies of the original texts. Therefore, it is quite possible that any Bible we pick up has some technical errors in it. It definitely has some missing portions of some original writings. And there could be some undiscovered writings out there that could and should be part of the very books that the church has declared to be the Bible. On the other hand, the church does officially assure us that our current versions of the Bible do contain the substantially correct, complete, and inerrant divine revelation.

How did it come about that the Protestants have a different canon than we do? It is a long story, but I quote this brief passage from *The Jerome Biblical Commentary*: "By the end of the first century A.D. there were in Judaism two canons, or lists of the sacred books, a shorter Palestinian canon drawn up by the rabbis at a city called Jamnia, and a longer Alexandrian canon represented by the *Septuagint* or Greek Translation of the Old Testament. The early Christian church adopted the Alexandrian canon; but the Reformers (early Protestants), following a minority view among the Fathers, decided to revert to the Palestinian canon. The respective results were the Catholic and Protestant canons." It is the Protestant canon that is included in the King James Version of the Bible used by many other Christians today.

I'm not sure that it makes any difference to fundamentalist readers of the Bible, be they Catholic or Protestant, which version of the Bible they read. You see, dear friend, it is not the book itself that causes fundamentalism; it is how we look upon, read, and interpret the book that makes the difference. For this reason, there have been and still are very many Catholic fundamentalists. It is my hope and prayer that all of us, Catholics and other Christians alike, can learn to use the Bible properly, and thereby come to know the beautiful light of the Word of God contained in the frail and utterly imperfect words of humans found there.

Can I be spiritually healthy without reading the Bible?

I find that I have come to know more about God's love for us through reading books and articles, sharing with others about personal faith, and especially just appreciating the joys of nature and the environment rather than by reading the Bible. It seems that I want to do less Scripture reading, because that doesn't satisfy my "thirst" as the other above activities do. I've almost abandoned regular Scripture reading. Is this spiritually healthy?

■ *Answer*

Your initial points and comments about Scripture as "a" source but not the "only" source of revelation are very well taken. Indeed, Scripture is *not* the only source of revelation. The other sources you mention, plus what our church calls "sacred tradition," are just as essential sources of revelation as is Scripture. And probably, for the very great majority of people over the ages since the beginning of humanity and even to the present day, the other sources you mention are more important because they affect everyone's life!

I refer most of all to the one you mentioned last: "...and especially just appreciating the joys of nature and the environment." Hopefully, for you (as for me) this includes your relationships and interactivity with other human beings. A succinct way of putting that would be simply "revelation through creation." I firmly believe that until we learn to recognize God's presence in revelation through our everyday lives and experience, the God who is revealed in Scripture or tradition will be an empty shell of a God.

Furthermore, there have been millions of people in the past and many living today who either cannot read or who have had absolutely no contact with the Bible, or, for that matter with Christianity. Many other millions never knew about what we have come to call "organized religion." If Scripture, then, were the only source of revelation, only a minute percentage of the human race since its inception would have had the benefits of God's revelation.

On the contrary, it is my conviction that the most basic method used by God to reveal Godself to us is creation—which includes our very selves, those with whom we live our lives, the communities in which we live, and all of creation around us, including the distant stars and planets (which in today's space age are becoming increasingly available as sources of God's revelation). So I definitely think you are right on track in seeing God's revelation all around you.

On the other hand, I would hesitate to conclude from this that the Scriptures can be almost discarded. The Bible has been given to us in and through our sacred tradition, and represents basically the same revelation as God is giving to us today through our own experience of creation. But it is even more than that. The Bible is an inspired summary of God's revelation to humanity from its very beginnings. Not that it was written at the very beginning, but that it contains the accumulated revelation experienced by humans from the very beginning.

And we as Catholic Christians believe that—provided it is read and understood properly—the Bible contains that accumulated summary of revelation in an inerrant way.

In other words, dear friend, I think it would be a mistake for us to discard the Scriptures as an unnecessary source of revelation. I suggest that it would be a mistake for you not to continue to read the Bible and not to recognize in those scriptural readings the confirmation of the very revelations that are made to you each and every day of your life through the other means you mentioned. Also, it is quite possible that our own everyday recognition of God's continuing revelation will fall short of that which is contained in the Bible. The Bible is a great gift to us.

We need God's revelation in all its forms and sources. The Scriptures are an excellent source of this. Let us use it, but let us use it well: with a full understanding of its background and purpose.

Prophecy

What will the last day be like?

I'm a student in the seventh grade in a Catholic school. My class-
mates and I would like to know: what will the last day on earth
(judgment day) be like?

■ *Answer*

In one way your question is very easy to answer, and in another it
is somewhat difficult. You see, my dear young friend, no one
knows what the last day on earth will be like, and if I wanted to
take the easy way out, I would stop my answer with that. But that
wouldn't be fair to you.

The difficult way is to handle your question in connection with
the passage in the gospel of Matthew (chapter 25, verses 21 to 46)
where Jesus speaks of the so-called "last judgment." I'm sure
you've heard the story before—how on the last day the good people (the lambs) would be put on one side and would go to heaven,
and the bad people (the goats) would be put on the other side and
would go to hell.

The big difficulty about dealing with this passage is that if we
look upon the passage as a *prediction* of what will happen on
"judgment day," then we're reading the Bible in the wrong way.
This is not a prediction about judgment day; it is a teaching about
how we should live our lives today and every day.

You see, my friend, what Jesus is trying to teach us in that passage is that we must always treat our parents, brothers and sisters,
friends, schoolmates, neighbors, and all other people as we would
treat Jesus himself. If we are kind to any other human being, we
are being kind to Jesus; if we are unkind to any other human
being, we are being unkind to Jesus. That is not something we
need to know to face "the last day on earth." It is something we
need to know today, and tomorrow, and every day.

But to make us all "sit up and listen," St. Matthew situates this story within a larger event in which Jesus is teaching about the last judgment. It sounds like a prediction, but really is not.

There are also some passages in other parts of the Bible dealing with this same subject. I really can't get into that here, except to point out that the purpose of those passages is not to predict what will happen on the last day either. The purpose of these apparent predictions in the Bible is always to teach us some valuable lesson about what we should be and do *today*—and every day of our lives. The Bible is not (and cannot be) wrong in what it teaches us in this way.

Finally, may I simply say that scientists tell us we don't have to worry about the "last day on earth" coming in our lifetime. Even someone as young as you are will never live long enough to see that day. So what are you to do? Learn well and put into practice the important lesson Jesus teaches us in this gospel passage. Live like that, and it really doesn't matter if the world ends tomorrow!

Explain "prophecy" as used in the Bible.

Please explain "prophecy" as it is used in the Bible. Is it a vision and foretelling of the future, or is it the ability to read the present? If not the future, then why the expression in the New Testament: "fulfillment of the Scriptures" in reference to the prophecies of the Old Testament?

■ *Answer*

In a rather lengthy article on prophets written for the *Encyclopedia of Biblical Theology*, the eminent German Scripture scholar Johannes Schildenberger says: "...the nature of the prophets' calling, which was to be sent by Yahweh in order to announce his words to the people, was such that it caused the Hebrew word *nabi* (prophet) to be thought of as a 'proclaimer' or a 'spokesman' of God...." Then he says: "The Greek word 'prophetess' also means not 'predictor of the future' but 'spokesman for someone' or, still better perhaps, 'crier,' or 'proclaimer.'"

Thus, without totally ruling out the concept of the prophet as "predictor," Schildenberger makes it quite clear that reading *predictions* of the future into the teachings of the prophets was more a matter of interpretation by the ancient Hebrews than it was the actual role of the prophets themselves.

The prophet of the Old Testament, then, was someone who was called by God to teach in God's name. Part of that teaching concerned the destiny of those who did or did not remain faithful to what God wanted his people to be or do. That teaching also revolved around the promised Messiah or Savior, through whom, the faith of the Hebrews assured them, they would be "saved" and fulfill their God-given destiny. Of course, when one speaks of "destiny," one is speaking about the future; but not so much by way of prediction as by way of a logical outcome of following the truth.

For instance, to cite an example from science, the truth is that, "if I put my hand in fire it will burn." Is this a prediction? Not really, but it is true and will indeed be the logical outcome if I play with fire.

Now when the prophets of the Old Testament taught about the coming Messiah, they were doing basically the same thing. As Schildenberger puts it, "The significance of the prophets consists chiefly in the following four factors: first, their superb exposition of the object of Israel's faith (Yahweh is the God of the whole world, the controller of world history); second, their demand that their hearers shall prove themselves true servants of God by maintaining righteousness, love of neighbor, humility, and trust in God; third, their deepening of the personal relationship between God and humans, a relationship the full force of which is to be made effective in the future; fourth and finally, their *portrayal* [emphasis added] of the messianic age to come."

But note that Schildenberger uses the word "portrayal" rather than "prediction." In other words, the prophets taught, rather than predicted, what the "messianic age" would be like if it was to live up to the truth.

Thus when the gospels speak of the "fulfillment of the Scriptures," or the "fulfillment of what was said by the prophets," they are not saying that "predictions" were made evident (as my burnt hand would be in the example I used above). Even more important, because the events the gospels were teaching conformed to the truth of the Old Testament prophets' teaching, the readers of the gospels could be confident that the Messiah and therefore the messianic age had indeed arrived. In other words, Christ did fulfill the Old Testament Scriptures and prophecies. He was and is the truth, and therefore if we believe in the truth of what is taught in the Old Testament, then Christ does indeed fulfill that truth completely.

The "prophecies" have been fulfilled.

Is the end of the world near?

Some of my Bible study group friends have been telling me that the end of the world is near. They point to the millennium of Christ's birth as the time when he will return to judge the living and the dead. They also tell me to look around at all the natural disasters (earthquakes, hurricanes, typhoons) and at the revolutions and upheavals all over the world as proof of his second coming, as he foretold in his prophecy in chapter 24 of Matthew's gospel. What do you think?

■ *Answer*

It's obvious from your question that you and your friends in your Bible study group need some informed and updated guidance in interpreting and understanding the Scriptures. Biblical prophecy really has nothing to do with "telling the future" (see the previous question), as is commonly held by fundamentalist Christian groups.

According to all sound Christian biblical scholars (Catholics and other Christians alike) biblical prophecy is simply speaking or teaching in the name of God. Thus the prophets of the Old Testament were simply teaching the people of their day what God wanted them to believe and know, and how God wanted them to act. In the biblical writings, their teachings are sometimes couched in terms that seem to be predictions, but those for whom these writings were originally intended understood them not as predictions, but as teachings. Thus, when Isaiah prophesies (teaches) that the longed-for Savior would be "born of a virgin," he is not predicting this as a future event, but rather teaching that the Savior, because of the very nature of his calling, would be a man born of a young woman of sterling virtue. This was meant to help the hearers of Isaiah and the readers of this written version of his prophecy (teaching) understand better the very special kind of person God intended as their Savior.

Similarly, the prophecies (again: teachings) of Jesus or those from the book of Revelation (which are so widely quoted by so many fundamentalists) about the end of time or second coming of Jesus were not intended by the writers of these books as predictions of when (or if) the world would come to an end or when the second coming of Christ would take place. They're meant to teach us about ourselves as human beings and help us see what we're to do with our lives in the face of adversity. Again they're couched in words that we are inclined to interpret as predictions; but they are not that at all!

I recently read a horridly fundamentalist little book about the so-called "messages of Medjugorje" in which, among other things, the author tries to interpret some of these so-called messages in light of these scriptural prophecies about the second coming of Christ and the end of the world. He makes the typical fundamentalist error: he looks upon the Scriptures as predictions rather than teachings, and he interprets the alleged messages as though they were proven facts and as though such private devotional experiences can and should be applied universally. We all need to grow out of such fundamentalism, and to grow into a mature faith that sees the Scriptures and all of God's revelation not as predictions of the dire results of our sins, but rather as the loving revelation of the goodness and love of God.

Finally, any summary study of the history of our world and humanity will obviously and readily reveal that the natural disasters and human turmoil going on in our world today have been occurring as they always have—no more and no less often or forcefully. None of this has anything whatever to do with when the second coming of Christ will take place, nor can we determine from such matters when or if this world will come to an end. The same kind of dire predictions were made throughout Christendom when the end of the first millennium was approaching. A thousand years have passed and still this world is very much here. I have no reason to doubt that when our successors in the human race approach the 2990s, the predictors of doom will have their third heyday; and a thousand years later their fourth; and so on for many more millennia.

So, dear friend, heed not the "predictors." They offer you only doom and gloom. Heed rather the prophets, who teach us that God is love, and that God creates us humans "in the divine image and likeness."

What is the truth about the "anti-Christ"?

I've been reading and hearing quite a bit lately about the "anti-Christ." It really scares me! What is the teaching of the church about the coming of the anti-Christ as predicted by Jesus and in the book of Revelation?

■ *Answer*

I think the first thing needing clarification in your question is the word "prediction." As I've said in the past few answers, neither Jesus in the gospels, nor the prophets of the Old Testament, nor the writers of the book of Revelation, nor any biblical author, nor any biblical character, was in the business of making *predictions*. Even when they preach about the future or use a phrase like, "It will come to pass," they simply aren't making predictions of future events. What they're doing is telling their listeners or readers something that is now true about ourselves as human beings, or about God, or about our relationship as humans with God. They do this by using a "literary form" or "manner of speech" that

seems (to the unknowing ear or eye) to be foretelling future
events.

If we read the Bible with an open mind and heart (and this is especially true of the book of Revelation), always willing to hear the message of God within the very human words and figures of speech
found there, we will learn eventually not to become disturbed by
apparent predictions in the Bible. What the gospels have Jesus saying
or what the writer of Revelation says about an anti-Christ doesn't
have anything to do with predicting the future! Those who heard
Jesus, those who have read those books of the Bible, those who read
them now, and those who will read them until the end of time, can
find a message *for the present* in those words.

Perhaps the "anti-Christ" is the sinful condition of the human
race (original sin); perhaps it is our individual sinful acts of the
past that still hold us prisoner; perhaps it is a tendency in us to do
evil; perhaps it is a person in our lives who is having some
unhealthy or evil influence on us.

Therefore, we don't have to wonder when the anti-Christ will
come, or what it will be like, or what kind of destruction it will
inflict on us. It came and went in the time of Christ. It came and
went on every day before and after that. It comes and goes today.
It will come and go every day from now on. What has the anti-
Christ done? All the evil that human beings have done since the
beginning of the world. What is it doing now? All the evil that we
human beings are doing right now. What will it do in the future?
All the evil that we human beings will do until the end of time.

So you see, dear friend, there is really nothing to fear. In telling
us about an anti-Christ the Bible is simply urging us to be constantly vigilant in protecting ourselves against evil. It is one of the
consistent themes of the entire Bible from the book of Genesis to
the book of Revelation: "Do good and avoid evil." There is really
nothing scary about that; so we can all "rest easy."

And the third millennium we are now in has no bearing whatever on the teachings about the anti-Christ in the Bible or in our
Christian Tradition. Only fundamentalists would disagree with
that. This year is like any other year, and we are free right now to

live up to our Christian faith, or to deny it by doing evil. God is with us. We need nothing more to be and remain at peace.

Fundamentalism

Must I be "a born again Christian" to be worthy of Jesus?

Being a Catholic, I've studied the doctrines thoroughly and I think I know my faith well. I have no difficulty understanding the term "born again." What bothers me is the fact that I don't "fall backward" at the touch of the hand of a priest or a preacher. I've been told that one is saved only if one is "slain in the spirit." In my situation, does my failure to succumb mean that I'm not worthy of Jesus?

■ *Answer*

I surely hope not, because if failure to "succumb" to the touch of a priest or preacher by "falling backwards" means that one is not "slain in the Spirit" and therefore not saved, then I'm afraid that I and millions of other Catholics, Christians of other denominations, and those who are not Christians would not be saved or "worthy of Jesus." But fear not, dear friend, salvation and the presence of Christ in our lives is certainly not dependent upon that!

Obviously, you've been caught up into the worst that fundamentalism has to offer. If you are, indeed, hearing such foolishness at events like the Jesus festivals and Bible study groups you are attending, your first decision should be to immediately discontinue any connection with them. "Succumbing" or "falling backwards" at the touch of an evangelist has absolutely nothing to do with Catholic teaching on being saved or being "slain in the Spirit." Salvation is a free gift given to us by God and has been expressed in numerous ways in the history of our church: faith, grace, resurrection, heaven, union with God, forgiveness, reconciliation, the presence of Christ, the presence of the Spirit, the indwelling of the Trinity, being "born again of water and the spirit," and, yes, even being "slain in the spirit;" to mention just some.

All these expressions, which have been used either in the Bible or in other writings, are an attempt to express the meaning of our faith in Christ as the Lord and Savior of humanity. To take any one of them as the one and only possible expression of that faith is to cheapen it. And worse yet, to tie that expression to some human ritual or gesture (such as a touch) and call that a test of our faith is to desecrate the very foundation of our faith itself.

And this is precisely what the fundamentalist "evangelists" have done. They take an expression like being "slain in the Spirit" and illogically establish an essential tie between it and a ritual like the one you describe. Then they have the pernicious audacity to question the very faith and salvation of those who don't fall (no pun intended!) for their machinations of the word of God.

I have said before and will say again that I consider fundamentalism to be one of the greatest evils of our time. It is far more dangerous to true Christian faith than such obviously hideous things as portraying crime, violence, or pornography, either in print or on the Internet. Let me make it clear that when I use the word "fundamentalism" I include fundamentalist religions, clubs, cults, ministries or study groups, fundamentalist priests, ministers, preachers, and evangelists, fundamentalist TV networks and programs, fundamentalist books, magazines, or newspapers—and all these no matter what their claimed religious affiliation. Some, of course, are even Catholic.

I can only plead with you, dear friend, and with every reader to disassociate yourself completely and immediately from such fundamentalist programs and influences. "Christ has died; Christ is risen; Christ will come again," we proclaim at Mass. He has done this for you, and for all humanity. This basic article of faith is often denied implicitly (and sometimes explicitly) by those who preach fundamentalism. Don't let them rob you of the security of this great gift.

Is fundamentalism really worse than pornography?

Do you really believe that fundamentalist religion and Bible interpretation are more dangerous than pornography? I must say that I prefer my grandchildren to attend a fundamentalist religious service than a porn movie. Don't you think we Christians should stop talking about fundamentalists as more lost to heaven than the hardened sinner? Why aren't we spending our time trying to convert the criminal mind to Christ and letting Jesus win over the fundamentalists?

■ *Answer*

I must say again that the fundamentalist interpretation of the Bible is, in my opinion, a false interpretation of the Bible. It can lead people into a false impression of who and what they are, who and what God is, who and what Jesus Christ is. In my opinion this leads inevitably to a false understanding of what religion and Christianity are all about. I'm firmly convinced that my view here is correct and in line with the official teaching of the Catholic Church. Because of that, I feel an obligation in conscience to tell people in an emphatic way to avoid fundamentalism and fundamentalist events. Having false conceptions about all these matters is more dangerous to individuals than the very great dangers and evils that I see in pornography. Pornography is so easily recognizable for the trash that it is. Fundamentalism pretends to be "of God" and many good people are fooled into believing that it is truly of God. That, in my opinion, is much more dangerous.

Let me say again, I do think pornography is evil and dangerous to anyone's faith. But I believe fundamentalism is even worse!

I have seen many good people hurt by trying to use faith and religion as an opiate for all their material, physical, and psychic problems. I have seen many people fall into despair because promises of "miracles" were never realized. I have seen many people live in perpetual fear of a lurking Satan to the point that they cannot have a moment of peace for fear that "the devil will get me." I have seen many people come to almost hate God because God becomes for them the "wielder of a big stick" rather than the loving Father of Jesus and us all. I see all of this as resulting directly from fundamentalist religious views and fundamentalist interpretation of the Bible.

Parenthetically may I add that our own Catholic church has been and is today far from immune from this problem. For instance, very recently I spent some time watching a so-called "Catholic" television show. A priest and a nun were giving people answers to questions over the telephone and on the air. Some of their advice and theology came close to being "criminal" in my view. If what they preach is truly representative of what it means to be Christian and Catholic, I would immediately have to look elsewhere for a meaningful Christianity.

Indeed we need unity. We need love. We need to honor the one true God. We must be understanding and loving to those with whom we disagree. We must be fully, totally, and unquestionably Christian. I am simply convinced that none of this is possible unless we are fully dedicated to the truth, and I am similarly convinced that the truth is not to be found in fundamentalism.

Were Adam and Eve the only people created by God?

I'm a member of a Bible study group in our community. A question arose about the story of creation in the book of Genesis. Some of us believe what the Bible says: that Adam and Eve were the only two people God created and then they "multiplied." Others believe that God also created other people at the beginning. If he didn't, where did the wives of Cain and Abel come from?

■ Answer

The Bible does not say that Adam and Eve were the only two people God created. The Bible says that God created and continues to create everything other than God's own self, and that includes both you and me. The Bible also says that God continues to be present to each of God's creatures, and that God's presence is by way of continuing the loving act of creation without which everyone and everything would immediately vanish out of existence.

I suppose you may be asking: "Where—in what book, in what chapter, in what verse—does the Bible say all these things?" The only real answer to that question is: "In all the books; in all the chapters; in all the verses!" In other words, it is only when the Bible is taken as a whole and with a full understanding of its origin, meaning, and purpose that we can truly understand what God is saying to us through this magnificent compilation of writings. Oh, I suppose I could quote hundreds of verses from the Bible that could be understood to support the point that I'm trying to make. But I would not then be using the Bible properly, because someone who holds a different view could probably quote as many passages that could be understood to support that view.

I will repeat here that the two stories of creation in the Bible, in the first and second chapters of Genesis, are not to be taken as historical accounts of how the world or the human race began. These biblical accounts are expressions of faith in the creative relationship between God and all of creation, including humanity. The Bible is not trying to tell us that God created two "starter" humans. Nor is the Bible trying to tell us that Adam and Eve were the names of the first humans, nor that Cain and Abel were the sons (much less only sons or only children) of the two first humans. The whole story of Adam, Eve, Cain, and Abel has an amazing wealth of divine revelation in it, but none of that wealth is wasted on the unknown historical details of when or how the initial creation of human beings came about.

While I strongly encourage you and all other Bible study groups to continue this effort to read, know, understand, pray from, and be enlightened by the Bible, I even more strongly encourage you never to look to the Bible as a source of solving the problems of human history. Historically, we simply don't know who the first humans were and how many there might have been, and the Bible doesn't attempt to answer that question. Similarly, we simply don't know if there ever were people named Cain and Abel in the early history of humanity, nor whether they had wives, nor who their wives might have been if they did have wives. However, none of that is important to our faith, which is what the Bible is meant to support.

What is important to our faith is that God is the loving creator of humanity. Therefore we owe all that we are and have to God. There is a loving relationship between ourselves and God, and that relationship is extended to the loving relationship that must exist among us as humans. Husbands and wives, sisters and brothers, and all members of the human family must learn to relate in love to each other. Otherwise the fracturing of that relationship (sin) will and can only lead to disaster for all of us. These are some of the basic revelations of the biblical creation story, and we would do well to dwell on it repeatedly so that the full implications of these realities might have an ever-growing opportunity to sink more deeply into our consciousness and our own real day-to-day life.

So dear friend, do continue to study your Bible. I hope the full impact of its wealth of God's revelation will continue thereby to be felt and make its impact on your life and that of your study group. Don't let these relatively unimportant historical questions blind you to the real message contained in God's Word. Then the Bible will become a great asset to your life rather than a book full of unanswered and unanswerable questions.

Why do people not follow the Bible about birth control?

Since God creates through us, how can a person have surgery to kill the seed of God in him? How can priests fail to speak out against such surgery and thus promote the killing of the sperm that gives life, and yet call themselves men of God who preach the Holy Bible?

What does the Bible say about a man who spilled the seed on the ground? It says that God killed the man on the spot for spilling the seed. How can these men be leaders in the church when they do not honor the commandment of God: "Thou shalt not kill"?

■ *Answer*

First, may I say to you, please make an effort to stop reading the Bible as though it were written word-for-word (and in English, no less) by God's own hand. The Bible is a collection of writings. The original languages vary, but many are ancient and barely understandable even by scholars. Literally hundreds of human beings were involved in writing the Bible over the course of thousands of years.

We firmly believe the Bible was written and passed on to us "under the inspiration of God." But please be aware that it cannot be read as a road map to every situation in life. It points the way for us by describing the kind of life God wants us to live, but it doesn't predetermine a response to every single life situation.

It is rather obvious from the wording of your questions that you, like so many of our people, have fallen under the spell of biblical fundamentalism. God's Word given to us in the Bible is a loving word, and revelation in the Bible is not a condemnatory one, as fundamentalists would have it. It is not a collection of repeated divine "warnings" to human beings, as fundamentalists seem to think. It will not reveal to us a despotic God "waiting on his heavenly throne" to cast big plagues of devastating illness and death upon every human who steps outside of his unflinching and uncaring collection of laws and commands, as the fundamentalists would have us believe.

Under the seemingly harsh and unattractive picture of God painted by a literal reading of the human words of the Bible, we can, if we read those words well, find the "real" God who, through his revelation and word, contained within and behind the human words, reveals himself as a God of love, as total mercy, as our totally loving parent who cares for us with an infinite love that God cannot and will not withdraw from us under any possible set of circumstances, and no matter how evil we might be. The God of the Bible is a God of love.

Briefly, I don't think the passage in the Bible to which you refer has any relevance or application to having a vasectomy, which is the surgery you describe. Furthermore, having a vasectomy does not "kill the seed of God" in a man. It prevents the seed from mixing with the seminal fluid and becoming semen. But I see absolutely no connection between such surgery and the commandment of God that we are not to kill.

I do see a real difference, however, between the great and loving God depicted in the Bible, and the tyrannical purveyor of vengeance that the fundamentalists see in this God.

There are better ways of conveying the "Word of God" than by simply quoting passages of the Bible totally out of context. Let us hope and pray that our priests and all those who teach in the name of God will preach the real God revealed in the Scriptures and in all creation.

Can't we trust in quotes of Jesus in Holy Scripture?

Our pastor recently shocked a number of us by telling us that some Scripture quotes of Jesus cannot be validly attributed to him. If you can't trust in the word of Jesus in Scripture, what can you trust?

■ Answer

Absolutely nothing! But indeed it isn't true that one cannot "trust in the word of Jesus in Scripture," and I am confident that your pastor did not mean to imply that at all! I am also confident that you are mistakenly interchanging the expressions "quotes of Jesus" and "words of Jesus." These are, however, two entirely different things.

You see, dear friend, the gospels are not a *historical* account of what Jesus said and did. There were no news reporters there, no one writing down Jesus' words as he spoke them. The earliest manuscripts containing the sayings of Jesus were written more than a generation after his death! Therefore we cannot accurately use the word "quotation" when speaking of the words that the gospels indicate Jesus used. A "quotation" is and must be an exact word-for-word duplication (or at least "translation") of what someone has actually said or written. In that sense the writers of the gospels do not even pretend to be "quoting" the words of Jesus.

But we can say that the gospels do contain the "Word" of Jesus, because when we say that, we mean that the words that the gospels attribute to Jesus accurately portray the substance of what

Jesus said. Any reputable Scripture scholar of today will insist upon this principle of reading and interpreting the Bible.

Thus, while not being historically accurate in all their aspects, the gospels are absolutely accurate expressions of the faith of the early Christian communities. They accurately express who Jesus was, and what he said and did. As such they express the *truth* of Christian faith, and give a true faith-impression of who Jesus was, a true faith-impression of what Jesus said, a true faith-impression of what Jesus did. Furthermore, this faith-impression is totally trustworthy, and we can be confident that they express the true and undeniable word of the one whom we know as Jesus Christ.

I think if you engaged in further conversation with your pastor about this, you would see that he was in no way demeaning the trustworthiness of Scripture. On the contrary, he was probably trying to help you realize that it is the truth behind the individual words of the Bible that is the "Word of God." If we can't overcome that "hurdle" in our efforts to use the Bible well, we are destined to fall into the fundamentalists' trap of reading the words of the Bible as though they were dictated as such by God himself. If that happens we have really lost the Bible, and what a loss that would be!

I could give you example after example of the "sayings" of Jesus as portrayed in the four gospels that would prove the contention that these are not quotations by any means. But just take, for example, the "Our Father" as we find it in the gospels of Matthew and Luke. (Mark and John do not present the Lord's prayer as such.) The same "Word" comes out of Matthew and Luke, but the individual "words" are quite different. If we insist that the gospels contain "quotations" of Jesus' words, then one of these accounts would have to be false. On the other hand, if we read these two passages as expressions of "faith" in what Jesus said, then they both give us the truth of his beautiful prayer.

Why did God choose to reveal himself through Jesus?

We know that before the time of Christ many different world reli-

gions had developed. There were many other religions from popu-
lous areas of the world 2,000 years ago. Why, do you suppose, did
God choose to wait thousands or millions of years from the time
of Eve and Adam to reveal himself to us through Jesus?

■ *Answer*

I have always had a difficult time with questions about God's
motivation in doing things, because such questions can only be
answered speculatively. For instance, who knows "why" God creates us and keeps us in existence? Who knows "why" God gives us
the powers of reasoning and free will? Who knows "why" God
continues to love us even when we sin? There are no real answers
to those questions, though we can speculate as a result of our faith
and God's revelation. So if we ask why God chose that time and
place to reveal himself through Jesus, I can only speculate, simply,
that he didn't. God *is choosing* in the ever-present now of eternity
to reveal himself through Jesus.

First we must realize that *our* perspective is based in time, but
God's is not! Every single moment is present to God at all times.
And we believe God has revealed the divine heart to every human
being that has ever lived, lives now, or will ever live. So for those
who came into the world before Jesus, for the contemporaries of
Jesus, and for those who came into the world after Jesus, there is
no difference from God's perspective. Again, for God, there is no
time; there is only eternity. Eternity doesn't have a yesterday, a
today, or a tomorrow. Theologians sometimes call it "the ever present now." So from God's perspective, God did not wait hundreds,
or thousands or millions of years to reveal himself. For God, the
earthly life of Jesus and the revelation that was given through him
are not a thing of the past. For God, it is still happening.

Don't feel bad if you don't understand what that means. I certainly don't understand it, and I think that those who do are relatively few. On the other hand I do believe that in this concept of
eternity lies the truth of God's revelation and salvation to all peoples of all times.

Somewhat more understandably, I hope, I would like to add

that it is not accurate that God revealed or reveals *only* through Jesus. Revelation is an ongoing process that began with the very onset of creation. It is the teaching of our church, I think we all know, that God reveals himself to us in many, many ways. Every one of God's creatures can tell us something about God if only we open ourselves to that revelation. This means that everything we know of and experience in life is teeming with God's revelation. In fact the existence of Buddha, of Mohammed; yes, and even of people like the ancient Egyptians, Greeks, Romans—the good and the evil alike—are all part of God's self-revelation.

Furthermore, events and aspects of nature, such as a beautiful sunset, a snow-capped range of mountains, the miracles of plant, animal, and human life, even seemingly evil things such as earthquakes, volcanoes, floods, and storms are all part of God's revelation. So we need not look only at Jesus to find the revelation of God.

On the other hand, it is a defined truth of our faith that Christ is the ultimate, total, and complete expression of God. He is the Word of God; to know him is to know God. But this truth in itself is an ever-developing truth. God, as we see him in and through the revelation of Jesus Christ, does not appear the same to us today as God appeared to people who were the personal relatives, friends, disciples, and even apostles of Jesus. Through the process of what might be called faith-evolution, which is that process whereby the faith develops as it is passed on as God's continuing gift from one generation to another, and understood in the light of each generation's progressive knowledge, the revelation of God in Jesus Christ and in all of creation is an ever-developing thing in our understanding and faith. The church teaches that the "deposit" of Christian revelation was closed with the death of the last apostle. That means that "it is all there." *But* (and this is a big "but") it is far from being fully "brought to light" or "out in the open." As Pope John XXIII said so eloquently, all that the gospel demands of us is not yet fully understood.

So let us not fret! God is not unjust to those who came before us, nor to us, nor will God be to those who come after us. God's revelation (as impossible as that might be for us to accept, much less understand) is open and accessible to all—from the first humans to see the face of this earth, to the last who will occupy it at the end of time.

Jesus Christ

Was Jesus really divine and human?

I have several questions about the teaching of the church that Jesus is both God and human. First, what are today's theologians saying about the divinity and humanity of Jesus? Is it true that some are saying that the humanity is more important than the divinity? How is it possible for someone to be God and human at the same time?

■ *Answer*

Wow, what a series of questions! They could "blow the mind" of even the best theologians and theology professors. Trying to answer them here, and make my answer at least somewhat intelligible, will be a monumental task.

First I must state very emphatically that there are no scientifically verifiable, historical answers to these questions. The science of history does not tell us that Jesus is God and human; only faith can tell us that. The science of philosophy does not allow for someone to be simultaneously human and divine; only faith can lead us to believe that. The science of psychology cannot delve into the mind of this human who lived 2,000 years ago and tell us what he actually knew himself to be; we can only have faith in this regard.

In brief, dear friend, let us all understand full well that there is precious little that the hard sciences can tell us about the human being whom we know today as Jesus Christ. What we do know from pure history is that in the early part of the first century A.D., there was a self-styled "prophet" named Jesus going around Galilee and

Judea. Other than that he was of Jewish heritage, his origins are unknown. He went around the countryside preaching; he attracted a relatively small number of Jewish followers; he was totally unknown outside of that immediate area; he was denounced by his own Jewish religious leaders; and he was finally crucified by the Romans as one-among-many insurrectionists or rebels of his time.

And that's it, as far as historical, verifiable fact is concerned.

Anything beyond that is not in the realm of scientific knowledge, but strictly in the realm of faith, which is still, of course, a very *real* realm. Even if all four gospels unanimously depict him as doing or saying certain things; even if the theologians of all ages since then agree about certain truths in connection with him; even if the church infallibly defines some truth about him; even if all this is true, we still have no more scientific historical knowledge of Jesus Christ than what I indicated in the previous paragraph. We might have (and I hope we do have) faith in all these teachings, but we do not *know* them as scientific or historical facts.

In other words, I don't *know* that Jesus Christ is God and human; I *believe* that. I don't *know* that he taught or said the things attributed to him in the gospels; I *believe* what those things are saying to me. I don't *know* that Mary was his mother; I *believe* that this is so. I don't *know* that he had a Last Supper with the disciples; I *believe* what this event in the Bible is trying to teach me. I could go on and on.

My point is, dear friend, that my response to your question isn't in the realm of science. It can't be proved in a scientific way. Nor is my response strictly limited to the defined or infallibly promulgated doctrines of our church. Rather, my response is a reflection of the true teachings of the church concerning the humanity, divinity, and consciousness of Jesus Christ.

What are today's theologians saying about this doctrine of our faith? I think they're telling us some rather interesting and faith-evoking things. Take, for instance, the series of books on Christology (the theological study of Jesus Christ) by the eminent Dominican theologian Father Edward Schillebeeckx. In his first volume, entitled *Jesus*, he concentrates primarily on the humanity of

Jesus. He goes to great lengths to demonstrate the consistent faith of the church throughout the centuries. We have always believed in the completeness of the humanity of Jesus. Schillebeeckx demonstrates beyond any shadow of a doubt that Jesus is indeed fully human, having every human characteristic other than sinfulness.

Many of us grew up with the *Baltimore Catechism*'s definition of who Jesus is, namely, that Jesus Christ is one person (the second person of the Blessed Trinity) possessing two natures: the nature of God and the nature of humans. But for most people, the stress of all this was on Jesus' divinity. His humanity was played down.

Schillebeeckx and other theologians are restoring balance to our beliefs. While his is an accurate repetition or translation of the words used at the Council of Chalcedon in 451 A.D. to define the church's teaching on this matter, Father Schillebeeckx skillfully and diligently points out that what the Fathers of Chalcedon meant by "person" and "nature" was quite different from our own modern understanding of these terms. It would be heresy, he reminds us, to believe that Christ was *not* a human person. If we believe that Christ has a full human nature, he reasons—and believes!—then Jesus has to be personally conscious of his humanity, which is another way of saying that he must be "personally human."

Can I understand how this can be so? Not really. But I do believe it with all my heart and soul.

Likewise, responsible modern theologians are stressing today that it is extremely important that we not forget the humanity of Jesus in our day-to-day relationship with him. Over the last several centuries especially, our church has had a tendency to emphasize the divinity of Jesus as the important aspect of his existence. It had gotten to the point among some people where the name "Jesus" and the name "God" were being used almost interchangeably. It was as though his humanity was just a human costume that God the Son took on to make himself appear to be human. Nothing could be further from the traditional faith of our church!

To counteract this, many of our most responsible theologians are stressing that we must recognize the importance and necessity of the humanity of Jesus, and that it is in his humanity that his role as savior or redeemer is carried out. So, while they would not say that his humanity is more important than his divinity, they surely are saying that in our faith, it is of the utmost importance that we restore his humanity to its proper place alongside our faith in his divinity. Jesus Christ is not first the divine Son of God, and second the human son of Mary. He is simply God and human; or just as simply and truly, human and God. Both are equally important elements of our faith in the one Jesus Christ. Neither can be put in second place.

So you see, dear friend, I just don't have definitive answers to all your questions about the humanity and divinity of Jesus Christ. All of us Christians have faith in the humanity and in the divinity of Jesus Christ. And in that confident faith, let us be at peace.

Was Jesus divine from his conception? When did he realize this?

Was Jesus divine (God) upon conception in his mother's womb? Can you tell me at what state in life Jesus realized he was the Son of God? What are theologians saying about this, and what is your opinion?

■ *Answer*

First let us establish again (as in the previous question) that these questions simply cannot be answered in a scientific or historical manner. There is no way we can go back 2,000 years and develop a scientific or historical profile of the human being Jesus of Nazareth. We really can't determine when he became aware of anything, not to mention when he became aware of his own divinity. Historically, we just don't know that much about him.

So, dear friend, we are obviously dealing here with a matter of faith. It is the common teaching of the church (though not defined doctrine) that the human knowledge of Jesus included an "awareness of" or "vision of" God. Exactly what such an awareness or vision means in our faith is a question that has baffled theologians down through the ages. They have no clear answer to it; nor do I.

I have recently read the thoughts of several responsible and believing theologians of our own time. But I find them restating the question, rather than trying to give an impossible answer. They express their faith in the divinity of Christ, and then emphasize the absolute importance of the humanity of Jesus and his likeness to us.

Then they ask new questions like: "If he is totally human, did he slowly learn human knowledge as we do? Or did he know everything through his divinity?" Or, "Were his sufferings and temptations just like ours, if he knew he had the knowledge and strength of God within himself to deal with them?" Or, "Was it so difficult for this man to face death, when he knew the full extent of the glory that was to be his beyond that death?" Or, "How can we aspire to be totally like him in our own human endeavors, if his own human endeavors were aided by knowing that he was divine and had divine powers and abilities?"

These are all unanswered (and probably unanswerable) questions that neither affirm nor deny the presence of divinity in Jesus or his awareness of that divinity at any point in his human existence. What these questions do accomplish, I think, is simply to move us in prayer to delve more deeply into the meaning of our faith in the defined doctrine of the church that Jesus Christ was and is fully human while also being fully divine.

Would answers to these questions, though, really help our faith? What nourishes our faith is not knowing the timing of this or that in Jesus' life, but that we know ourselves to be made holy as a result of encountering Jesus Christ in our own lives.

So you see, dear friend, I just can't give a definitive answer to your question. All Christians have faith both in the humanity and divinity of Jesus Christ. Each of us must let our faith in his humanity permeate the very fiber of our being. We must be confident, too, that his divinity is ever within us by the very creative power of God. By virtue of both his divinity and his humanity he has declared all us humans as daughters and sons of God. We can and should call God by the same name that Jesus called him: "Abba"..."Father." To me this is the wonder of the doctrine of the incarnation: not so much what it means to Jesus Christ, but what it means to us!

Did Jesus ever laugh?

I've got a question that I think might stump you. Did Jesus ever laugh?

■ *Answer*

Dear friend, whether your question stumps me or not, I think it reveals something very pertinent and important about your faith; or better yet, about *our* faith. Our faith in Jesus Christ is a faith that sees in him every possible facet of human existence; everything that can possibly be an aspect of human existence (except sin, of course). We do not, as do most fundamentalists, allow the divinity of Christ to overpower, overcome, or negate his humanity.

And isn't laughter—genuine, heartfelt, joy-inspired laughter—part and parcel of what being human is all about? Can you even imagine liking or admiring any human being who never "cracked a smile" or had a good "belly laugh" once in a while? Can a real human being go through life without any "light" moments; or better yet, without expressing joy, satisfaction, or exuberance through laughter?

Unfortunately, no contemporary of Jesus saw fit to leave us with a historical record of his life or of his social personality. The history of his life will always remain an unfathomable factual mystery. But the accounts we have of him in the gospels paint a magnificent "faith-picture" of a man who had every possible human asset. For instance, the stories in John's gospel about his friendship with Mary, Martha, and Lazarus could possibly have been written precisely to reveal the utter warmth of the humanity of the man. Although there is certainly no reference whatever to it in the gospels, I can just see the four of them (or the three of them, as Martha washed the dishes) sitting down after a meal in the evening and having a friendly and loving laugh as Jesus related stories of the sometimes ludicrous reaction of the disciples to what Jesus said or did.

In a similar (though unhistoric) manner, I can see him smiling with "tongue in cheek" at a befuddled Simon Peter who could not understand his repeated questioning of Peter's love. I can see the smile on his face as he might have thrown a manly arm over the shoulder of the confused Nathaniel while saying: "Do you believe just because I saw you under the fig tree?" I can see him laughing with the children whom he insisted be brought to him after a long day of preaching. Yes, I can even see an impish grin on his face as he asked his parents, "Didn't you know I must be about my father's business?"

Please understand, dear friend, that I am not saying that the gospels portray him as smiling or laughing on any of these occasions. What I am saying is that the gospels portray a faith-image of a man who could and would smile or laugh whenever the occasion called for it. The man called Jesus acted like a man. His divinity in no way inhibited or restricted his humanity. There was no "halo" floating over his head as he walked the dusty roads of Galilee or the filthy streets of Jerusalem. He sweated not blood but plain old human sweat in the heat of the Palestine countryside. He relieved the tension of many a moment, I am convinced, with a hearty laugh at himself.

He cried and, yes, he laughed. He, thank God, was as human as you and I. So thanks for asking. I would never have thought of such a delightful question!

Did Jesus really die?

What is the position of theologians today on the actual death of Jesus on the cross versus a clinical death on the cross? I read somewhere that current Scripture experts are claiming that Christ was only clinically dead, and then was revived in the tomb. What is your opinion?

■ *Answer*

It is my sincere hope that as a result of this response, all of us will be able to follow your example and delve more deeply into our faith as well as our understanding of Scripture.

I certainly do not claim to be knowledgeable of all the theological and scriptural opinions abounding within the church today, but I must say here that I'm not aware of even one Catholic theologian or Scripture scholar who would hold that Jesus did not experience total human death on the cross. Further, it is a matter of our defined doctrine that Jesus did experience a true and total human death on the cross, and not simply some sort of feigned death or "clinical" death as you describe it. It's also a matter of defined doctrine that the resurrection of Christ was not simply a revival of a seemingly-dead-but-actually-still-living body, but was a completely new life into which this dead human being entered "out of" death.

As I've said before here, we need to begin to realize and accept the fact (as we should!) that the gospel accounts of the life, passion, and death of Christ are not meant to be factual descriptions. They're an expression of faith in the meaning of the Christ event. There have been novels and historical fiction written about the life and death of Jesus, which take their facts from sources outside the Bible. If we're not careful, we may fall into the error of accepting these other accounts as though they're the factual descriptions that the gospels are somehow lacking. No matter how plausible or believable a work of fiction or an attempt at history might be, there is no better expression of the truth of our faith than what is in the gospels.

My opinion on the matter, then, is that Jesus did indeed experience the totality of human death on the cross, and was not simply "clinically" or "seemingly" dead.

In other words, dear friend, Jesus did die, exactly as we all will! And our hope as Christians is that we will share his resurrection.

Did the dead body of Jesus really come back to life?

A member of my Bible study group told us that she heard a priest say that the empty tomb on Easter morning does not prove the resurrection. He also said that the resurrection of Jesus did not mean his dead body came back to life. We found these things hard to believe in view of all the evidence in the gospels. Does the church teach that Jesus really had a bodily resurrection?

■ *Answer*

Thanks for an excellent question, which will give me an opportunity to guide you and all my readers to a very valuable little book (only 133 pages) entitled *The Virginal Conception and Bodily Resurrection of Jesus*, by the eminent Scripture scholar, Father Raymond Brown, published by Paulist Press.

Yes, the church does teach that Jesus did experience a bodily resurrection. But, as Father Brown so clearly explains in his book, this does not mean that his dead body simply came back to life again or was resuscitated. Father Brown points out that there is a vast difference between the risen Christ and the people raised back to ordinary life by Jesus in the gospels (Lazarus, the daughter of Jairus, and the son of the widow of Naim). The gospels have these people rising or being resuscitated to ongoing, normal human life; in other words, the same composition or combination of physical elements of which their bodies were composed before death were brought back into "composition" to form the same body again. It is evident both from the Scriptures and from sacred tradition that the resurrection of Jesus was in no way like that. As Father Brown puts it: "Jesus was not restored to ordinary life; his risen existence is glorious and eschatological, transported beyond the limitations of space and time; and he will not die again."

If this weren't the case, we would worship Lazarus, wouldn't we, as the one of the first people to experience resurrection?

Father Brown speaks of three sets of believing theologians who have the following different views on the "how" of resurrection.

1) There are those theologians who believe precisely what the church teaches about the resurrection of Jesus and who are convinced that the body of Jesus did not corrupt into dust in the tomb, but who feel we need some better expression than "bodily resurrection" to describe the complete transformation to glory that we believe took place.

2) There are those theologians who believe precisely what the church teaches about the resurrection of Jesus and who are not sure whether or not the body of Jesus corrupted to dust, but, like

the first group, their main concern is that we should have some more meaningful language than "bodily resurrection" to express our faith, and they feel that both Scripture and tradition give us examples of such better language.

3) There are those theologians who believe precisely what the church teaches about the resurrection of Jesus and who are absolutely convinced that the body of Jesus did corrupt into dust in the tomb, and that the stories of the empty tomb were simply a "primitive and theological way of describing a victory over death that totally defied human description and experience."

None of these three groups, however, would consider the resurrected body of Jesus as the resuscitated corpse that was placed in the tomb on Good Friday. Please note, dear friend, that all three groups are described as believing in the church's teaching on the resurrection, and that includes the definitive teaching of the church that the resurrection of Jesus was indeed a bodily resurrection.

The reason I so belabor this point is that so many of us are so ready to cry out "heresy" whenever we hear some truth of our faith expressed in a way to which we are not accustomed. There is great value in thinking about the resurrection in all three of the above ways, as there are drawbacks in each method of thought. We lose so much when we insist on only one method of expressing the truth. What we really need to do is to study and pray over each method of expression, and I am fully confident that each will lend strong support to the real truth from which they arise.

I warmly recommend to your Bible study group that you obtain Fr. Brown's book and study it carefully. By the way, don't pass over the introduction, which contains extremely important "ground rules" for the proper reading and interpretation of Scripture from one who is a master. It will throw new light on what the entire Bible is really all about.

What were Christ's last words?

Today there seems to be contradictory opinions about the "last words" of Christ on the cross. Some are contending that Christ was praying when he said, "My God, my God, why have you forsaken me?" Others are saying that momentarily he was forsaken by the Father. What's your opinion?

■ *Answer*

My opinion is that those two contradictory opinions are a result of a fundamentalist manner of reading and interpreting the Bible. Solid Scripture scholars of today would not speak about what Christ might have meant by these words (because they would agree that none can know whether they are a historically accurate record of what Christ said on the cross). Rather they would speak of what the *author or authors* of that particular gospel passage meant by using these words in that passage.

There are many gospel texts that speak eloquently of the humanity of Jesus Christ. The text you cite in your question is surely one of them. To me the evangelist is teaching us the ever-important lesson that Jesus was and is indeed a human being in every possible meaning of those terms—"like us in all things, except sin," as St. Paul puts it. Throughout his earthly life Jesus had committed himself in faith totally to God, his Father, and to the mission that he had accepted as his own. He was bent on inaugurating the reign of God on earth. Thus he had given himself totally to God and to his fellow humans.

At this moment on the cross, he is actually praying a psalm from memory, as any good religious person of his day would have been able to do. The psalm is number 22. Look it up in your Bible. It begins with this terrible sounding lament, as though God has rejected or abandoned him, but lo! It ends in victory!

Of course the evangelist as he writes knows that out of the apparent defeat on the cross, God would bring resurrection: recovery, victory, new life, success, renewal, and glory.

The point, good friend, is not to determine if Christ actually said these words. The Bible was not written for God's benefit, nor were the gospels written to record or justify the life, words, and actions of Jesus Christ. There were no news reporters on the scene.

The Bible was written for us humans, and the gospels, as part of that Bible, were written to help us learn the "message," the "good news" that Christ brought into the world, with the hope that this message will penetrate every facet of our existence and support us as we attempt to live out our human existence as Jesus did his. If we use them in that way, we will find them very supportive, and we will know that the ever-faithful "Yahweh" or "Abba" will no more fail us than he did Jesus himself.

What did Jesus mean by "Let the dead bury the dead"?

Please explain the passage in Matthew 8:18–22 in which Jesus says, "Follow me and let the dead bury the dead." I realize it shouldn't be taken literally. Is the Lord saying, "I am No. 1; forget any other obligation"? Do we not have an obligation to our spouse, children, and elderly parents? Thanks in advance.

■ *Answer*

No, I do not think our Lord would want us to "forget any other obligation" in order to follow him. It simply isn't possible to take one single passage out of the Bible and interpret it as though the rest of the Bible did not exist. To do so is to be mistaken. You obviously realize the literal reading of the Bible is not appropriate.

What we must do in interpreting this or any other passage of the Bible is to be as conscious as possible of all other biblical references to the same topic. Even more important, we must use our intelligence to determine what the true "Word of God" is concerning the matter. Now I'm sure you would agree that the God we meet in the Bible, especially the Father of Jesus, would never want you to abandon anyone you love.

I think that this passage in Matthew's gospel is simply an effort on the part of the evangelist to emphasize the importance he sees in following "the way of life" that Jesus had taught. The gospel writer was using exaggeration to bring home the importance of the point being made. When you get right down to it, we all do basically the same thing in our everyday life. For instance when someone (even someone whom we love very much) has offended us in some way, we have a tendency to say something like: "If I get my hands on him I'll kill him!" Now when we say such things, especially if past experience has made it clear that we love this person very much, I don't think anyone would ever draw the conclusion that we intend to commit murder. But they would understand that we are hurt by what this person has done, and that's what we really mean by the expression: "I'll kill him!"

Throughout the gospels Jesus says things that would be basically inhuman if they're not taken in context. It's easy for us to give in to the temptation of thinking that Jesus' humanity was totally overpowered by his divinity, and that therefore everything that he said or did was simply the word or act of God himself. But that is simply not so. He was a human, and he thought like a human, spoke like a human, and acted like a human. Furthermore, he was a Jewish man of his own time and was subject to the same cultural and environmental influences as were all his Jewish brothers and sisters.

So when we read something in the gospels that is preceded by "Jesus said," and it doesn't seem to make sense to us in relationship to our other human and God-given responsibilities and obligations, we should immediately look for a deeper and perhaps less literal meaning of the passage.

Sacraments and Liturgy

The Mass

Why do I have to go to Mass every Sunday?

Why do I have to go to Mass every Sunday? I feel as though I can talk to God just as well at home, perhaps better.

■*Answer*

Please know that you are not alone in feeling you can "talk to God just as well at home." I would venture to say that this may be true of many people. But talking to God at home has nothing to do with why the church urges you to "go to Mass" on Sunday.

You see, dear friend, the purpose of the Mass is not to give us a better opportunity to "talk to God." On the contrary, our participation in the Mass presupposes that we are "talking to God" throughout our lives in all that we think, say, or do. When we gather with our fellow Christians to celebrate the Mass, we come to join with them in thanking God for being present in our lives every moment. There is a human need to share this sense of gratitude with others in a community. As Catholics we do this in the way that Christ asked us to when he said, "Do this in remembrance of me."

At Mass, Christians gather to hear together the Word of God in the Scriptures, to share this Word with each other, and to express their common faith in that Word and in the Christian way of life. Christians gather to join with other Christians in the eucharistic meal. Jesus Christ, ever present in the Christian's life, is present in this gathering of Christians. "Where two or three are gathered in my name, there am I in the midst of them."

Therefore, it's precisely because we're able to "talk to God" at home that we have reason to attend Mass weekly. It's where we relate to our brothers and sisters in faith. Mass is where we share our own personal experiences of God. It's where we allow others to share with us. It provides a cadence in life, like the drum in a marching band, assisting us to walk always in the light.

You see, the reason we "have to go to Mass" on Sunday is not because the law of the church says we must. On the contrary, the church's law says we must because "we need to." Our faith, after all, is *personal* but not *private.*

How can Mass be made more meaningful for all?

When I participate at Sunday Mass, I often feel like I am really not contributing anything to the Mass itself, as the priest, the lector, the song leader, and other liturgical leaders do. How can we, as the congregation, help the priest to make the Mass more meaningful and enjoyable for all?

■ *Answer*

First let me point a finger at myself and say that we priests, as the principal celebrants (or presiders) at the Mass, are sometimes quite lax in doing our part well. At a recent seminar on liturgy, the role of the priest was beautifully described as "the gatherer" of the Christian community in prayer. It is the community, or the congregation, that prays the liturgy; it is not the prayer of the priest, or of the lector, or of the song leader, or of any of the other liturgical leaders. It is not that the congregation takes part in the leaders' prayer, but that the leaders take part in the congregation's prayer. The role of the priest, then, must be an "enabling" role. He must enable the congregation to pray by being the catalyst for gathering them in prayer.

If that is so, the priest must be in constant contact with the worshiping community, keeping it together in the prayer they offer. This requires a steady effort on his part through persistent eye contact, gathering and embracing gestures, and an outreaching posture. You might say the presider must have good "body language."

It is an attitudinal thing, I guess, as much as anything. By that I mean that the priest must have a constant awareness of his true role in this eucharistic celebration. If he deems his role to be one of upstaging everyone else; if he makes the mistake of considering the Mass as "his" Mass or "his" prayer, rather than that of the community, there is no way that the community will be enabled by him to be a community at prayer.

While it's true that the leaders (especially the priests) can "make or break" the celebration, the congregation or community can also do so by not doing its part. If you just sit (stand or kneel) there with little or no interest in anyone or anything that's happening, then indeed you are not contributing anything.

Allow yourself to be "gathered" in prayer by the priest. Really enter into prayer when he says: "Let us pray." Open your eyes and heart to the Word of God as proclaimed in the Scriptures and homily. Join yourself with the community symbolically offered in the form of bread and wine. Eat and drink of the living Christ when you approach the eucharistic minister. In other words, if you actively pray the Mass, then you indeed are contributing as much to that celebration as anyone else in church.

Shouldn't the church be a "welcoming community"?

A recent column in a Catholic newspaper speaks of the need for Catholic parishes to be more loving and better at welcoming. As one who has visited different parishes in our diocese, I must admit that all aren't as loving or as welcoming as they should be. Could you give us your thoughts as to how we can all strive to have warmer and more inviting faith communities?

■ *Answer*

For a very long time now I have bemoaned this very problem within parish life in our church. When I was an associate pastor in a New Orleans parish years ago, I very much admired the practice of the rather elderly pastor who spent at least fifteen minutes before each Mass on Sundays in front of the church offering a warm welcome to people as they approached the church. He was there again at the end of Mass to wish them well as they left. When I became a pastor myself, I made a point of following this excellent example, and always encouraged other priests in the parish to join me.

Obviously, though, this was far from being enough to make our parish celebrations "welcoming" events to those who came to participate. In the liturgical reforms resulting from Vatican II, a new ministerial role emerged for the people we used to call our "ushers." The ushers were now designated as "ministers of hospitality." As a pastor, I urged our ushers to live up to this new ministerial role by greeting people warmly as they entered the church and by encouraging them to engage in friendly conversation before Mass with both parishioners and strangers alike. Many other pastors have so encouraged their ushers. But there remains a general reluctance among some of the ushers themselves to really accept that designated role. They seem to prefer the traditional role of showing people to an empty pew and taking up the collection.

I really believe that our problem is much deeper than the reluctance of our priests and ushers to make people welcome, though. I think the root of our rather unwelcoming church environment stems from a practice urged upon our people for centuries by church officials "from the pope on down." I refer to the practice of not talking in church. Talking in church about the people and events of our lives was seen as unholy. It was seen, in fact, as a sign of disrespect for Christ present in the Eucharist. Because of that, we urged people to use the time before Mass for private prayer and devotions. These practices were so ingrained in people over the years that many are literally shocked when they hear others "chatter" in church and feel the need to apologize, and sometimes confess it as a sin when they dare to say anything but prayers in church.

Please note that I don't blame these good people for feeling this way; they are only living by what they were taught (by me and others, but wrongfully in my opinion!) for the greater part of their lives. They believe it is the law of God and the church.

May I offer a suggestion for a possible beginning: could not we priests and other parish staff members mill about within the body of the church fifteen to twenty minutes before each Mass chatting with people as they come in, getting into light but warm conversations with them about the events of the previous or coming week; offering a welcome to those whom we do not recognize? It seems to me that if our people saw us doing this, they might be moved to participate in this effort to bring a welcoming atmosphere within the church. Then after Mass, we could all linger (inside!) a few minutes and wish each other well as we face another week of life reinvigorated by the warmth of Christ's life and love that we have just shared with one another.

And we really need *not* think that we are showing any irreverence to God or the Eucharist. On the contrary, we'd be giving witness to our faith in the presence of God in one another. We'd be demonstrating our living realization of Christ's presence "when two or three gather" in his name. We'd be showing our respect and love for God by showing love and respect to his daughters and sons (as Christ calls us). We'd be practicing our faith as a eucharistic people. And most important, we'd be welcoming in God's and our own names those who might not otherwise think we even care.

Without this kind of "scenario" before the formal celebration of the Mass begins and after it ends, we have lost one of the essential elements of Eucharist—that it is a gathering of people of Christian faith. With each person quietly entering a pew, kneeling in silent private prayer until the formal liturgy begins, and hardly noticing and seemingly not caring whether anyone else is there, and then hurrying out to beat the traffic at the end, we really do not have a gathering of faith-filled people, but rather what might be called a "bunch of warm bodies." I know we can do better than that. I think we should.

Should people socialize and talk when in church?

I was always taught that the church was a place to worship the Lord, and one should respect it as such by not talking unless necessary. The Mass I attend is like a social gathering—that is, before Mass starts, the people just talk almost like at a football game. Is that proper?

■ Answer

Indeed the church is "a place to worship the Lord"; so also is your home, your yard, a shopping center, a football stadium, a factory, an office, or anywhere else we people gather.

In other words, dear friend, the proper place to worship the Lord is everywhere, and we should be worshiping him every moment of our lives by everything we think, say, or do.

The church is a place where we gather to worship him in a very special way: as a Catholic Christian community, and specifically through the celebration of the Eucharist in keeping with the request of the Lord at the Last Supper when he told us to "Do this in memory of me." What is it that we are doing "in memory" of him? First, we gather, just as he and his disciples gathered for the Last Supper. Can you really imagine that they were in silent and individualized adoration of their God as they came into that room for the Last Supper? Of course they weren't! Like any group of people gathering they were talking to each other about what was happening in their lives. Maybe they were talking about the things Jesus was doing. Maybe about the problems with the Roman occupation of their country. Maybe about how good or bad the fishing had been lately. Maybe about their families. Or maybe even just about the weather. Who doesn't talk about the weather from time to time?

I can think of no more accurate and proper description of what a church should be like before Mass than the one you gave: a social gathering. Oh, I realize full well that you (and I!) were taught as children that we should not talk in church, and I must admit that I even confessed that as a sin in my younger days.

But Vatican II reformed and restored the Mass to more closely resemble that gathering which Jesus had with his followers. The church now teaches that the Mass, like all liturgical celebrations, is indeed a social gathering of Christians. As such it is not only proper, but also important that we "socialize" with each other as we gather. This helps the social aspect of the Mass be more than merely an artificial thing, but a true and worship-full expression of what we actually mean to each other. In the hand shaking, hugging, and visiting that goes on before Mass begins, we recognize that our daily relationship with each other is a most (perhaps *the* most!) important aspect of our communal and even individual relationship with God.

You see, dear friend, when we were taught in the past that we were not to talk in church, the church building was looked upon as a place for private prayer, and therefore something that goes on between an individual and God. Actually a much more proper place for that kind of prayer is our own bedrooms, a walk in the woods, the privacy of a Blessed Sacrament chapel, or some other more private place. But unless we go to church when there is no one else around, the church cannot be considered a place for private prayer.

I realize that for some of us who were reared with the idea that to talk in church was disrespectful to God (and in those days, there may have been good reason for that), it will take some time to overcome this idea. What we need to realize, though, is that this old idea is really rooted in a heresy known as Jansenism. That heresy is what kept so many of our parents, grandparents, and great grandparents from ever knowing the beauty, warmth, and true delight of full participation in every Mass we attend.

Jansenism was that horrid heresy that overemphasized the "unworthiness" of us humans to have a relationship or even be in the presence of God. It concluded that we weren't worthy to stand, much less speak, in the presence of God. It held that we weren't worthy to receive communion unless we had gone to confession immediately before Mass. As such, Jansenism failed to recognize one of the most basic teachings of Christ, which was that we humans are so important to God that God considered himself our Father and we his children.

Fortunately, the force and beauty of the truth as developed and taught by Vatican II has corrected these errors. Let us thank God that we can now share the vibrant beauty of our humanity as we gather in church to express our oneness with God and each other. No, let's not cut out the "socializing" in church; on the contrary, may it become more and more prevalent in our churches each time we gather as a Christian community to worship God by celebrating who and what we are.

Does the church have an official set of directives for liturgy?

I'm on my parish liturgical committee and thus am frequently involved in preparing parish liturgies (usually with others). Since none of the committee members have had formal training in liturgy, we must constantly seek the advice of our parish priests about various matters. They don't always agree on what is proper. Is there any one official set of directives put out by the church on what is or is not good liturgy?

■ Answer

Yours is not an unusual question, but it is a very important one. There really is no "one" official source because, in addition to the official books (such as the Sacramentary for Mass), the church has promulgated any number of official directives to supplement and sometimes update what is in the official liturgical books without at the same time issuing completely new and revised sets of directives. Perhaps, though, I can give you a few helpful suggestions.

The first two chapters of Vatican II's *Constitution on the Sacred Liturgy* is always a good place to begin an effort to comprehend the basics of good liturgy, since in those chapters the church outlines the highest ideals of good liturgy and also offers a number of practical steps toward implementing the new liturgy.

A firm foundation for good eucharistic liturgies cannot be attained unless we are thoroughly familiar with the Foreword and General Instruction of the Roman Missal, published in 1969. Another must is the Introduction to the Lectionary published in 1982 and contained in the revised lectionary now being used in parishes. Please understand, dear friend, that I am not saying here that you must follow each detailed step indicated in these books. What I'm saying is that these books give us the basis or foundation for what good eucharistic liturgies should be. But there is much room there for adaptation and for your own ingenuity and imagination, and also for "localizing" and "personalizing" the liturgy so that it will be meaningful and appropriate for the particular celebrating community for whom you are preparing it.

What is of extreme importance in these documents is the outlining and distinguishing of the roles of the various ministers of the eucharistic liturgy, as well as of the choir and the people "in the pews." So many liturgy planners lose sight of the diversity of these roles and the importance of this diversity, with the result that roles are combined and people shut out of their proper parts in the celebration. A most common error in this regard is allowing the choir to usurp the role of the congregation in singing various parts of the Mass. No matter how beautiful a "performance" might result from this, it is not beautiful *liturgy* unless and until each person or group of persons contributes properly to the unity in celebration. In other words, what might lack some musical quality might be much better and more beautiful liturgy if the singing is being done by those properly assigned to do it.

A number of additional general instructions on liturgical worship have also been issued by the church. Among them is the very important *Third Instruction on the Correct Application of the Constitution on the Liturgy,* which was published by the Congregation for Divine Worship in 1970; and the *Instruction Concerning Worship of the Eucharistic Mystery,* published in 1980. Then there is *Music in Catholic Worship,* published by the United

States bishops' conference in 1983, giving some good guidelines for music in our liturgies.

Finally, let me commend you for your obvious understanding of the importance of good liturgical celebrations and for the efforts you are making toward that goal. So many of us, even those of us in leadership positions, are often satisfied with the "humdrum" same old Sunday Mass week after week after week, whether or not it bears any resemblance to what a true eucharistic liturgy is supposed to be. Don't lose your enthusiasm: we, the church, need it—and you!

What is the place of music in the liturgy?

I've got a few questions about music in the liturgy. What is the official instrument of the church? Hasn't it been and shouldn't it continue to be the organ? Should we allow worldly music in the church, such as Nashville sound with strumming guitars, drums, piano, bass guitar, and featured vocalists throughout the service? Should we forget about or throw out Gregorian Chant? What is the fundamental songbook to be used in church? Should we emphasize entertainment and many non-professionals rather than prayer?

■ Answer

Whew! You've asked a complex and important question. I grew up in the seminary during the 40s and early 50s when the pipe organ, Gregorian chant, polyphony in Latin, and male choirs were the only approved forms of music within the liturgy. By the time of my ordination in 1954 I was convinced that nothing else was worthy of our sacred worship. It very much seems like you, dear friend, are precisely where I was then. Your series of questions suggests that you are reluctant to breathe the "breath of fresh air" with which Pope John XXIII tried to revive the sleeping church by calling Vatican II. It sounds as though you won't allow yourself to move forward with the church as she tries to implement liturgical reform and restoration.

Let's face it, friend, we cannot continue to live in the same past that enveloped us for hundreds of years and led, unfortunately, to an unrealistic church trying to insist that her people exercise their communal worship of God in a manner that was no longer meaningful to them. Yes, the organ was and is a magnificent musical instrument, and still plays a major role in liturgical music. But this does not mean that other musical instruments are not similarly appropriate for the expression of musical prayer (or prayerful music, if you will). Over the last 30 years or so, I have come to a much greater appreciation of what various other musical instruments can add to prayerful music. And I thank the church for officially recognizing this possibility and for encouraging modern composers of sacred music to offer to our liturgies a full course of musical instruments to enhance our liturgies.

I don't know what you consider "worldly" music. I do know that in the past anything "worldly" was officially frowned upon by the church. But (thank God!) we have grown within our church to realize that we live in the "world" and we are "of the world." We have reached the point, again thankfully, where we are beginning to learn that Christ did not come to reject the world, but rather perhaps to absorb it. And yes, to absorb it with all its God-given (or God-created) goodness and gifts, many of which are best expressed in the music which that same "world" produces.

I loved Gregorian Chant when I was in the seminary, and still do! But that beautiful chant is, in my opinion, inextricably tied to the Latin language and loses so much (frankly, almost everything!) in translation. For that reason, I find it very difficult to find a place for it in today's liturgy in the average Catholic parish. To impose the unfamiliar Latin tongue upon the prayer life of today's people is to take away from them the very purpose of liturgical prayer: the expression of the common faith of the community. I hope that Gregorian Chant will be preserved for our enjoyment and prayer in monasteries, seminaries, convents, and other religious establishments within the church.

An official song book for the church? Horrors, no! It would be a tragedy, I think, for the church to adopt any such collection of music as the only official hymnal. I have heard and sung some magnificent new pieces of liturgical music. So let's keep the doors and windows open so that we'll never be deprived of God's wondrous gifts to the musicians of our day.

No, we certainly do not want to stress "entertainment"; in fact, entertainment has no part in liturgical music. I might point out that the old Gregorian Chant was also sometimes just that, however. And unfortunately some (but certainly not all) professional musicians who participate in liturgies today give me the impression that they're more intent on entertaining than on praying.

The documents of Vatican II and subsequent official decrees on the liturgy emphasize the ultimate importance of *participation* by the worshiping community in *all* aspects of liturgical worship. Special stress is given to participation in music. I don't think we need "performing professionals" at our liturgy. I do think we need those professionals to help us bring liturgical music to the minds, hearts, and lips of all our people, so that they can properly express their prayer in song.

Would Christ object to using grape juice instead of wine?

Do you think Christ would object to the substitution of grape juice for wine at the Mass?

■ *Answer*

Some people cannot drink wine. Period. From the bottom of my heart, dear friend, I regret that many people seem insensitive to this, and do it in the name of Christ. This despite extremely eloquent testimony to the contrary in almost every chapter of each of the four gospels!

Indeed our faith is that Christ instituted the sacraments, and the gospels tell us he used wine at the Lord's Supper. But we don't read the text of these Scriptures literally, do we? If we did, then we would also have to insist that baptism by immersion (in the River Jordan, at that!) is the only valid method; that forgiveness of sins must be done by physical healing; that a bishop could only ordain by saying to a group of (probably married) men reclining around a table: "Do this in memory of me"; and so forth.

I certainly don't mean to suggest we should disregard the rich symbol of wine used at Mass. But Christ himself would certainly not have deprived anyone of this rich symbol. The Eucharist is Christ's gift to a living and loving community. Wouldn't it be tragic if we prevented anyone from participating fully on the basis of a technicality?

I am convinced that if you gave this matter serious thought in the light of what the message of Jesus Christ so strongly teaches (kindness, mercy, healing, forgiveness, peace, unity, and love), you would come to realize that no one, including alcoholics, should be deprived of the full impact of this "good news" of the gospel! And I hope that someday the law of the church will reflect that.

Is Christ present in a host received by a non-believer?

If a non-believer entered a church during Mass, joined the line for communion, and received communion, would Christ be present in the host the unbeliever received?

■ *Answer*

The official teaching of the church states that we Catholics believe that Christ is eucharistically, substantially, objectively, and really present in the consecrated bread and wine, regardless of the faith of the receiver. It is also the official teaching of the church that one who does not share our faith in the Eucharist cannot be considered to have shared in the faith dimension of receiving communion.

Your question reminds me of the "old theologians tale" about a mouse that gnawed its way into a tabernacle and ate all the hosts; the "theological" question was: "Did the mouse receive communion?" Of course, the answer is "no," despite the fact that we hold to our faith in the real presence of Christ in the consecrated bread in the tabernacle. The point of the story is to demonstrate that taking part in the Eucharist and receiving communion requires a faith-dimension that a mouse certainly lacks, and that is also lacking in the "nonbeliever" of your question.

Speaking about the eucharistic presence of Christ in this way, however, strikes me more as a magical thing than a matter of faith. What purpose does it serve to find a conclusive answer to such a question? If we're not careful, we could easily become superstitious about it. It's this kind of thinking that has surrounded the "sacred species" with an aura of glamour and glory and puts them in the almost "untouchable" category.

This attitude toward the Eucharist in the past had led to certain now-defunct regulations. For example, only priests and deacons could touch the "sacred vessels" or "sacred linens." If a host dropped on the floor, no one but a priest or deacon could pick it up. Chalices had to be made of—or at least plated in—gold.

In our much healthier outlook on the Eucharist today we give it no less glory, and we certainly approach it with no less faith. But today we realize that, while Christ is certainly present in the bread and wine, Christ is also present in the Word we break open at Mass, in the assembled faithful there to pray together, and in the priest who leads us.

Therefore, rather than consider the average person unworthy to touch the containers of the consecrated bread and wine, we invite everyone to take the host and chalice into their own hands before eating or drinking. There is a vitally important warmth and closeness in our attitude and relationship with Christ in the Eucharist that did not exist prior to the reforms following Vatican II. It's the kind of warmth that allows us to look upon Christ as our brother. Like us, Christ is a child of God. And like Christ, we now call God "Abba," Father.

Let us be ever thankful that Christ, present in the Eucharist, is again ours!

Why did the church discard the symbolism of breaking bread?

The gospels tell us that at the Last Supper Jesus broke bread, told the apostles how his body was to be broken, and asked them to remember his presence among them in the future whenever they would break bread during the meals they would continue to share out of love for one another as a community of brothers and sisters with one mind and one heart. Why did the church, somewhere along the line, discard this powerful symbol of Jesus' body being broken for us?

■ *Answer*

What a beautiful question! Frankly, I think your question is so well worded that it almost evokes its own answer from our church. Unfortunately, though, it may never be heard by the official teaching authority of our church, and thus the official answer may never arise. Alas, I must attempt my own answer.

In the course of the Dark and Middle Ages, the communitarian and paschal aspect of the Eucharist came to be de-emphasized, and the church's eucharistic focus was placed almost totally on the real presence of the "immaculate and perfect Son of God" in the spotless round "host" at the "miraculous" moment when the priest repeated the words of Jesus: "This is my body"; and in the consecrated wine contained in the golden and bejeweled chalice when the priest said: "This is my blood."

How better, we thought then, to demonstrate the presence of the Godhead in those elements than to lift them high precisely at that moment "amid trumpet blasts and cymbals and bells." And it is this emphasis of what is (at least essentially) our true faith that we have inherited today in that part of the Mass.

In all fairness to the ritual as we have inherited it, the separate consecration of bread and wine and the recognized presence of Christ under these separate species is meant to be symbolic of the death and therefore "brokenness" of the Lord. Similarly (and more effectively, I think), the "brokenness" is symbolized in the simultaneous and dramatic lifting of the separate species at the end of the eucharistic prayer ("Through him, with him, etc."), which, I think, would be a much more proper place for bells if we are to have them at all. But as you point out in your question, the symbolism seems to be lost in the perfection and spotlessness of the host, and the same could be said of the "richness" of most chalices containing the consecrated wine.

For this reason I strongly agree with those liturgical theologians (such as Fr. John Melloh, S.M., and Dr. Tad Guzie) who teach that what we know as the "elevation" in the Mass should be de-emphasized, and the church should reintroduce into the Mass what they call a strong and very obvious "Fraction (Breaking) Rite." If we could find a practical way to consecrate one loaf of bread and one cup (or container) of wine even at Sunday liturgies, and then, amid much fanfare, break the one loaf so that it can be eaten by all; and then pour out from the one container of wine several cups to be shared by all, then the full impact of the broken and emptied reality of the sacrificed Christ could more readily be experienced at our Masses by those who are committed by their Christianity to that same "brokenness" for others.

Yes, we do have a remnant of a fraction rite in our Mass at present. It takes place during the singing or praying of the "Lamb of God" prior to the distribution of communion. Unfortunately, we priests have a tendency to almost hide the breaking of the host and allow the words being said or sung to occupy the forefront of the assembly's attention.

Actually, the "Lamb of God" is supposed to be an "accompanying" song to the "breaking of the bread" and the "pouring of the wine." While I do not begin to suggest that this almost insignificant and brief rite is sufficient to demonstrate what you so beautifully and properly derived from the gospel accounts of the "brokenness" of Christ in the Eucharist, I do think it would help if we priests dramatized the breaking by lifting the consecrated bread in full view of the people, breaking it clearly in their sight, and replacing it on the altar in its broken form. Likewise, when we do share the cup with the faithful at Mass, we should at this point of the Mass dramatize the pouring out of the consecrated wine into the several cups that might be used.

In the New Testament, the words consecration" or "elevation" are never used in connection with the celebration of the Eucharist. It is usually called "The Breaking of the Bread." With you, I'd love to see more evidence of that in our Mass today.

When did magic enter the eucharistic celebration?

I'm curious to know when all the "magic" entered into the eucharistic celebration. On the night before he died, when Jesus broke the bread in the usual Hebrew fashion, he asked his followers that whenever they did this same ritual during a special meal, they recall his own body being broken and destroyed for their sakes. There was nothing magical about that. When the early Christians celebrated Eucharist after his death they simply "devoted themselves to the apostles' instruction and the communal life, to the breaking of bread and the prayers" (Acts 2:42). Again, no magician zapping Jesus' body down from heaven. What was important to them was that they experienced his presence in their midst during that ritual—as if he were actually there.

Feeling the presence of someone we love is a profound experience. A love letter, a souvenir, a photograph—the presence of one of these objects is the presence of the loved one. A relationship exists there, a spirit, a force. We hold these precious items close to us as if we were actually holding that person, bodily.

I don't think priests are magicians; the apostles and early Christians were not. Styles of living can be improved throughout the centuries, but how could the church have changed that simple, symbolic ritual Jesus himself gave us into something that bears no resemblance to it now? We have to get back to seeing and hearing bread being broken on the altar, recalling Jesus' body being broken, and becoming aware again of his presence among us out there in the pews.

■ *Answer*

Were it not for a couplet of little two-letter words that appear twice in your letter: "as if," and your use of the souvenir concept to describe the eucharistic presence, I think I would have confined my response to another quite familiar little colloquial couplet: "'nuff said!" You express some magnificently beautiful and meaningful insights into the real Eucharist.

You see, dear friend, I thoroughly agree with you that we priests are not magicians and that no magic takes place at Mass. I agree, too, that the apostles were not magicians and that a clear expression of the brokenness of Christ for all humanity is an essential element of the Eucharist. However, I must point out my conviction and that of the church (which I think is yours also despite the weakness of human language) that we are, in the Eucharist, celebrating our experience of the real presence of Christ—not "as if" he were actually there, but precisely because our faith-experience assures us that he *is* actually there. The risen Christ is present, really and truly present, within the Christian community. Because that is true and because he asked us to "Jewishly" remember (which means make present again) and express our faith in that presence by breaking, pouring, eating, and drinking bread and wine, he is indeed truly present in that eucharistic action. So again it's not "as if" he were there; he actually *is* there.

While I very much appreciate your drawing a simile between the presence of Christ in the Eucharist and relating it to the presence of loved ones brought about by souvenirs, photographs, and remembering profound experiences, I think that this simile is valid only if we use it as a "stepping stone" to the total faith-reality of the real presence of Christ in the Eucharist. Despite the fact that it "limps" in the need to use "as if" to express the quality of presence produced by those remembrances, the similarity is there and all we need do is go beyond that and realize that even that does not express it all.

After all, it is a mystery, and by that I do not mean that we cannot understand it, but rather that we are still reaching, and will continue to do so until the end of time. We are reaching out with the probes of our faith to gather up from the depths of this faith-reality all of the greatness and goodness that it contains. Your reaching is, therefore, valid! Reach on!

Shouldn't people kneel after receiving communion?

I've noticed lately in our parish Masses that many people sit down immediately when they return to their pews after receiving communion. I'm 60 years old, and I was taught as a child that the respectful thing to do after receiving communion is to kneel down and thank the Lord for coming to us. What's going on now in our parish seems disrespectful to me! After all, our God is in us at that precious moment, and it seems to me that we should be kneeling and adoring him instead of sitting down and just looking around at who's going to communion after us. What do you think?

■ *Answer*

I think that it's perfectly natural and very much in order that we return to our places and *sit* after receiving communion. However, I certainly do not fault you for feeling the way you do about this, because, just like you, I was taught as a child that the proper posture before, during, and after communion was kneeling!

But let's reconsider the whole matter for a moment. When you and I were children, our entire church, but especially the church in this part of the world, was really steeped in customs that had their foundation, not so much in church doctrine, but rather in a heresy known as "Jansenism." In part this led to a highly exaggerated idea of how "unworthy" we were to be in the presence of God, of Jesus Christ, of the saints, and, yes, even of church officials such as priests and bishops. That was a frightfully unfortunate development in our church. The church, after all, sprang from the beautifully *opposite* concept that, in Jesus Christ, God revealed that he is very much present not only in our world, but *within our very selves*.

We may be unworthy, but not in God's eyes! God has chosen to overlook that! It's hard for us to imagine such magnificent and boundless mercy and love!

Through the teachings of Jesus, we are able to look upon God as a loving and intimate "Father," who doesn't live in some distant "heaven" light years away from us. No, Jesus opened our eyes to see that God lives in the very fiber of our being. Christ did not come to rule over us, but to be one of us. He wants us to look upon him much more as a brother than as "Lord and God." He tried to teach us the great dignity that we all share as human beings. We are, after all, created "in the image and likeness of God."

But somehow over the centuries, we Christians lost sight of this and concentrated almost entirely on the divinity and lordship of Christ. As the centuries went by, we have distanced ourselves from him by looking beyond his humanity and always thinking and speaking of him as God. There were myriad reasons for this, but most of the blame can probably be placed squarely on the backs of church leaders over the centuries. Many priests, bishops, and popes came to look upon themselves as better than the "average" Christian. Thus they began to horde for themselves any sort of intimacy with God or Jesus Christ.

It was in this atmosphere that the practices that we were taught as children came to be known as the only "proper" way to relate to God and Jesus Christ. Thus it was only natural that while we clergy did stand during and after communion, the laity were taught to kneel, as though they were unworthy of anything else.

Even in the aftermath of Vatican II, which did so much to counteract the Jansenist practices that infected the church, we still have some remnants of them. Did you ever notice at concelebrated Masses (where there are several priests participating) that, after we priests have received communion, we return to our places and are *seated* immediately; while at that same Mass, the laity return to their places and *kneel* until the communion rite has been completed? How odd! Because at that point in the Mass we are certainly more equal than not! Christ doesn't have favorites, even if they're ordained.

Communion, after all, is the ultimate expression of unity with each other in Christ.

Can sinners be eucharistic ministers?

My wife and I are eucharistic ministers. However, we don't agree with (or obey) the pope and the church authority in several areas. Our disagreement (dissent?) does not cause us discomfort in our role as eucharistic ministers, nor as members of our faith community. We do feel, though, that the "church" would not approve of us. Given the choice, I think we would rather give up our ministry than compromise our principles in the matters where we disagree with church authority. Can you clarify the church's stand on this kind of situation?

■ *Answer*

From the contents of your letter, I am relatively certain that you are fully and totally dedicated to living a Catholic Christian life to the point that you would give up this very fruitful ministry if you felt that the church demanded it. I really don't think that the church would demand that of you, however. I won't even try to determine for you whether your "dissent" and "disobedience" are morally wrong or not. That is something that I must leave to your informed conscience and perhaps to personal counseling. But even if I could judge that you were guilty of sin in the matter, I could never rightfully conclude that you are, therefore, unworthy to participate in this ministry.

You see, dear friend, if the church required sinlessness of anyone who performed some ministry within the church, not one human being on this earth would qualify for church ministry. I sincerely hope, for instance, that no participants in a Mass where I am the presider think for one minute that I am innocent of sin, or that I am more worthy of being the presider at this celebration than the worst sinner in that congregation.

At the very outset of the Mass, each of us clearly and openly acknowledges our sinfulness. This is no mere pious gesture! It is a real and incontrovertible fact!

If those to whom you are ministering the Eucharist do not understand or cannot accept that, then they need to understand better the true meaning of the Eucharist. You see, at Mass we celebrate the presence of Christ in all of us sinners. And, more important, we accept his presence in us! In this we are fully aware that he brings with him into our hearts and lives, those very people sitting around us who have just acknowledged their own sinfulness. The Christ of the Eucharist is not just Jesus of Nazareth; the Christ of the Eucharist is the entire Body of Christ, which includes all us sinners.

May God continue to bless you and those to whom you minister.

Do we need saints and priests to communicate with God?

I think of devotion to Mary and the saints as an option, but by no means a requirement for my communication with God. Would this be grounds for exclusion from the church? Also, I believe that ultimately everyone has a direct line to God and that my own in-depth search and spiritual journey ultimately requires no priest. Can I still be a Catholic if I don't attend Mass?

■ Answer

The church does not consider having devotion to Mary or the saints a "requirement" for communication with God—or even for enhancing that communication. Indeed the church, very rightfully I am firmly convinced, has always encouraged us to honor, pray to, and emulate our Blessed Mother in view of the major role she played in the life of Christ. He is, after all, the one by whom and on whom the church is founded. We also honor her because of her exemplary life. Similarly, the church encourages us to honor, pray to, and emulate those who have been officially recognized as "saints" because of their having lived exemplary Christian lives.

But we must not conclude from this that the church is somehow telling us that we cannot or should not communicate directly with God. On the contrary, it is one of the oldest teachings of the church, based upon the gospel accounts of the public ministry of Jesus, that "when you pray, you are to say, 'Our Father...'." We are invited to address God personally, with familiarity like that which exists between a parent and child. This would hardly support any thought that Mary, or the saints, or anyone for that matter, could possibly be considered by the church as "required" channels of communication between Catholics and God. Therefore, if an individual such as yourself does not find it possible or desirable to pray to the saints, there is no teaching or law of the church that requires you to do so.

Your question about the importance and necessity of participation in the Mass as a requirement for Catholics gives evidence of some misunderstanding of the role of the priest and the nature of the Mass. You see, dear friend, the Mass is not a mediation between us and God. And we priests are not mediators or lines of communication between Catholics and God! As stated above, all of us can very readily communicate directly with God: for that purpose we need no priest; we need no Mass.

Catholic teaching is that the Mass is a "gathering" of people with a common faith. At Mass we are intimately related in the Christian faith. This gathering is for the purpose of expressing, celebrating, and strengthening this bond of unity and faith as Jesus asked us to at his own Last Supper. "Do this in memory me," he said. And so we do!

The priest at this gathering is not our "mediator." He is the "presider." He is the official representative of the entire, universal church. When we gather with a priest like this, along with the Word and the Bread and Cup, what happens is like nothing else in human existence. Christ is present in the assembly, in the priest, in the word, and in the consecrated bread and wine. Quite a miracle indeed!

Now, while it's certainly true that we all have our "direct line to God," it's also true that we are social beings. We need to relate to other humans as we pursue our purpose and goals in life. Further, this "direct line to God" is invariably and essentially embroiled in our relationship with each other and with all creation. In other words, dear friend, we cannot live in a vacuum as though only "God and I" existed. For us to live at all requires the relationships and support of family, friends, neighborhood, and a "community of faith." We call this community of faith, "the church." It is this set of relationships that calls us Catholics to Mass.

At Mass we do communicate with God, not only with our own "direct line" but also within the "communications network" of what we know as liturgical eucharistic prayer.

No, the Mass is not our "pipeline" to God. It is our gift from Jesus Christ. It is a marvelous gift and a challenging responsibility. Let us thank God that we have it.

What do you think of "priestless Sundays"?

My question is about Sunday liturgy without a priest. A friend of mine in Texas says that it happens in their area, and this confuses me. How are such services performed without a priest? Is a layperson allowed to read the gospel, give a homily, and follow the exact format as an ordained priest, excluding only the consecration?

■ *Answer*

Your friend in Texas is obviously already facing what Catholics have long faced in places like South America, Africa, and China. An increasing number of places in the United States have also been facing "priestless Sundays" for some time. Don't think it won't happen soon in your own diocese. The shortage of priests is not a rumor; it's a matter of fact.

Under such circumstances, the church encourages people to try to participate at a Mass in another parish if that isn't too difficult. Barring that, a leader in the parish (it could be a deacon, a religious sister or brother, or any layperson) would be assigned by the bishop to conduct a service for the benefit of the people on Sundays when no priest can be there for Mass. What are these services and what is included in them?

Well, first of all, we must make it clear that they are not Masses, since our church requires that Mass may not be celebrated unless there is an ordained priest there to preside. Usually there is common prayer, readings from Scripture, a homily on the Scripture passages given by the one assigned to lead the celebration, and usually the distribution of communion. Please understand, though, that this is not meant to be considered (and is not!) a priestless "Mass," or a "Mass with everything but the consecration." As I have already indicated, it is simply not a Mass at all. In fact, those who plan and lead these services are advised to arrange them in such a way that they would not parallel the Mass sufficiently to be considered a "Mass with the consecration left out."

In other words, it should be clear from the very nature of and procedure within the celebration that what this congregation is doing at that moment is something other than the Mass. Thus, for instance, while it might be quite appropriate to use the identical readings assigned by the church for Masses that day, I think it would be inappropriate to use the same prayers and rites as in the Mass (such as the opening prayer, prayer over the gifts, and closing prayers, the prayers and rite of the "preparation of the gifts," and certainly not the eucharistic prayer).

On the other hand it would be quite appropriate to use the usual format of the communion rite in the Mass in the distribution of holy communion, since if all else is done properly as indicated above, it should be quite clear to all by that time that they are indeed at something other than the Mass.

Having said all this, then, let me add that these "priestless" services should not be considered as useless, nor as simply another form of private prayer. After all, the community is gathered there, and therefore Christ is there "in the midst of them," just as surely and just as really as if it were a Mass. He promised us as much! Further, the individuals of the community gathered share themselves and Christ with each other by their presence, by their prayer, by their song, and through receiving communion.

In other words, there is a real religious dynamic taking place there. This "priestless" service, while not a Mass, is certainly not something to be just ignored in the absence of the Mass. We are gathering in his name; and that is magnificent within itself. We cannot fully abide at that moment with his request that we "do this (the Eucharist) in memory of" him. But we are remembering him; and remembering him well!

Can we go back to the old ways?

I've been a Catholic for many, many years, and I don't like any change. I hate the changes in the Mass and wish we would all go back to the Latin Mass and quit all that noisy singing with guitars and all that. Why can't we just have a beautiful organ and choir to listen to while we pray at Mass and follow the Mass in our missals like we used to? Also, I hope I never see a woman priest. That will be the end of my religion, or at least I'll find another church to go to. Why can't things be like they always were?

■ *Answer*

Dear, dear friend, by the way you worded your question you seem to be a rather elderly person who was taught the faith (as I was!) by the example of your parents, by memorizing the questions and answers in a catechism book, and by listening to "hellfire and brimstone" sermons at Mass or at those old parish missions of yesteryear. Realizing all that, I can and do feel for you and hope that somehow our faith and the way it is carried out and celebrated at Mass now can be meaningful and helpful to you in your remaining years with us.

The church, which is all of us who make it up, owe so very much to the very history to which you are holding on so dearly, and to good and faithful people like yourself who keep reminding us of our roots. So please know that what I write here in response to your questions and statements is in no way meant as criticism of you or anyone who may share your views.

Like you, I grew up with the definite view that the church does not and cannot change. I can even remember being taught that in school. Probably this impression was taught because there indeed was relatively little change and development in the teachings and laws of the church for the 400 years or so before our lifetime, that is, since the Council of Trent in the sixteenth century. For the three and a half centuries before this one, there was no one alive who could remember many significant changes in the teachings of the church, in the laws of the church, in the manner the sacraments were received or celebrated, or in the Mass which was then (and continues to be for many today) the main point of contact with the church.

But it was not always so! All we need do is read a little church history and we will find that the church of our youth and of the last four centuries was far different from the church of the first, or the third, or the sixth, or the tenth, or the twelfth, or the fourteenth, or the fifteenth, or even of the early part of the sixteenth century. The Catholics of those early centuries would not even have recognized much of what we became during the last four centuries before Vatican II.

For instance, Greek was the official language of the early church long before Latin took over. At the beginning there were no church buildings as we know them today. There were no tabernacles. Even the rosary did not come into existence until the thirteenth century. The sacrament of penance did not take the form we grew up to learn as "confession" until the eleventh and twelfth centuries. The requirement of priestly celibacy was not even heard of in the very early church, and became mandatory in the Western or "Latin" church only in the twelfth century. Even today, our "Roman Catholic Church" still allows (or approves) marriage for priests in the "Eastern Rites" of the church, which, by the way, are just as "Catholic" as we are.

What I'm getting at here is that change has been an absolutely essential part of what has become the Catholic church today. It really cannot ever be "like it always was" because it just was not always any particular way. Without change, we would never have had our Apostles and Nicene Creeds; without change, we would not have any church laws; without change, we would never have had the Latin Mass. Without change, we would never have had our church buildings. Without change, we would never have had dioceses or parishes. Without change, we would never have had our Catholic schools. Without change, we would never have had priests, or nuns, or brothers. Without change, we would never have had novenas, and the rosary, and devotion to the Blessed Mother. Without change, we would never have had a pope in Rome. And I could go on and on and on.

With the Second Vatican Council, the church has vigorously promoted again the process of change and development that had lain almost dormant for the four previous centuries.

Whether that development will ever lead us to recognize and accept the call of women to the priesthood, I really don't know, but I am fully confident that this will not happen in your or my lifetime. If and when it does come, I sincerely hope that our Catholic people of that time can see this as another giant step forward within our church, the same kind of giant forward step that, over the last 2,000 years, brought us the kind of changing and developing church that we love so dearly now.

Must we become like Protestants after Vatican II?

I really find our church hard to take since the Second Vatican Council. Ever since then all we get is change, change, change—and more change! I'm sick of all these changes, especially the ones that we "stole" from the Protestants. And I'm not alone, believe me! Not all of us want to be "Protestant Catholics." I grew up learning about novenas lasting nine hours or nine days and always getting good results. Now most parishes don't even have any novenas, and some have banned them. Why should it be that way?

■ Answer

Dear friend, I wish I could arrange a personal visit with you at your home so I could share with you some of the magnificent joys and hopes that I and many other Catholics have experienced precisely because of the changes in the church that seem to be causing you and (as you so correctly state) many others so much distress. I say it would take a personal visit because when someone is hurting as you seem to be, just hearing it in a sermon or homily, or reading it in a newspaper or magazine just doesn't seem to get to the "heart" of the matter.

And there (that is, in the "heart") is where the crux of the matter lies. I am relatively certain that no words I might use here and no homily or sermon that you might hear in your parish would effectively help you to understand and feel comfortable with, much less appreciate, the changes in the church and its liturgy resulting from the Second Vatican Council.

But if someone who has experienced the beauty, warmth, and joy of the changes in our new liturgy, especially if it is someone whom you love and respect, would have the opportunity and the ability to share with you his or her own experiences, perhaps such a personal touch would reach through to what is obviously your beautiful heart, to your steadfast faith, and you too could begin experiencing the real value of the new liturgy in our church. But since such a personal visit doesn't seem possible, I can only write a few words here that perhaps might lead you to seek out someone who does appreciate our modern liturgy and can help you to share our joy in it.

First, may I very kindly and respectfully point out that you were probably misled by well-meaning parents, priests, or religious to think that before Vatican II prayers offered nine times (called novenas) would somehow be more effective than those offered once, or twice, or three, five, or ten times. The fact is, there never really was anything "magical" or miraculous about saying or doing prayers nine times. God listens to us out of love, no matter how many times we pray.

It's true that our church has for centuries encouraged "novenas" (and still does!), and the purpose of that was to encourage *perseverance* in prayer, not to establish a way to insure results. But because the very word "novena" is inextricably tied in with the number "nine," people only naturally concluded, even when they were told otherwise (which was rare, unfortunately!), that there was a value in doing something precisely nine times, and even that doing it nine times was almost a guarantee that we would be granted whatever we might be petitioning of God in the novena.

The Second Vatican Council really did not change the value of devotions such as novenas; nor did it even discourage them. What the Council did and what the church has done since then is to place proper emphasis on the official liturgies of the church, and in particular the celebration of the Eucharist. Then in their zeal to help people understand and accept this proper emphasis, many zealous priests and religious leaders perhaps went a bit too far and almost completely dropped any type of unofficial or non-liturgical devotions from the life or schedule of the parish church. But these devotions really still have the same value as they always did. The problem is that they used to be over-emphasized, and perhaps they are now under-emphasized.

Let us hope that the spirit of Vatican II will bring about the *proper* emphasis on such devotions.

Baptism and Original Sin

Do we still believe in original sin?

I read in a parish bulletin an item entitled "Renewal of Faith," in which the writer poses the question, "What is Baptism?" and goes on to explain: "...through baptism, we believe that original sin (which is passed on from generation to generation) is removed and that we are welcomed into the body of believers known as Christians."

Frankly, I am quite disturbed by such statements, especially in "official" church publications. I didn't think this old, outdated kind of theology was still being taught. And even more unfortunately, parishioners are invited to partake of more of this "high cholesterol" theological diet during one-hour seminars at the church on specified dates and times.

Would you kindly comment on the church's theology vis-à-vis baptism and "original" sin?

■*Answer*

Well, here we go again! Another one of my dear friends is inviting me to sit on the end of a dying tree branch and saw it off between the trunk and myself. But here goes, as I pray with the temptations of Jesus in mind, asking (as he refused to do!) that his angels come and support me that I "may never stumble on a stone!"

There has been, for centuries, so much readily available fundamentalist "junk" about what we have come to call "original sin" that it's almost impossible to respond briefly. You see, dear friend, what you read in the parish bulletin can also be read in thousands of old, new, and still being written Catholic theology books, newspapers, and magazines. It has been, is being, and will be heard in Catholic classrooms, homilies, and at many mothers' knees. And do you know why? Because that statement is a true statement! It's even an accurate statement of a truth that has been part of Catholic faith since its inception, and part of Jewish faith even before that.

The problem is not that it is *false*. The problem is that most people read and understand this statement in its literal or *fundamentalist* sense. That makes this understanding of a traditional doctrine of our church extremely detrimental to faith itself, and particularly to our faith in what humanity really is.

According to the doctrine of our church, "original sin" is not and cannot be something that we "inherit" in conception. Original sin is not something "in the genes" of our parents; it is not a "stain" on our parents' soul (or body, for that matter!) that can be passed on like racial characteristics, hair or skin color, etc. It is not something "generated" in the human reproduction process. But that's what the words used in your parish bulletin (and thousands of other places) make it sound like.

To understand the sacred truth contained in those words we've got to look behind our tradition and find there the "Word of God." What is the sacred truth behind those *imperfect* human words? Perhaps it could be expressed this way: Every person is born into a human family damaged by sin, and each of us is affected by that damaged human condition. Each of us is inclined toward darkness. Each of us is sometimes caught up in sinfulness. Baptism is the celebration of our entrance into the saving mystery of the Christ event. Through it we accept our place within the Body of Christ, sometimes called "the church." In the church we are "reborn" into the "new Adam," the new humanity, the new human condition of grace. This grace changes that part of the human condition that leans toward darkness. It leads us to the Light, Christ the Lord.

But you see, dear friend, our entrance into human life was not "stained" with the guilt of our "first parents." We were not "guilty" of anything, and so even if the guilt of sin could properly be described as a "stain on the soul" (and it cannot!), there would never have been (by Catholic doctrine) such a "stain" to be "removed."

So, has our church "debunked" the doctrine of original sin since Vatican II? Of course not! What she did do, however, was ask us to look beyond the words expressing that doctrine to the beauty of the truth that lies behind them. I hope these few words help you do that, too.

Was St. John the Baptist born without sin?

In a recent homily our pastor said that St. John the Baptist was born without original sin, because he was absolved from it while still in his mother's womb. I've been a Catholic all my life and I don't remember ever having heard this teaching before; nor have several of my friends ever heard of it. My understanding was that Christ instituted the sacrament of baptism, which removes all sin. How could John have been cleansed before the coming of Christ?

■ *Answer*

First let me say, dear friend, that I have never heard of such a teaching either. However, in discussing your question with some acquaintances of mine, I learned that each of them remembered being told in their childhood about an ancient legend that St. John was freed from original sin when he leapt in his mother's womb in the "visitation" scene of the infancy narrative of St. Luke's gospel. How I missed this legend in all my years of Catholic education I don't know, but we must recognize that it is no more than that: a legend!

We should also realize that the entire infancy narrative in Luke's gospel is not meant to be factual history, but a narrative created by the early Christian community to teach us something of what it means to believe in Christ as the risen Lord. Our church does not teach that the conception and birth of Jesus actually happened as it is literally narrated in this gospel story. Therefore, it certainly would not be a "teaching of our church" that this legend about John the Baptist is a historical fact, since it is based on something that itself is not taught by the church as a historical fact.

Second, dear friend, you refer to the sacrament of baptism as the agent for "removing" or "cleansing" from original sin, as though this sin were some sort of physical appendage that needs removal (like a tonsillectomy), or a stain that had to be cleaned away at a given point in time. Unfortunately, many of us older Catholics grew up with that concept of baptism and original sin through our study of the *Baltimore Catechism*, the basic religion text of the time, and many of us still cling to that description as though it were the teaching of the church.

But you see it just isn't that way, and never really was! While it is possible to use words in that way to teach what the truth is, we must not fall into the trap of thinking that those words were themselves the truth.

Baptism indeed is the sacrament in which we celebrate in an effective way Christ's victory for each individual over the state of sin existing in the world in which we are born. It is this "sinfulness of humanity" that we call original sin. Each of us is certainly born into that, and each of us would suffer from it much more than we do had Christ not won his victory over sin for us. But original sin is not something that any individual is guilty of or needs forgiveness for; it is not something that is attached to us that needs to be removed, or a stain that needs to be washed away.

When we used to say that baptism "removes" or "takes away" original sin, all we were really saying is that the Christ-event (his life, passion, death, and resurrection) won a victory for each of us over this "state of sin" in the world, and in baptism we "realize" (make real) in our individual lives that his victory is our victory! In baptism, then, it can be properly said that original sin is overcome; it is removed; it is gone. Our world is no longer a world of sin, but a world of grace!

Now to ask whether it was possible for John the Baptist to be born without original sin prior (in time) to the coming of Christ is simply to ask the wrong question. You see, dear friend, St. John certainly participated somehow (as did the people before him) in the victory over sin won by Jesus Christ. We really don't know (and it really doesn't matter) at what point in his life this victory became effective for him and for others before him. We do know that God does not have to depend on time to "straighten things out." He lives and acts independently of time.

Therefore, if the Christ-event constituted or accomplished the victory of humanity over original sin (and all sin), then God can (and did!) make that victory as effective in the lives of those who came before Christ as for those who came after him. At what historical moment in the life of John did this take place? I assure you, no one knows! Did it take place? You bet it did, just as surely as it does for you and me! And that, dear friend, is the beauty of our faith!

Confirmation

What happens if you refuse to be confirmed?
Is it true that if you refused to be confirmed when it was made available to you as a teenager that you can no longer marry in the church or receive the last rites?

■ *Answer*
The theology of the sacrament of confirmation is rather vague, especially when it is separated from the other "sacraments of initiation," namely baptism and the Eucharist. To some it represents the maturing of an individual in the faith; to others it is the personal commitment of the individual to active membership in the faith; to others it is the personal ratification or acceptance of the commitment made for one by one's parents at baptism; for others it represents the so-called "baptism in the Spirit."

All these concepts are all well within the official teaching of the church. For myself, I am not absolutely sure which one of these I would adhere to, and probably it would be a combination of them all. Each of them has its place under the circumstances of each individual's life. So it would be rather difficult for me to make a presentation on this sacrament that would be meaningful or helpful to any number of people.

On the other hand, I think I can very readily respond to the practical questions you pose about it. First of all, confirmation is not required by the church before marriage or before the last rites of the church can be received. And, although you didn't ask this, it is not required for Christian burial, either. Confirmation has always been a sacrament that an individual must be allowed to choose to receive or not receive, with no penalties ever being attached to not receiving it.

It is true, however, that the church strongly encourages the faithful to accept this sacrament. Over the course of my life, it has been given at various stages of life. I received it when I was in the sixth grade; it later was given to children in the fourth grade; later it even went down to the second grade; then it was returned to the sixth grade; then it went up to the seventh; then the eighth; then the ninth; in our diocese now, it is given in the tenth grade; in some places it was and is being given in the twelfth grade. All of this "movement" from one grade to another is representative of the various theologies of this sacrament.

There are those who advocate that confirmation should be reserved to adulthood, or at the minimum age of 21. Others, however, feel (and I tend to agree with them) that the celebration of this sacrament should not be confined to age or school grade levels. These believe that it should be totally optional as to whether or when it is received. Under this notion, there would be no more so-called confirmation classes. Rather, when an individual felt ready to ask for confirmation, he or she would petition the Christian community for this privilege. Provided there were no obstacles in the way, this individual would become a candidate for this sacrament at the next celebration of it in that community.

Under such a system it is rather obvious, I think, that many, and perhaps a majority, of our people would never be confirmed. I really see nothing tragic about that. I believe the present system produces a much greater tragedy. People now receive this sacrament because of parental, peer, or community pressure. Some even receive it out of the same misguided fears you have had—about not being able to marry or be buried in the church.

However, if it were received by personal choice, then its recipients would experience it in a more favorable and Spirit-filled way. Also, the celebrations of this sacrament would take on an entirely new significance for the local parish. All who participate in the celebration of confirmation would do so in support of the free choice of each candidate. And the assembled community would joyfully support its decision to grant their request and accept them as confirmed Catholics.

Reconciliation

Why do we have to tell our sins to a priest?

Why is it we have to go to confession and tell a priest exactly what we have done before God can forgive our sins?

■ *Answer*

I can't answer "why" this is so, precisely because it is *not* so! There is no doubt whatsoever that God offers us loving forgiveness long before we even think about going to confession, and it has been the consistent teaching of our church that there are many means other than confession by which our sins can be forgiven. I hold firmly to the belief (and I think this is really what our church teaches) that God is so loving a Father that he offers us forgiveness at the very moment that we fall into sin, and that he never withdraws that offer. All we need do to actually be forgiven by God is to "let his forgiveness in," that is, open our hearts to his offer of forgiveness and just let it be ours.

Please understand, dear friend, that I am not saying that we do not have to submit our sins to the great ministry of healing in the sacrament of reconciliation. That sacrament for us is a vital part of God's whole plan of reconciling us to himself and each other in and through Jesus Christ. In fact, it seems to me that this process of reconciliation (more frequently called redemption) is what Christ came into the world to do. He came to teach us by his own life, death, and resurrection that our God was and is a loving God; a forgiving God; a God who "does not count our transgressions against us" (2 Corinthians 5:19); a God who forgets the evils of the past, and who holds his arms out to us constantly in loving, embracing forgiveness (remember the Prodigal Son?).

But you see, dear friend, God wants us to be like him in all things. He creates us in his own image and likeness. He wants us to share this loving, forgiving characteristic of his, and to transfer this forgiveness to each other. St. Paul puts it so beautifully in 2 Corinthians 5:17–20: "The old order has passed away; now all is new! All this has been done by God, who has reconciled us to himself through Christ and has given us the ministry of reconciliation. I mean that God, in Christ, was reconciling the world to himself, not counting our transgressions against us, and that he has entrusted the message of reconciliation to us. This makes us ambassadors for Christ, God as it were appealing through us."

Does that sound like a God who doesn't forgive us until we go to confession? I certainly don't see it that way! What it is saying, though, is that we, the church, as ambassadors and assigned ministers of reconciliation, use this sacrament to exercise that ministry and to proclaim effectively the "message of reconciliation" entrusted to us by God. In and through the sacrament of reconciliation we, the church, become what God wants us to be. We become like him by bringing to each other, through this sacrament, his loving message of reconciliation and forgiveness.

So, dear friend, while we might not do our part in the whole process of forgiveness until we participate in the sacrament of reconciliation, we do not believe that God must wait on anything or anyone, and certainly not on one of our sacraments, in order to give us forgiveness. But one of the reasons the sacrament of reconciliation is so important is precisely because in it we experience (make our own) that very forgiveness by which God constantly forgives our sins.

What about those who confess to God only?
I have a friend whose 15-year-old son, born and raised a Catholic, has decided he doesn't have to go to confession anymore. He feels he can just confess to God. What do you think of this?

■ *Answer*

If the 15-year-old son of your friend had been living in the time of Jesus, or probably any time in the first few centuries of the church's existence, he would have had no choice but to "confess to God." Confessing one's sins to a priest was unheard of at that time. It is only because there have been changes, many and constant changes, in the church over the centuries that it finally became a common practice and then a law that we confess our sins to a priest in the process of celebrating what has become the sacrament of penance or reconciliation.

I think it is highly unfortunate that this great sacrament, through which we are meant to celebrate and share with each other the infinite, unbounded, and ever loving mercy of our God, has evolved over the last few centuries to the point that we have come to call it "confession." It is true that confession of one's sins is part of the process whereby this sacrament is celebrated. Under the current discipline of the church it is an essential requirement for our participation in the celebration, but the confession of our sins is certainly not the principal component of what takes place in this sacrament.

Similarly, the practice and teaching of the church over the last few centuries (although this is not and was never the official teaching of the church) has led most of us, especially before Vatican II, to believe that God offers forgiveness of our sins only if and when we confess them individually in the sacrament of penance and that serious (or so-called "mortal") sins would not be forgiven by God at all unless and until they were "confessed."

The fact of the matter is that the consistent official teaching of the church, founded upon the gospels themselves, is that God's loving mercy and forgiveness is *never* withheld from us, even at the moment of the most serious sin that we might commit. In the sacrament of reconciliation this magnificent truth is brought home to us. There we celebrate this forgiveness. And there the church officially makes God's forgiveness her own. The church officially conveys her forgiveness to us within the context of the Christian community. The church officially declares and celebrates our acceptance of that forgiveness. And, very important, I think, the church gives us an opportunity to celebrate our forgiveness of each other.

In that sense it's quite true to say that in the celebration of this sacrament we "receive" forgiveness. It is also true that by church law we are required to submit seriously sinful or "mortal" sins to this sacramental celebration before receiving other sacraments. But church law does *not* say that such sins cannot be or are not forgiven until we do so.

So, what do I think of your friend's son and his decision to "confess to God"? I think it is rather unfortunate that he has lost, as perhaps the great majority of Catholics have, the true sense of the meaning and purpose of this sacrament, and the great value that it could have for him. Anyone can "confess to God." I'm fully confident that whether we do so or not God will not withhold his love or forgiveness from us. But if we who are Catholics do not also celebrate the sacrament of reconciliation, we are missing out on something that can and should be of great help to us; we are perhaps cutting ourselves off (by church law) from other sacramental opportunities; and we are withholding our participation in the Christian community's official forgiveness of others.

I think it would help a lot if the confession part of this sacrament were greatly de-emphasized by the church, and the celebration aspect of it stressed. I wish we would stop calling it confession. That might help us all to get a better hold on what it really is.

Must I tell my sins to be forgiven in a penance service?

I recently attended a penance service in our parish. When the time came for private confession I was told by the priest that I only needed to confess "sinfulness" and not verbalize any particular deeds. Did I really receive absolution? Or was it just a "blessing" I got that day?

■ *Answer*

I presume your question refers to a communal celebration of reconciliation that includes individual confession and absolution. We call that "form two." (Form one is private confession outside a communal setting, and form three is communal reconciliation with general absolution.)

With that in mind, let's take a broad look at this situation. First, let's presume that you went to this celebration to be an integral part of everything that is meant by the sacrament of reconciliation. In other words you went because you'd done something that you were personally convinced is sinful, you were sincerely sorry for having done this, and you were firmly determined to reestablish this relationship and to commit this sin no more.

Further, let's assume that you believe in the ever-loving mercy of God. In light of this, your decision to repent already welcomes that loving mercy and reconciliation into your heart. But there's more. You felt the need for some kind of official affirmation of this reconciliation and also for the expression of this reconciliation from the community. God has entrusted such official things to the church through this sacrament. And finally, you felt a need to celebrate that reconciliation within the context of the community.

Please note that you are entering from the very beginning into a celebration of the sacrament of reconciliation. The welcome that we hope you will get from and give to your fellow sinners (including the priest) at the very moment of your arrival is how the sacramental celebration begins. Then there is usually an opening hymn or prayer, some pertinent Scripture readings, a suitable homily, a careful examination of conscience, perhaps some suggested procedures for correcting our sinful ways (penances); a communal expression of our sinfulness and a mutual expression of forgiveness; the individual confession of sins and expression by the priest of reconciliation (absolution); a joyful exchange of a sign of peace among the participants; and usually a concluding hymn.

Note that all of this is the celebration of the sacrament of reconciliation (not just confession and absolution), and it is to be hoped that when the celebration is concluded all the needs that brought you to it will have been well fulfilled. You leave the celebration with the assurance that the damaged or broken relationship has now been healed; you have been reconciled; your sins have been forgiven.

In that context, I think that no priest has a right to tell you that you need not "verbalize" any particular sin. You have come not only because you, like other humans, are a "sinful being." You have come because you committed a particular sin or sins and you may very well need to verbalize them. The law of the church says that you must indeed "verbalize" in confession any sin that has totally destroyed the grace-relationship with God and the community (mortal sin). I think this law is simply recognizing a basic human need at such a moment. Furthermore, there may be many situations involving much lesser sins where the need of an individual may very well *not* be satisfied by a simple expression of sinfulness. Not that your forgiveness will depend upon this verbalization, but that your total need at the moment may not be fulfilled without that verbalization. But you as penitent, and not the priest, must judge that need to verbalize, just as only you can judge whether or not your sin has totally destroyed the grace-relationship and therefore is "mortal."

Absolution does not "zap" your sin away. The whole process heals you. It fills your need for reconciliation.

Why are priests so disrespectful to penitents?

I was helping out at the rectory after confirmation by waiting on table for the priests who had stayed for dinner. I was really shocked and dismayed when I heard the priests making fun of people who had been to confession to them. They didn't reveal anyone's sins, but I just don't think it's proper for priests to make jokes out of other people's unfortunate sinfulness. What do you think?

■ *Answer*

My initial response is that you were quite rightfully disturbed and offended by what some of us priests have done by making light of what we have experienced in hearing confessions. There is no excuse for that, and each of us priests needs to make a new resolve that we will never participate in such idle and destructive talk.

To attack this problem from a different perspective, however, I would like to express a few thoughts on the method whereby the sacrament of reconciliation has been "celebrated" in our church since about the twelfth century. In fact, the church, in its disciplinary declarations, still holds that this is the "only ordinary method" available to the faithful for the celebration of this sacrament. I am obviously referring to what we have come to call "private auricular confession," usually in the anonymous setting of the "confessional" (and still usually anonymous in most reconciliation room settings).

The church has always insisted (and still does) on the social dimension of sin, and each of us Catholics should clearly see that the most secret of all sins has its inevitable effect upon the entire Christian community and even all humanity. In sin we introduce disorder, disorientation, chaos, and destruction into our lives. Our lives, however, are never purely private but are unalterably related to all of creation around us. We do not and cannot live in a vacuum, and therefore our every thought or act—indeed our very continuing existence—affects either positively (in the case of virtue) or negatively (in case of sin) the very core of society and all creation within which we live. So *no* sin is really private or without its social effects and dimensions.

Further, the church has also always insisted (and still does!) that God is infinitely loving and merciful, and would therefore never withhold his love or forgiveness from even the greatest of sinners. Repeatedly in the gospels Jesus is depicted by the evangelists as having come into this world not for the just but for sinners. Yes, his mission on earth was to reveal the love of the Father for even the likes of the traitor Judas, the denying Peter, the doubting Thomas, the tax-collecting Matthew and Zacchaeus, the adulterous woman, the thieves on the cross, and the persecuting Saul (Paul). And here I've mentioned just a tiny percentage of the sinners whom he encountered in the gospels. To them all he offered loving mercy and grace-filled forgiveness *before* there was even any thought in their minds of repentance, and certainly before they saw fit to make any sort of "confession."

For these reasons (the social dimension of sin and the continuing love and forgiveness of sinners by God), I am fully convinced that we Catholics need to participate in, and the church must come to approve and encourage, *communal* celebrations of the sacrament of reconciliation. It isn't enough to merely offer "penance services" before "confession." The point is that we humans need to admit our guilt publicly before the community (without the necessity of naming individual sins). We need to make God's love and forgiveness our own. We need to share that love openly with our sisters and brothers, who are sinners like ourselves. We need the declaration of God's unending love, made in our church by the priest, sinner though he be, on behalf of us all as he touches us in the beautifully forgiving presence of that community with the unbridled loving mercy of the church's (not his!) absolution.

That, folks, is "celebration!" And in that type of setting I assure you that there would never again be a temptation on the part of anyone to make jokes about whatever might be said or done.

I accept the wisdom of the well-known axiom "confession is good for the soul." I see and have experienced for myself what an open unburdening of oneself to another can do for a human being. I understand and accept that this is greatly enhanced by the grace-filled atmosphere in which it takes place when the confession is part of the sacramental celebration of reconciliation. We must never deny our Catholic people (or anyone for that matter) this magnificent opportunity to sacramentalize such a moment. Because of this, I believe we should forever retain the one-on-one (penitent and priest) method of celebrating this sacrament as an *option* for us all.

However, I am deeply convinced that much of the magnificence of such a moment of grace is lost in the anonymity of the confessional. Even the use of modern reconciliation rooms still provides too much anonymity. However, I have never failed to experience the marvel of grace-filled reconciliation when I have participated in the communal celebration of the sacrament. May the church open wide that door without delay.

After Vatican II, must we confess before communion?

On the Feast of Corpus Christi, I heard a homily on the Eucharist. The priest said that people should not feel unworthy to come to communion, that Vatican II had changed our thinking about whether we had to go to confession before going to communion. He talked about the "new theology," which views us as a "eucharistic people." He seemed to imply that even if you are in a state of mortal sin, you should still come to the Eucharist because "none of us is without sin." Is this true? Did Vatican Council II change things this much? And what does it mean to say that we are a "eucharistic people"?

■ Answer

First I guess I should make it clear that Vatican II did not change any doctrine or dogma of the church. What it did do was restate our faith in modern terms and rid us of certain customs that were not in keeping with the inner nature of the sacraments themselves. In doing this, it freed us to change our thinking about a lot of things without bearing the stigma of not following the teachings of the church. Vatican II looked at the same truths taught by the church through the ages and enabled us to see them in a breathtakingly beautiful new light. I emphasize the words "free us" and "enabled us" because I see Vatican II as a freeing and enabling development in our church rather than a dictatorial one like the Council of Trent (with all its "anathemas").

No, Vatican II did not change the law of the church that requires us to submit our "mortal" sins in the sacrament of penance before receiving communion. Even the revised Code of Canon Law retains that law. What the spirit of Vatican II did do was lay the groundwork for rethinking the meaning of what we've traditionally called mortal sin. It also allowed us to rethink the relationship between the sacraments of reconciliation and Eucharist.

As a result of Vatican II, for instance, we came to a universal realization that the total break with God and the church known as mortal sin is a rather rare occurrence in the life of the average person.

Second, the role of the Eucharist as the prime sacrament of reconciliation has been greatly highlighted as a result of Vatican II. Third, in coming to a more realistic vision of the sinfulness of all humans, we realize now that "worthiness" should not even be a consideration when approaching the Eucharist (since none of us is worthy). Rather the healing and reconciling elements of the eucharistic celebration are embraced by all of us in full recognition of our sinfulness. Finally, since Vatican II the sacrament of reconciliation, sometimes still called penance or confession, has become much more a celebration and sharing of the reconciliation won for us by Christ rather than a means of "making peace with God" (See 2 Corinthians 5:16–20).

Why are we called a eucharistic people? Do you remember the story in the gospels about the nourishment of thousands with a few loaves and fishes? One point often overlooked in that story is that, with the relatively insignificant possessions of an even more insignificant unnamed young boy, the needs of a great multitude could be met. Similarly today, through the power of our faith in Christ, our own insignificant gifts are transformed into a powerful force for good in today's world, a force that can and does meet the needs of a multitude much greater than that of this gospel story.

This, I think, is what Christ meant to teach us in giving us the Eucharist, through which we celebrate his living presence among us. But we can truly do this only because we're participating with him in today's "nourishment of thousands with a few loaves and fishes." This gives us the power to satisfy all the various hungers in our world today.

In other words, we can celebrate the Eucharist effectively only if we are totally giving of all that we are and all that we have to our fellow humans, just as Christ gave his all. He asked us, our faith tells us, to symbolize this presence by "doing this in remembrance of me." Out of this request grew what we know today as the Eucharist.

So we are a eucharistic people because we, like the resulting Eucharist we celebrate and participate in, are the living presence of Christ in today's world. Without his living presence in us, there could be no presence in the eating and drinking of the consecrated bread and wine. We must be a eucharistic people in order for there to be a Eucharist to celebrate. A eucharistic people must be present with Christ in the Eucharist. Otherwise it could not be what it is meant to be!

Sacramental Celebrations

Are the sacraments "celebrations" or just "services"?
I recently read the book *Morality and Its Beyond* by Dick Westley, a lay Catholic theologian from Chicago. I found the book not only very informative but also uplifting and hope giving. For instance, Westley says: "Sacraments are not so much the sources of grace for believers as the celebration by believers of graces freely and already given to all."

It seems to me that this statement is full of exciting possibilities if taken seriously and put into practice. Is it possible, since such statements are becoming more prevalent by responsible Catholic theologians, that we can expect changes in the attitudes and official teaching of the church in such matters?

■ *Answer*
It certainly seems to me that the vision of and emphasis on the sacraments primarily (though not exclusively) as celebrations of "graces freely and already given to all" by a bounteously loving Father, who thus shares himself with all humans as he creates them "in his own image and likeness," is indeed becoming more widely held by the better theologians of the church; and with you I would hope that this vision and emphasis will soon become the vision and emphasis of the official teaching or magisterium of the church.

It is obvious to me that Mr. Westley's moral theology is based on a worldview, a Christology, and an ecclesiology that our magisterium embraced in the official documents of Vatican II. I have noticed, however, that certain church leaders have rather promptly (over a short span of some 20-30 years) "backed-off" from

Vatican II's focus in favor of the individualized, authoritarian, exclusive, personal salvation type of theology upon which the Council of Trent insisted. In its own time the Council of Trent was certainly correct. It imposed its thinking unflinchingly and unwaveringly upon the universal church, and really upon all humanity, throughout the 400 years between Trent and Vatican II. But, as Pope John XXIII so clearly articulated, the theology of Trent was fine for its day and for many years thereafter, but is simply out of date for modern needs.

I agree with you, with Mr. Westley, and with many excellent Catholic theologians of today that salvation is a *gift* that has been offered to *all* of humanity. Thus salvation (or God's love, or God's grace, or God's creative presence) is not the exclusive preserve of the Catholic church to be "dispensed" to people through the sacraments. In other words, the church and the sacraments are not nearly so much the *means* to salvation, but rather they are and should be the means given to us by Christ *to proclaim and celebrate that salvation.* We are called to celebrate the love, the grace, and the divine presence in all those created in God's own image and likeness. And that includes everyone, every single human being.

Priesthood and Ministry

Priesthood and Celibacy

Will priests ever be allowed to marry?
Will the Catholic church ever allow priests to be married?

■ *Answer*
Let me first clarify the issue: in the Western (or Latin) rite of the
Catholic church (as opposed to the Eastern rites) married men are
not allowed to become priests, and in all rites of the Catholic church,
priests are not allowed to marry after ordination. I make this distinction because I would not want our readers to become confused at
some time in the future if they should encounter someone who is a
married Catholic priest of one of the Eastern rites. Also, the church
has lately allowed some married ministers of other churches to be
ordained as Catholic priests and retain their married way of life.

Will the church ever change this discipline of celibacy? I really
don't know, but every indication now is that it won't be changed
for a long while. The magisterium of the church is firmly committed at this time to celibacy as an absolute value and need, and the

authority of the church (vested in the pope and bishops) would hardly act contrary to this conviction.

The theory is that, as a celibate, the priest is able to devote himself more fully to the work of the Lord and the church, since he is thus "unencumbered" by the responsibilities and care of a wife or family. This thinking is based (in a somewhat fundamentalist fashion, I fear) on the passage from St. Paul's first letter to the Corinthians, 7:32–35.

It is the conviction of many in the church (including me) that everyone, both married and unmarried alike, must be totally devoted to the Lord and therefore to the church. The married person does this in a different way from that of an unmarried person, but both the married and unmarried face their own difficulties. If we maintain that the celibate person is, by his or her celibacy, better enabled to devote his or her entire life to God and the church, we are thereby placing the noble vocation of the married below that of celibates. I feel that this is a crying shame and grave injustice in view of the magnificent dedication and saintly commitment to God and the church made by millions of married people in their daily living of the Christian life.

Should priests be allowed to marry?

Do you think the church *should* allow priests to be married?

■ *Answer*

Yes, I do. When I say this I don't mean to deny the value of a celibate life, or of a celibate priesthood. Surely God will always call celibates to the priesthood. I simply feel that there are many persons who could make excellent priests and who could do wonders for the church, but these same persons want and need the blessings of marriage for their own personal fulfillment, and also to enable them to best minister as priests.

The point is that the intimate personal relationship that exists in marriage can be a tremendous advantage to the priestly ministry.

Priestly ministry, if it is to be truly effective, requires a distinct ability in the priest to establish good, healthy personal relationships with many people. The establishment of such relationships can be greatly assisted, in my opinion, by the relationships experienced in any good marriage. Also, in and through the experiences gained in the family relationships (husband, wife, and children), the priest would be enabled to better assist others in facing their own relationships.

You see, dear friend, I don't think that your questions can be answered with a simple "yes" or "no." Both answers have far-flung implications. What I have written above is only a brief background of what such decisions could be based on, and I can assure you that it will take many years of deep deliberation and prayer by thousands of theologians and bishops, and probably the next several popes, before a theologically sound and practical decision is made in this matter. All I can give you here is my own thoughtful and prayerful opinion.

Is there any valid argument left favoring celibacy?

Do you believe there is any valid argument left for imposing mandatory celibacy upon the priesthood? While there's a shortage of priests almost everywhere in this country, in our diocese it's reaching crisis proportions. (Please note the enclosed excerpt from Father Edward Schillebeeckx's book, *The Church with a Human Face*).

■ *Answer*

While I share your doubts (and those of Fr. Schillebeeckx) about the value and need of mandatory celibacy for all who want to embrace the priesthood in our church, I cannot share your obvious hope that a simple reversal of this requirement by the church will necessarily resolve the priest shortage with which we are currently faced and which is growing more serious every day.

First, let me thank you for enclosing that excerpt from Fr. Schillebeeckx's book. Even in this brief excerpt, Fr. Schillebeeckx puts the entire matter of clerical celibacy in its proper perspective. He demonstrates very convincingly that the law of celibacy was not explicitly promulgated until the Second Lateran Council in 1123! It was based on an ancient liturgical law and practice of "ritual purity" whereby one was to abstain from sexual intercourse the night before presiding at the Eucharist. Then, he makes the magnificently significant point that it was not until the Second Vatican Council that the church officially tied the concept of clerical celibacy to the scriptural concept expressed in Matthew 19: "...and some have freely renounced sex for the sake of the kingdom of God."

This gives me all the more basis for my conviction that mandatory celibacy for priests is a result of the pervading (somewhat Manichaean) official attitude in our church toward human sexuality. It is as though the body and sex are our "lower" or "baser" parts and therefore we should reject them as much as possible as sources of evil in our lives, as though the only real good in us is that which is "spiritual."

It's because of this conviction that I cannot agree that the simple lifting of this obligation in connection with the priesthood will alleviate the shortage of priests. What needs to be lifted is the attitude that marriage and sexual relationships are "unworthy" of the priesthood. I think our people are having problems with the attitude that celibacy in and of itself lifts one above the plane of the "average person" and that through celibacy the priest is better able to "dedicate his life more fully to God and the church" than can one who is married.

As for the vocation crisis to which you refer, I don't think most of our young people want to be part of that kind of separation from their peers. They aren't asking for that kind of "better-than-thou" thinking. I do see young people emerging as leaders in our communities, but their view of leadership is not the kind that might be viewed as "domination by heroes." Rather, they want to incorporate their total humanity into their leadership. They see themselves as holy and also as sexual (yes, sexual!) humans.

Furthermore, I don't believe that Jesus himself had any other view than this. Note that there is every evidence that the people he gathered as leaders were married! He did not gather a group of celibates around himself.

There is obviously room in our modern society for those who

choose to live in celibacy, no matter what their role might be within the Christian community. I know many wonderful laypeople, for example, who have freely chosen celibacy. It's equally true that the married have as much to offer and can be equally dedicated to God and the church—and I know many, many more of them than I do celibates. But to make celibacy a condition without which one cannot serve the community in the ministerial priesthood is, I think, a remnant of one of the gravest errors in discipline that has ever affected our church. When that error and its basis is eradicated, I think then the church will see a revival of interest in the ministerial priesthood as a meaningful form of life in service to the Christian community.

Can a priest celebrate Mass while in the state of sin?

I recently watched a rerun of the *Thorn Birds* mini-series on television and was struck by the reality that priests, including cardinals, need human love. Oh, don't get me wrong, I know priests are human. It's just that it was not until I saw this movie that I realized how celibacy, however good a virtue it may be, may be obsolete as a discipline in this day and age. My question is: if a priest has "affairs," and if he believes this to be gravely or mortally sinful, must he first seek the sacrament of reconciliation before celebrating Mass?

■ *Answer*

First let me thank you for the initial comments before you posed your question. I, too, watched the *Thorn Birds* and thought it was a magnificently conceived story, and equally magnificent in its portrayal on television.

A priest is bound by the very same laws and moral principles as are the laity. His priesthood in no way gives him the right to commit sin, or to be excused from the consequences of that sin. Furthermore, he has no more special "avenues" for forgiveness than does the layperson. Therefore, if he judges himself guilty of a sin that is of such magnitude or seriousness that it totally shatters the grace-relationship between himself, his fellow humans, and God, then indeed he is bound by church law to submit this sin in a celebration of the sacrament of reconciliation before church law would allow him to preside over the celebration of Mass.

But let me remind you, as well as all my dear readers, that this same law applies to all Catholics, and that it has no absolute connection with the celibacy of the priest. Any Catholic who judges himself or herself guilty of sin as serious as that described in the previous paragraph is bound by the very same law. And it doesn't matter whether there is a vow or promise that is broken. Celibacy is not the exclusive focus here. In other words, it is not being unfaithful to his promise of celibacy as such that makes this law applicable to the priest who judges himself guilty of fornication or adultery, it is the gravity of his sinfulness (which can be judged only by him). If he committed a sin of injustice that he judged to be similarly grave, he would likewise have to apply the same law to himself, as would any Catholic.

It has long been obvious to me (and your question is something of an example of this) that the church is "caught up" with the morality or immorality of acts that have any kind of sexual connotation. For instance, in this particular story, I doubt seriously that the greatest evil in "Father Ralph's" life was the breaking of his promise of celibacy. Were we asked to judge his life, I think that, rather than concentrating on his momentary sexual lapses, we should look much more at his almost uncompromising ambition for power. We would consider how he placed this ambition far above the loving needs of the woman he was rejecting throughout his life—and all this to allow him to attain the stature in the church that he deemed his destiny.

But in the public response to this film, I have never heard the sinfulness of that blind ambition—and the people it hurt—raised as an issue. I think that's so unfortunate. I'm personally convinced that many, many more grave and grace-destroying sins of injustice are committed each day by people in all facets of our human society (including us priests, to be sure) than have been or will be committed in the area of human sexuality from the beginning to the eventual end of the human race. I have seen or read of so many people, be they popes, bishops, priests, or laity who very blatantly commit acts of injustice toward individuals or groups— and the question so seldom comes up as to whether their acts were immoral or not, much less whether these people had obligations to "go to confession" or not before receiving the Eucharist.

But "look out" if sex is involved. The immediate outcry is "Immorality!"

To answer your question more directly, may I simply state that if a priest (or anyone!) has "affairs," with all the connotations of that word, *and he believes his sin to be gravely evil,* he would indeed be required by church law to bring that sin to the sacrament of reconciliation before celebrating Mass. But the key words in your question are those I have emphasized by putting them in *italics.* Without those key elements, I would have to answer your question in an entirely different way.

Shouldn't priests be able to marry?

I'm now firmly convinced that the Catholic church is committing a great injustice by keeping priests from marrying. I don't think this way because I am looking for a way to ease the clergy shortage. I truly believe that it is inhuman to require men to be celibate. What do you think?

■ *Answer*

I was happy to note that your opinion on these matters is not based on the current shortage of priests. For most people, I think, this is the one and only reason they would give these two subjects any thought at all. With you I feel that it's more a matter of principle that should be addressed by church authority regardless of the number of priests and regardless of how well or how poorly these priests are meeting the priestly ministerial needs of the church.

I was ordained in 1954. In the course of all these years as a priest I have personally experienced, both in my own life and in my relationships with my brother priests, both the advantages (yes, there are some!) and disadvantages of mandatory celibacy. It would be useless to list them here since they're of no practical significance to the question at hand. I have also experienced in myself and seen in my brother priests some distinct deficiencies resulting directly from the lack of a "partner" with whom we could seek holiness and live our lives. I honestly think we celibate priests cannot relate to other humans as most others can because we don't have the basis for such relationships in our own lives. In my opinion, that basis is married love.

I have heard the argument hundreds of times that celibacy allows us to commit our entire lives to God and the church in that we are not "bound down" by the responsibilities of a spouse and children. That may be true in some cases, but I really don't feel that I or any priest I know gives himself more to God and the church than many dedicated husbands, wives, fathers, and mothers in the church.

Furthermore, my own experience tells me that many (some would say "most"; others would even say "all") of us celibate priests have a very difficult time relating well to others, especially to the majority of people in the world: the married. This is true because we have not experienced the intensity of the intimacy of that relationship (and I don't mean just sex here!) out of which can grow a facility for relating to others.

I do realize that the majority of marriages these days fail and end in divorce, but that does not minimize the intrinsic value of what a sound marriage relationship can and does do to help humans reach their ultimate potential in relating to others as Christ would want us to, and thereby make him present to ourselves and others. It seems to me that having a married priesthood would benefit everyone, including the institution of marriage itself.

You see, dear friend, I really don't think that mandatory celibacy is so much an injustice to us priests. I think rather that it is an injustice to the church, the people of God, who need priests who can understand them, relate to them, and minister to them out of the same experience within which the very great majority of them are living: the married life. I think the church does need celibate priests, too, so that there will be some who can relate and minister better to those who, like them, might freely choose the celibate life.

Priesthood Today

What should the "new priesthood" be like?

I'd like to challenge you to follow up on a statement I heard you make where you called for an intense study of the priesthood to determine whether the priesthood as we know it today is relevant to the needs of both the church and society. You also called for "surgery" to be done on the meaning, goals, purposes, and role of the priest in the church and society today. Can you give us some thoughts on what the "new priesthood" should be like?

■*Answer*

Since I don't have advanced theological or sociological education or expertise, I'm really not properly equipped to draw any solid conclusions as to how the priesthood can be made more relevant and attractive as a vocation.

But what I can do here is present some areas that I feel need to be studied, and perhaps some ideas as to what might be considered possible changes for the priesthood in the future. Even as I write this I have no *firm* convictions about what improvements to the priesthood are realistic. I simply feel that, unless serious consideration is given to these ideas, we may very well continue to have priests who are increasingly irrelevant in today's church and society.

I would like to see an international study undertaken *without foregone conclusions dictated by Rome* regarding the modern priesthood. Among the points or questions for this study would possibly be the following:

- the very nature of the priesthood as initially established in the church;
- the development of the nature of the priesthood over the centuries;
- the type of priesthood needed by the church today;
- the necessity of its consistency with the priesthood of our tradition;
- the relationship between priests and bishops and their mutual roles in the organizational structure of the church;
- the relationship between the so-called "ministerial priesthood" and the priesthood of the laity;
- the restriction of the priesthood to males;
- the requirement of celibacy for priests;
- the role of the priest as the primary leader in the parish (for instance, is it necessary or best that a priest be the executive of the parish?);
- the necessity (or lack thereof) of the current legislative and determinative Roman edicts regarding the priesthood and priestly life.

Again, this list is certainly not exhaustive, and each of these items for review will necessarily lead to others that may be even more important and play a greater role in determining the future of the priesthood in the church.

It is my hope and prayer that someone of much more competence than I have, and especially of much more influence within the current power structure in the church, will take up this charge as essential to furthering God's kingdom on earth.

Why do we need priests at all?

There's a lot about our new pastor that we don't understand. For example, he has a day off during the week. Shouldn't he take care of his personal business on that day? Then, we frequently have substitute priests for weekend Masses, especially during football season. Further, he never has time for anyone in the parish. He always gives the excuse that he has to go to a meeting. In one case he spent only 15 minutes at a wedding rehearsal because he had to "go to a meeting."

If other things are more important than Mass and your parishioners, especially the young people, what do we need a parish priest for? The bishop could come once a week, consecrate the hosts, and we could have a communion service.

Also, what vows does a priest take? Maybe it would help if I knew that he hadn't promised to be humble, meek, and unworldly.

■ Answer

First may I very respectfully point out that it is rather harsh to expect anyone to take care of all personal "business" on his one day off in a week. I don't think anyone in any profession or calling should be so restricted, and very few people whom I know are. It is another matter, of course, if one spends a major amount of "work time" at one's personal business or in other personal things such as recreation. I certainly wouldn't want to make a judgment on this in connection with your parish priest's life and ministry. But certainly he can and should!

Second, presiding at the celebration of the Eucharist, especially on Sundays, is of primary importance in the role of a priest. But we cannot reduce that responsibility to merely the consecration at Mass. That responsibility and role is carried out in every part and parcel of the entire Mass, from welcoming people before Mass to wishing them well afterward and everything in between. And, even if he gets someone to replace him, he can't excuse himself lightly from this important weekly responsibility. Again I can't make a judgment for him with regard to the instances you mention—but he can, and must.

Diocesan priests, aren't required to take any vows. Those who become members of religious communities such as the Franciscans or Jesuits, do take solemn vows of poverty, chastity, and obedience. Diocesan priests are simply required to make a solemn and formal commitment to priestly ministry among the people of God, to be obedient to their bishop, and to live in a state of celibacy.

What is a priest supposed to be and do? A priest is chosen by the church to be the primary one who brings "holy order" into community life, to organize and coordinate the many gifts given by God to the people. A pastor calls or gathers the people for worship and then presides over the public prayer of the church. That's part of establishing good, holy order in the parish. A pastor is also designated by the church to serve the religious needs of the parish. He's also expected to work steadfastly toward the establishment and growth of the "Reign of God" within the community he is assigned to serve. Likewise, he is responsible for nurturing the Christian life in individuals and in the community as a whole through prayer, faith development, teaching, celebration of the sacraments, and the continuation of every aspect of Christ's ministry on earth. Pastors are also required to provide the necessary buildings, equipment, and supplies needed for the proper functioning of the parish.

If the priest in your parish is failing in one or more of these areas, then he indeed needs to make some changes in the way he exercises his priestly ministry. Your letter and, I hope, this response will give him food for thought and prayer, and I pray with you that he will find it within himself to change any aspect of his life that is not in keeping with the commitment he has made in accepting the gift of the priesthood.

Why is so much emphasis placed on the priesthood at the annual Chrism Mass in our diocese?

Holy Week is almost upon us, and I'm trying to decide whether I should go to the Chrism Mass on Holy Thursday again. I've gone for a number of years now, and each year I've been left quite confused. How does it relate to other Holy Week ceremonies? Are laypeople as well as clergy really invited to be part of it by renewing their commitment to the church?

Why is there always so much emphasis on the priesthood in the Chrism Mass? I thought Jesus had shared his priestly mission with all of us. Doesn't the rite of baptism say that we all share in the priestly, kingly, and prophetic mission of Christ? Didn't Vatican II say that to us very clearly?

■ *Answer*

After a bit of research, prayer, and some sobering thought I can clarify for all of us some of the issues you bring up. I hope this will help to make the Chrism Mass more meaningful for us in the future. Please note that I say for "us" intentionally, because I have shared many of the same problems as you do in participating in the Chrism Mass over the years.

The Chrism Mass (as a separate liturgy from the principal Mass of Holy Thursday) only came into being with the reforms of the Holy Week liturgies instituted by Pope Pius XII in 1955. From approximately the seventh century until 1955, there was really only one liturgical celebration in each church on Holy Thursday, and at the cathedral church of each diocese this celebration included the consecration of the oils to be used in the diocese during the forthcoming year in the celebration of the sacraments of baptism, confirmation, the anointing of the sick, and holy orders.

With the restoration of the evening "Liturgy of the Lord's Supper" by Pius XII in 1955, an entirely separate liturgy at the cathedral church was initiated for the precise purpose of the consecration of the oils by the bishop. The liturgical emphasis on Holy Thursday was placed almost entirely (very properly, I think) on the evening liturgy as a celebration of the institution of the Eucharist with its essential connection to the paschal mystery of the life, passion, death, and resurrection of Jesus Christ. Further, in and through the now official (but not mandatory) inclusion of the washing of the feet in that celebration, emphasis is similarly placed on a rededication of the Christian people of God (including priests, of course) to the same priestly ministry of "service" that John's gospel tells us Jesus demonstrated at the Last Supper in the washing of the feet of his disciples.

It is only within the last few years (perhaps ten or so) that the church has given the Chrism Mass an ever-growing emphasis on the rededication by priests to their priestly commitment. Perhaps it is based more on a "pious tradition" rather than any theological principle that Christ "ordained" the apostles at the Last Supper when he said: "Do this in memory of me." Be that as it may, Pope John Paul II has made a point of sending a Holy Thursday message to the priests of the world and requesting that on this day all priests renew their commitment to priestly service. I'm not sure when or how this came about, but as a result of it, a rededication of priests to priestly service has become an official part of the Chrism Mass liturgy, and it has become almost a "sacred duty" for priests to gather around their bishop at this particular Mass to rededicate themselves as a body of priests to their priestly ideals, mission, and commitment to service.

I personally believe that the Chrism Mass is the wrong place and time for this. It is much more meaningful when we as priests, gather with our "priestly people" during the evening Liturgy of the Lord's Supper and rededicate ourselves as the entire pilgrim people of God to be of service to one another and thereby personify the uniquely service-oriented priestly ministry of Jesus Christ as depicted at the Last Supper.

Although there certainly is a clear distinction of the roles and purposes of the sharing in Christ's priesthood by the "unordained" and the "ordained," I see absolutely no reason why we cannot and should not jointly and with one voice renew the pledge of our baptismal, confirmation, or ordination commitments to live out our share in Christ's priestly ministry of service rather than doing so by separately voiced commitments. And because the Chrism Mass is not where the majority of our people are in their liturgical observance of Holy Thursday, it seems to me that we are more one with our people if we priests make this joint recommitment with our people at the commemoration of the gospel event that typifies our priestly ministry as one of service: the evening celebration of the Lord's Supper.

Can an illegitimate person become a priest?

I'm a parish secretary. Today a young man called requesting his parents' marriage certificate, stating that he needed it to establish his legitimacy, which is a requirement for entry into the seminary. With some misgiving about this legitimacy requirement, I complied with his request and sent the certificate.

However, I immediately decided to write to you and ask whether church law indeed makes illegitimacy of birth an impediment to the priesthood. And if this is so, I wonder what would happen if the illegitimate children of the married priests (or bishops!) who are so much in the news these days would apply for the priesthood.

Probably if the priest would not admit paternity, the boy would be out in the cold, but if clerical paternity were admitted, the church would bend the rules or redefine the law to accommodate sons of clerics. What do you think?

■ *Answer*

"Legitimately" or not (pardon the pun!), I think there is "a little sliver of wood between your neck and your upper arm" concerning the disciplinary and procedural law and practices of the church. My suspicions are perhaps somewhat incited by a bit of "sawdust" that I occasionally find on my own shoulder. Tut tut!

Getting back now to at least a modicum of seriousness, I was all set to quote what I was absolutely sure was the law of the church, that those born illegitimately are, indeed, impeded from entering the priesthood. But lo and behold, after two thorough readings of the pertinent canons in the 1983 revised Code of Canon Law, I discovered that there is absolutely no mention in any of these canons (thank God, and those responsible for this revision of the law!) that legitimacy is a requirement for ordination, or that illegitimacy is an impediment thereto. We are making some progress in this church of ours!

Going back to the "old" code of 1918 (which is no longer in force), I found that illegitimacy is mentioned there as the very first of the irregularities or virtually "permanent" impediments to ordination. Strangely enough, however, the primary method of "removing" this irregularity and thus becoming eligible for ordination, was to first take "solemn vows" as a religious (the other ways are by the subsequent marriage of the parents or by a rescript or dispensation from the Holy See)!

While the pre-1983 code did prohibit illegitimate men without the proper remedy from ordination, I have known any number of men who were indeed illegitimate and ordained, presumably after the proper dispensation was given. I can seriously and confidently assure you that none of these were "sons of clerics." Contrary to the implications in your question, my conviction (for what it's worth) is that, if illegitimacy was still an impediment to orders, the church would be far more reluctant to grant a dispensation (or "bend the law," as you put it) if the father of the candidate were a cleric.

Frankly, I find the continuing castigation in society of those who are born out of wedlock to be totally out of step with the message of the gospel. It should be obvious to all (especially after twenty centuries of Christianity and many more than that of supposed civilization), that no one is the instigator of his or her own conception/creation. So, just like God in the book of Genesis looked upon his new creation and found it all to be good, so does he obviously find every human being to be good, no matter what the conditions of his or her birth. I find no valid reason why we should not do the same.

Women and Ministry

What is the role of women in the church?

As a woman, I think it's clear that, in the course of its history, the church has held on steadfastly to the dominant role of males in society, and has done little or nothing to even absorb within its structure the advances made by women in society, not to mention

the total lack of leadership from the church in this field. I think
we women have proven that we have equal ability to men. We can
and want to take leadership roles just as men do. But this doesn't
seem to be recognized by the church.

What are your views on the role of women in the church today?

■ *Answer*

As a man (male, that is), I am absolutely amazed at and ashamed
of the failure of us men over the ages to recognize the God-given
and essential roles of women in society. I, with you and so many
of our outstanding women (and some outstanding men) in the
church today, cry out to this church of ours to withdraw the many
barriers that make it impossible for women to effectively offer
their many gifts to the church and, through it, to society. By not
doing so, we have wasted billions and billions of human lives and
the talents that could have offered so much that no male could
possibly offer.

There are some specifically feminine characteristics and abilities
that are lacking in most males, just as there are specifically masculine characteristics and abilities that are lacking in most women.
Therefore, what our church has done, in essence, is ignore and
reject that wealth of feminine characteristics and abilities that was
readily available to it, in favor of using only the masculine characteristics and abilities in all areas of major church leadership, management, and ministry. What a pity!

Please don't misunderstand me, dear readers. I am not saying that
we men must allow women to replace men as leaders in the church.
What I am saying is that until the church places women and men
side by side and employs the fullness of human gifts and abilities in
all facets of church leadership, management, operation, and ministry, we are doing our church and society a grave disservice.

Thus women must not only have an equal voice in the church,
but they must have their distinctively feminine equal voice and
role in the church, which until now they have not had. All we
have heard and been required to live by is what has evolved from
the masculine dimension of leadership in the church, and I am

firmly convinced that this is a major factor in the failure of the official church today to comprehend and make its own the major advances for women that have already taken place in society.

God creates us, after all, male and female, and as such, according to Genesis, "in God's own image and likeness." Thus we are not being led and developed in a fully human way until and unless we allow the fullness of humanity to have its effect on us. The essence of humanity is in its likeness to the divine; that likeness can only be achieved if we allow—nay, see to it—that both the male and female characteristics of humanity are imbedded in the very fabric of our being.

Why can't women be ordained?

I believe that it is unthinkable that in this day and age the church would want us to believe that women should not be priests. Tell us your opinion about this.

■ *Answer*

I have expressed myself on many occasions and in many forums on this point, and need only say that I am absolutely convinced that our church is doing her people a grave disservice by not allowing women to choose the priesthood. Further, our Holy Father has dictated that this subject is not "up for discussion," and that we are to believe that it is the will of Christ himself that only men be priests. Be that as it may, I think the people of God are being done an injustice by being deprived of what only women priests could possibly do. The women of our world and church have been suppressed far too long, and it is our world and our church, rather than our women, who have suffered most from this suppression. The world seems to be waking up to and correcting this sad state more and more each day; unfortunately, as I see it, our church continues to lag behind!

Maybe some day? I sure hope so!

Should women be in the washing of feet on Holy Thursday?

The washing of feet at the Holy Thursday celebration was the center of controversy in our parish last Holy Week. It was announced that those interested in participating should contact the pastor. Women who called were told by the pastor that "women need not apply," because Jesus had only washed men's feet. The women were hurt and angry. The pastor was firm in his decision. What do you think of this?

■ Answer

I consider the attitude of this pastor typical of the official position of the church until the Second Vatican Council brought renewal. For many, it remains their steadfast position despite minor advances in the place of women in the church.

There is no doubt that it is perfectly permissible under current church law and ritual for women to participate actively by having their feet washed at the Holy Thursday celebration, and I know of very few parishes that still ban women from this role. I find it quite disturbing to hear that some still do. Perhaps even more disturbing to me, though, is the reason your pastor gave for not allowing women in this role. His reason gives evidence that he, like many (including official leaders) in the church, still holds fast to the fundamentalist notion that the gospels can be read literally as historical accounts of the life and teachings of Jesus. Otherwise, how can he possibly know that Jesus did not wash the feet of women in the course of his life among us? For that matter, how could he know that there were no women present at the Last Supper? Oh, the first three gospels clearly state that he sat down "with the Twelve" or "with his Apostles" to eat this meal, but they do not indicate that no one else was there. And John's gospel, the only one in which the story of the washing of feet appears, says little about who was there except by using the expression "the disciples," which can readily be understood to be much broader than simply the twelve apostles. I am not saying, however, that John thereby tells us that others were present besides Jesus and the apostles. On the contrary, to draw such a conclusion would be as scripturally unsound as its opposite.

More important, though, the beautiful, faith-filled, and true stories of the Last Supper, which appear in all four gospels (each, however, with some significantly different details!), are not necessarily historical or factual accounts of this event. They certainly were not written to tell us historical facts; they were written to share with us the Christian faith, and these particular passages concerning the event of the Last Supper are beautifully rich in faith. The preponderance of solid scriptural evidence indicates that the gospel writers made a point of restricting this meal to Jesus and his closest disciples. This is a key element in expressing the faith of the early Christian community. Jesus entrusted his message of faith to this select group of followers in a very special way.

But to jump from this message of faith to the specific historical conclusion that Jesus as a matter of fact explicitly excluded women from participation in any facet of church life and practice is to belie the very message of faith contained in these passages. The message of the Eucharist as expressed in the institution narratives of the first three gospels, and the account of the washing of the feet in the fourth, are simply meant for everyone, period.

For centuries, we males in church leadership have cited these passages and treated them in a fundamentalist way in order to dominate women. It's past time for this to stop.

Lay Ministry

What is church's view of the vocation of marriage in the light of the Council?

I'm a single Catholic, but I've come to believe that Christian marriage is designed to be a sacred and powerful vocation from which flow rich and beautiful gifts for the church in fulfilling its mission. That a man and woman are sacramentally united in this vocation, just as religious vocations are sacramentally celebrated, seems to affirm the marriage vocation as equally essential in the life and work of the church. Is this what the church teaches and believes about the vocation of marriage? What is the church's view of marriage in light of Vatican II and the redefined role of the laity in today's church?

■ *Answer*

First, let me address the concept of marriage as a vocation. Actually I don't see it so much as a vocation, but rather as a "way of life" that people choose as appropriate for them to live out their purpose in life. I think the work we do, the profession we've chosen, is where our vocation lies. To use a readily understandable example, people in the medical profession have a God-given *vocation*. Doctors, nurses, medical technicians, and other medical people (consciously or otherwise) carry out, extend, give witness to, and make present in a visible way the healing love of God for his suffering people. That, I think, is their primary vocation, rather than their decision to marry, remain single, or commit themselves to the priesthood or religious life. My point is that their state in life is not really their vocation; their work or their profession is their vocation.

On the other hand, their choosing of the single, married, or celibate religious life will have a distinct effect on their vocation of ministering to the sick. To be his or her best, an individual doctor may find it necessary to remain single; for another, marriage may be an essential element in bettering his or her effectiveness. For another, vowed celibacy may be essential; for still another joining a religious community may be the key to being a great dispenser of God's healing love. These various "states of life" provide the framework within which the doctor exercises his or her vocation of healing.

A bit of research indicates that, while Vatican II speaks eloquently about marriage—its value, purposes, and goals within the total divine plan for humankind—it does not call marriage a "vocation" but rather a "state of life." For instance in its *Decree on the Church in the Modern World* (par. 48), we read: "The intimate partnership of life and the love which constitutes the married state has been established by the creator and endowed by him with...various benefits and with various ends in view: all of these have a very important bearing on the...personal development and eternal destiny of every member of the family, on the dignity, stability, peace, and prosperity of the family and of the whole human race."

That same document goes on to express quite beautifully how Christian marriage is essentially connected with and is a living and active symbol of the unity in love that exists between Christ and his church. If that is indeed part of our faith (and I am absolutely convinced it is), then this sacramental character of Christian marriage makes it (to use your words) indeed "equally essential in the life and work of the church" as is the state of life of celibates and others who may not be married. (By the way there is no sacramental celebration of celibacy as there is of marriage).

But again, I think it's important that we not depict the priesthood or religious life as alternatives to marriage. What each person must do is determine what unique gift he or she has to offer. That determines our vocation. A second step is to determine in what state of life he or she can best carry out that vocation. This leads us to choose either marriage or the single life (with or without a vow to celibacy). Of course we must be practical. Under current church discipline, when we determine that the priesthood is our life work, we may only choose celibacy as the way of life in which we live out that vocation.

Here I will concentrate on what you call (very appropriately) the "redefined" role of the laity in today's church. To do this, I will depart somewhat from my usual style, which entails few direct quotations, and "compose" most of my response through direct quotations from the Vatican II *Decree on the Apostolate of Lay People*.

Indeed, the church can never be without the lay apostolate; it is something that derives from the lay person's very vocation as a Christian....

In the church there is a diversity of ministry but unity of mission... the laity are made to share in the priestly, prophetic, and royal office of Christ; they have, therefore, in the church and in the world, their own assignment in the mission of the whole People of God.

From the fact of their union with Christ the head, flows the lay person's right and duty to be an apostle. Inserted as they are in the Mystical Body of Christ by Baptism and strengthened by the power of the Holy Spirit in Confirmation, it is by the Lord himself that they are assigned to the apostolate. If they are consecrated a royal priesthood and a holy nation (cf. 1 Pet 1:4–10), it is in order that they may in all their actions offer spiritual sacrifices and bear witness to Christ all the world over.

The apostolate is lived in faith, hope and charity poured out by the Holy Spirit into the hearts of all the members of the church. And the precept of all Christians to work for the glory of God through the coming of his Reign and for the communication of eternal life to all, that they may know the only true God and Jesus Christ whom he has sent (cf. Jn 17:3).

On all Christians, accordingly, rests the noble obligation of working to bring all peoples throughout the whole word to hear and accept the divine message of salvation. ...for the exercise of the apostolate (the Holy Spirit) gives the faithful special gifts... so that each and all, putting at the service of others the grace received, may be "good stewards of God's varied gifts" (1 Pet 4:10), for the building up of the whole body in charity. From the reception of these charisms...there arises for each of the faithful the right and duty of exercising them in the church and in the world for the good of all and the development of the church, of exercising them in the freedom of the Holy Spirit...and at the same time in communion with his brothers and sisters in Christ....

Now for a few words of my own. Please note that nowhere in these quotations is there even the slightest implication (much less any positive indication) that the role of the laity in the work of the church is to *assist* the clergy in doing "their work of Christ and the church," which is so often heard as the reason for the apostolate of the laity. On the contrary, the decree specifically states that by their very membership in the church the laity share in the right and obligation to bring the gospel to all people. So while their role in the total effort of evangelization of the world is different from that of priests, and bishops, their role is not subservient to that of the clergy. Likewise, laypeople do not derive their place in the apostolate of the church from that of the clergy. The fact is that laypeople are called to service by virtue of their baptism. Lay ministry is as essential to the apostolate of the church as that of any other ministry.

Obviously, then, in the light of Vatican II, the role of the laity (married or otherwise) is absolutely "essential in the life and work of the church." And if marriage is essential (as it most often is) to an individual's best "performance" in that apostolic vocation, Vatican II obviously encourages us in that direction.

Should laypeople be "ministering" within the church?

Should laypeople be "ministering" within the church? I thought this was the realm of clergy and religious, and that (even according to Vatican II) the apostolate of the laity was to be "in the world."

■ *Answer*

Yes, laypeople should be ministering within the church today, as laypeople have been doing throughout the history of the church. "Ministry," after all, is a very broad word, and includes (in the church) anything one might do to bring the message of the gospel home to individuals, families, parishes, communities, and special groups of people. Thus the work the laity has been doing for centuries in the field of catechetics alone, for instance, constitutes a magnificent ministry of service. Parents in their own homes have throughout the history of the church been ministers to their children, not only when they teach them the truths of our faith, but also in every act of caring for them in physical, educational, or social ways. All of this, when given a faith dimension, is ministry within the church, and there is no way that this should be restricted to the clergy and religious.

Second, I think Vatican II officially (and at long last) paved the way for us to get away from considering ourselves apart from "the world." If Vatican II says that the ministry of the laity is to be "in the world," that is because our church, the people of God, exists in (and only in) the world. For too long, I think, we have separated our physical or bodily life from our "spiritual" or religious life. We do not have two lives. We have one life, a human life, and that human life is lived in the world. Our life (and therefore ministry) cannot be exercised separately in the "church" and "in the world." People live in the world; they need our ministry where they are. We (clergy, religious, and laity alike) must minister, therefore, in the world.

It is true that the gospels portray Christ as saying, "I am not of this world," and our penchant for distinguishing between "the world" and "the church" is based on this. But the important word in that passage is the preposition "of." That passage was equating "the world" with the "forces of evil." Christ was simply saying that he was separating himself from the forces of evil and allying himself with the forces of good. But we have tended to forget that fact in the course of these twenty centuries, and have come to set ourselves apart from (and above!) the real world around us as though the world (God's creation) were evil. That is simply not so.

Your question brings up another matter: the "calling forth" of the laity by bishops and priests has largely been a call to volunteer ministry. Except for the non-clerical religious (sisters and brothers) we have for the most part failed to give serious thought to the concept of what might be called "career" lay ministers. Oh, we have of late (mostly because of the current shortage of religious brothers and sisters) employed the laity to teach in our Catholic schools; some have been employed as parish directors of religious education; others have been given secretarial or business positions.

But how much "recruiting" do we do to obtain and provide training for dedicated laypeople to become full-time (and therefore paid) home and foreign missionaries, catechists, social ministers, family ministers, youth ministers, liturgical ministers, evangelists, theologians, and administrative ministers?

Such people, it seems to me, are needed to put their own expertise and experience specifically as laypeople to work to meet the needs of people in the world (the church) today. We cannot go on expecting wives/mothers or husbands/fathers to "make a living" for their families through their professions, and then to take themselves away from their families to volunteer their preciously little remaining time to ministry in the church. It is primarily for this reason, I think, that the revival of the permanent diaconate has been significantly *ineffective*. The dedicated men who've become deacons were trained and are working only on a part-time, volunteer basis. The demands made upon them are far beyond the capabilities of any human, if they are also to maintain their roles as husbands and fathers in their families. The same is true for any layperson who wants to devote herself or himself to ministry in the church today.

I grant that it is an idealistic goal; it may never be realized. But I am convinced that unless and until this real problem in our church is faced squarely and realistically, we will fail to adequately call upon the ministerial capabilities of our people and thus fail in our Christ-given task to "bring the gospel to all peoples."

Shouldn't only priests and deacons give the homily?

On a recent Sunday, a laywoman (or she might have been a nun) read the gospel and delivered the homily in our parish. I thought only a priest or a deacon was allowed to read the gospel and to preach a homily at Mass. Am I right?

■ *Answer*

It is clear from Canon 767 of the Code of Canon Law that the preaching of a "homily" is "part of the liturgy itself and is reserved to a priest or to a deacon." Canon law is less specific regarding who shall be permitted to read the gospel *at Mass*. But it's still clear there that an ordained cleric is designated to proclaim the gospel reading at Mass. I suppose if the only clerics present were unable to do so, a layperson could be so designated.

The General Instruction of the Roman Missal also makes it clear that either the presider or a deacon is to read the gospel, and that one of these is also to give the homily. However, both canon law and the General Instruction of the Roman Missal allow for "special occasions or circumstances" under which someone else may "speak" or "give an exhortation or instruction on a particular matter" of special pertinence to that community after the reading of the gospel. Certainly all of us have experienced those occasions when "experts" or especially skilled persons in various fields are asked to speak after the reading of the gospel to a community gathered on a Sunday for the Eucharist.

Nonetheless, it is clear from both of these sources that, when these special occasions arise when such a "talk" by a layperson or religious is appropriate, the term "homily" should not be used to describe it. In church rubrics and law, the term "homily" specifically describes "the application at Mass by a member of the clergy of the gospel reading of the day (and, perhaps, the other Scripture readings) to local and contemporary Christian faith, life, and practice, and to pertinent issues of the day." In this light, it would seem, dear friend, that the occasion you describe could have been totally within both the letter and spirit of the law only if the priest or deacon had read the gospel and if the talk had not been described as a "homily."

Having thus exposed the ritual and canonical "rules" on the matter, let me add a few of my own thoughts. I know of situations similar to the event you describe. I must say that, given the skills, theology, and faith commitment of the people normally invited to give "talks" at Mass, I certainly support this growing movement within the church.

It may be true that a cleric should have read the gospel and the address should not have been called a homily. But why should we be deprived of the tremendous gifts that so many of our dedicated laity and religious can give us, sometimes most efficaciously, within the context of the Sunday liturgy? Because of his special position in the community of the church, I do understand that the priest is the presider at our eucharistic liturgy. I can even understand why priests are assigned the special role of presenting the homily.

However, knowing my own weaknesses and limitations as a priest, and having experienced the strength, speaking skills, and faith commitment of many religious and laypeople over the years, I think that church leaders should amend the rules and make it possible for such people to give the homily at Sunday Mass. It is only in this way that the very great majority of our people could have the opportunity to share in the faith insights of such talented and faith-filled people.

Don't we all have the "Gifts of the Spirit"?

I'm very interested in the Catholic church's teachings on the gifts of the Holy Spirit, most especially the gift of healing in 1 Corinthians 12:9–11, 28–31.

However, someone told me that these gifts were only for that time in history while Jesus was alive and teaching. If that is so, then the Holy Spirit was only working during that time frame also. Then what was the point of the gifts if we couldn't use them today and tomorrow?

Is it wrong of me as a Catholic and a Christian to believe that God imparts the gifts of the Holy Spirit, all the gifts, to those earnestly seeking them prayerfully for the greater glory of God and for our fellow humans?

■ *Answer*

You are indeed correct in believing that the "gifts of the Spirit" as described by St. Paul are as available to us today as they were to the very first Christians! For that matter, these gifts have been available to every human being from the beginning of time and they will continue to be available until the end of time.

The problem, as I see it, is that most human beings in the history of humanity have not found it possible to recognize these gifts. Because of that, they have generally failed to use them well. Thus, for the most part, they remain unknown.

You see, dear friend, the "gifts of the Spirit" as described by St. Paul in the beautiful passage to which you refer were not anything "new." They're nothing more than the very gifts given by God (the Spirit!) to all humans during the creation of the world. But for many millennia until the coming of Jesus into our world, humans simply didn't realize they had these gifts for their own benefit and that of their fellow humans. It would not be wrong to say that one of the principal revelations in the life and teachings of Jesus Christ (and therefore of the New Testament writers) was that simply being fully human is filled with great dignity and "power." Human beings, after all, are endowed by the Creator with these tremendous gifts that Paul describes as "gifts of the Spirit."

Not that the Old Testament was lacking in this revelation! On the contrary, the very story of creation in the book of Genesis speaks of our creation "in the image and likeness of God," and who would dare to say that God in whose image we're created was lacking in these "gifts of the Spirit." Further, the story of "the fall" in that same biblical book gives evidence of the insight of its ancient writer that even in its primitive state humanity was endowed with tremendous gifts and powers.

Then, over and over again throughout the Old Testament "magnificent" or "wondrous" deeds are done by humans, usually attributed to "special" powers or favors from God, but nonetheless done by human beings.

Then the very wonders that were done throughout human history as attested to in secular history of human civilization—learning, architecture, and yes, even non-Christian religions—give evidence that humans have been endowed with the Spirit—gifts of wisdom, expressing knowledge, faith, healing, miraculous powers, prophecy, power to distinguish one spirit from another, tongues, and interpreting tongues. And as Paul concludes: "But it is one and the same Spirit who produces all these gifts, distributing them to each as he wills" (1 Cor 12:8–11). And he could have added: "...and when he wills!"

Indeed these gifts of the Spirit are still with us, and we see them manifested in many ways in our daily lives. Just go to any hospital and see the marvels of healing that take place there, hundreds of thousands of times each and every day. Some (even some who are exercising them!) don't recognize this healing as "the gift of healing," but it is!

Go to any school or any institution of learning and see the "gift of knowledge" and the "gift of prophecy" at work! Go to a session of the United Nations and see the "gift of interpreting tongues" working its magic, or should I say miracles. And I could go on, and on, and on!

God is good! God always has been! God always will be! And God shares that goodness (gifts!) with us! Therein lies the truth that we have come to call the "gifts of the Spirit."

PART FOUR

Church Teachings

Authentic Teaching

Which is the ultimate authority: tradition or Scripture?

If church tradition and sacred Scripture conflict, which one is the ultimate authority?

■ *Answer*

The Catholic church does not view tradition and Scripture as "authorities," much less as authorities that are vying for precedence against each other.

The Catholic church teaches that there are several "sources of divine revelation," the principal ones of which are sacred Scripture and sacred tradition. Even as sources of revelation, one does not take precedence over the other, and actually they are never in conflict. What may "seem" to be a conflict at times is simply a misunderstanding of one or the other (or both). God, we believe, uses these two means (along with others) to reveal the truth to us. We do not believe that God would reveal one thing in the Bible and something different in sacred tradition.

The real question is: Who has the ultimate right to interpret the true meaning of either source of revelation? The Catholic church has maintained that she has this right by virtue of the mission she bears from Christ to "Go forth and teach all nations whatever I have commanded you." This in no way restricts the right of any individual (Catholic or otherwise) to his or her own opinion about the interpretation of God's revelation. However, when the church does officially give an interpretation to a particular passage in Scripture or a particular part of tradition (which would rarely, if ever, be done in any kind of final way), Catholics would be bound to accept this teaching of the church whether they do actually agree with it or not.

Another important point in the relationship of Scripture and tradition (or perhaps I should say tradition and Scripture) is that sacred Scripture is basically the *written* tradition of God's people: the Old Testament being the written tradition of the ancient Hebrew People of God, and the New Testament being the written tradition of the early years of the Christians. The point is that in the history of the Bible, we find that tradition is the initial method used by God in the revelatory process. This tradition is then put into writing and becomes a second source of the *same* revelation.

So you see, dear friend, we need not pit God's wondrous sources of revelation against each other. They complement each other quite beautifully. Let us use them both to their fullest and thus learn of the marvels that God is constantly revealing to us.

What do you believe in?

I've heard you preach and read some of your writings. It's obvious you don't believe that the stories in the Bible are historically true; you don't believe in the revelation that come to us in private visions; you don't have much faith in devotions like the rosary. Miracles and wonders seem to "turn you off." So really, what do you believe in?

■ *Answer*

I believe in one God, the Father the Almighty, maker of heaven and earth, of all that is seen and unseen. I believe in one Lord, Jesus Christ, the only Son of God, eternally begotten of the Father, God from God, Light from Light, true God from true God, begotten, not made, one in Being with the Father. Through him all things were made. For us people and for our salvation he came down from heaven: by the power of the Holy Spirit he was born of the Virgin Mary, and became human.

For our sake he was crucified under Pontius Pilate; he suffered, died, and was buried. On the third day he rose again in fulfillment of the Scriptures; he ascended into heaven and is seated at the right hand of the Father. He will come again in glory to judge the living and the dead, and his kingdom will have no end.

I believe in the Holy Spirit, the Lord, the giver of life, who proceeds from the Father and the Son. With the Father and the Son he is worshiped and glorified. He has spoken through the prophets. I believe in one, holy, catholic and apostolic church. I acknowledge one baptism for the forgiveness of sins. I look for the resurrection of the dead, and the life of the world to come. Amen!

Surely you recognize all this as the "Profession of Faith" or "Creed," which we Catholics proclaim when we participate at Mass on Sundays. That, dear friend, is what I believe with every ounce of "believing power" within me. It is what my parents believed, and their parents, and their parents before them. This is what all Catholics believe and have believed down through the ages; it's the heart of the rich tradition that has come down to us, as well as of the Scriptures that rose up out of that tradition.

The challenge is for each of us as individuals, and each generation of individuals through the ages, to express what that faith means to us and to understand clearly how it is applied in the day-to-day lives we each lead. The particular expression that we use on Sundays evolved out of the faith of our church Fathers in the great Council of Nicea in the year 325 A.D., almost 1,700 years ago. We cannot deny that it is a true expression of our unchanging faith, but it certainly is not true that it's the only possible expression of that faith, nor that the words in which this Nicene Creed expresses our faith can never be changed; or that our faith cannot be expressed or explained in different words and through different concepts to meet the continually changing needs of believing Christians through the years.

Be that as it may, I can and do use that ancient expression of our beloved faith each Sunday precisely because I do believe that our faith is truly and properly expressed in these words. On the other hand, I find a need to take these same articles of faith and "translate" them into something that is more meaningful and relates better to the world as we see it and know it as we begin the third millennium. I must dig behind these words of the ancient Fathers of our church, as I must dig behind the words of the human authors of Scripture, so that I can find in today's concepts, language, and world, the right way to express and live those same eternal truths of the Nicene Creed in which I do believe and will always believe.

Why don't you refer more people to the Catechism of Catholic Church?

When people ask you questions, why don't you refer your readers to the *Catechism of the Catholic Church* for their answers? Why doesn't every religious education teacher have a copy of the *Catechism of the Catholic Church* as a reference to teach from? The Catechism is an authentic reference text for teaching Catholic doctrine for those who want to know what the Catholic Church believes.

■ *Answer*

Dear friend, you are so right in referring to the *Catechism of the Catholic Church* as a reference work, for that it is, and indeed a very valuable one. Those of us actively involved in teaching Catholic doctrine and moral principals find it a valuable reference tool.

However, the emphasis must be on the word *"reference,"* because in promulgating the Catechism, His Holiness, Pope John Paul II, clearly describes it as a "reference" and "source" book as distinct from a "teaching" or "textbook" manual.

The Apostolic Constitution *Fidei Depositum* (*The Deposit of Faith*), announcing the publication of the *Catechism of the Catholic Church,* reveals the pope's intentions and hopes with regard to the Catechism. Among other papal intentions described there, the pope indicates that he wants the Catechism to serve the church by providing a statement of faith that will "strengthen the bonds of unity" in the church. The pope expects the *Catechism* to accomplish this task by its being used as "a sure and authentic source book for the teaching of Catholic doctrine and especially for the composition of local catechisms."

The Prologue to the *Catechism* itself makes it clear that the *Catechism* is intended primarily for bishops in their role as teachers and pastors. Through the bishops, the *Catechism* is also addressed to all others responsible for instruction in the faith, which is where religion teachers (or "CCD teachers" [the old Confraternity of Christian Doctrine] as many still call them) get the responsibility of using the *Catechism* as a source and reference tool for their teaching.

But nowhere in the document itself, in the Apostolic Constitution promulgating it, or in its promulgation by the National Conference of Catholic Bishops (NCCB), has anyone referred to it as a book to which we should refer people for answers to their questions about the teachings of the church. It is for this reason, then, that I would never stoop to the level of using the *Catechism of the Catholic Church* as though it had the ready answers to the questions posed to me by those who write.

It is, however, incumbent upon me, if there is doubt in my mind about any teaching of the church, to use the *Catechism* as one of my sources or reference works. Note that I emphasize that the *Catechism* is only "one" source at my disposal; there are many others which, depending upon the subject matter, can be equally valuable in my continuing effort to "absorb" into my very being the full faith and teachings of the church, so that I can properly exercise my Christian and priestly ministry of evangelizing (bringing the gospel to) and sharing my faith with all with whom I come into contact through my writing and otherwise.

In other words, dear friend, I feel it would be irresponsible on my part to simply refer people to passages in the *Catechism* or any other source for the answers to their questions. On the other hand, when appropriate, I wouldn't hesitate to refer someone to an article in the *Catechism* as part of their overall search for truth. But I would do so only because in that particular instance I felt they could help themselves thereby to reach into their *own* faith to develop the answer they are seeking.

The *Catechism of the Catholic Church* is not a "Question and Answer" book. As you yourself say: "The *Catechism* is an authentic reference text" for teaching the Catholic faith. I and all others who participate in the teaching mission of the church should use it precisely as such. Christ came to live among us, I remind you, as a *person*—not as a theological system or catechism book.

Encountering the person of Christ will save us. A mere handbook of questions and answers can't.

Don't certain theologians teach heresy?

I was absolutely dumbfounded by your response to my question recently concerning a certain theologian's book on the sacraments. How any leader in our church can say that he agrees with everything that man says in this book is beyond my comprehension. If someone expresses an opinion that is opposed to the official teaching of the church, isn't he or she teaching heresy? And if so, how can a Catholic agree with such an opinion?

■ *Answer*

First let me assure you and all my readers that I did not state that I agreed with everything that theologian says in the books he wrote on the sacraments. I not only did not say that, but as a matter of fact I can state quite categorically that I do not agree with every position taken in those books, and that theologian would be the first one to assure me that he did not and does not expect me or anyone to agree with everything he says there.

To me this theologian seems quite strong in the position that every individual human being should, and indeed must, have the freedom to dutifully and responsibly form her or his conscience.

You see, dear friend, it is not necessary that we humans or we Catholics agree on absolutely everything. That's a false notion that has plagued the church for centuries—in fact, from its very beginning. Expressions of valid disagreements among us can be found in the gospels, in the Acts of the Apostles (a biblical account of the life of the early church), and in various other New Testament books. It can also be found, perhaps even more dramatically, in the books of the Old Testament.

The fact of the matter is that intellectual, practical, and experiential differences can, if rightly perceived and lovingly shared, be the lifeblood or source of extreme richness in human society and in the church. Indeed, it would be a doleful church and world if absolutely every one of us were identical, and all agreed on every matter that might come before us. Oh, that would be fine if there were indeed a chance that each of us humans as individuals could reach the apex of total and unlimited knowledge of all things; total and unlimited mutual love; total and unlimited perfection in life. But then each of us would be God! And we are not meant to be God (only *like* God), and we certainly will never reach that pinnacle.

In the meantime, what we do need is to share with one another, as this theologian does in his books, the full scope of our own knowledge, experience, and love, and thus bring humanity as a whole ever closer to its goal of its creation "in the image and likeness of God."

It is for this reason that I am not offended in the least (in fact, I rejoice) when I am told by some that they disagree with some positions I take. What horrifies me is those who take the position that I should not express (and should be admonished if I do) my own convictions, life experiences, and faith, unless I do so in words identical to those used in official church documents or statements, or unless I do so in words or concepts that are identical to those which they would use. In other words, for some it seems that the truth can be found in only one place and in only one expression.

The Bible itself, from Genesis to Revelation, puts the inevitable lie to that because, while we all know the absolute truth and inerrancy of the Word of God in that collection of books, certainly we also know the thousands of innate contradictions in the human words, expressions, convictions, and experiences that are recounted there to express that Word.

Do I agree with everything this theologian says or writes? Definitely not! Do I appreciate and hail what he has done in expressing his convictions, faith, and life? Very definitely yes! And a mountain of thanks for it.

Can't the church come up with a better answer than "mysteries"?

As I grow older, I become more and more impatient with our church's teaching about mysteries. It seems that every time the church is given a question to which it doesn't know the answer, she immediately tells us: "Well that's a mystery, so you'll just have to accept it on faith." More and more that seems to me like a "cop-out." This question may not be worth your while, but can't we come up with a better answer than that?

■ *Answer*

Thanks for an excellent question, and it very definitely is worth my while.

My understanding of the meaning of the word "mystery" goes back to a book that we used as a religion text when I was in my first year of college at the seminary. I still remember it so well, even though that was over fifty years ago. The name of the book was *Theology and Sanity*, by Frank Sheed, who was a prominent lay theologian of the time. Mr. Sheed described a mystery as the combination of two truths of faith—two separate truths, about each of which we are certain either through faith or through our reason (or both). But as confident as we can be about the certainty of the individual truths, we somehow cannot see with our human reasoning power how both of them can be true at the same time.

For instance, we can be absolutely certain (some think by reason; others say only by faith) that there is and can be only one God. At the same time our faith in Divine revelation given to us in Scripture and sacred tradition tells us that there are three Divine Persons: the Father, the Son, and the Holy Spirit, and that each of these is equally and totally divine; that each is therefore God! It is the combination of these two truths that is described in what we call the "mystery" of the Blessed Trinity, since neither our human reason nor even the strength of our faith can understand how these two great truths can be simultaneously true.

Similarly, we can be quite certain from both history and faith that a human being named Jesus of Nazareth was born of a young lady named Mary about two thousand years ago. We can also be certain in faith that this same Jesus of Nazareth is the one whom we call Jesus Christ, and that this Jesus Christ is also the divine "Son of God" or, as he is sometimes called, the "second Person of the Blessed Trinity." It is again the combination of these two truths that is described as the "mystery" of the Incarnation, since neither our human reason nor even the strength of our faith can understand how these two great truths can be simultaneously true.

But our lack of ability to understand the combination of these truths does not make these combinations or mysteries any less true. Mr. Sheed expresses it something like this: a mystery is not a vast void of darkness that our minds cannot penetrate. On the contrary, he says, a mystery is more like an unending tunnel of light, through which we need to continually move, always absorbing more and more of the inexhaustible beauty and wonder of its truth. Thus a mystery is not so much something we cannot understand, but rather it is something that we can never finish understanding. As we travel through the tunnel of its light, more and more of it becomes part of us, ever enlightening us and making us part of itself, thus ever increasingly enriching our very existence.

For instance, we need to enhance our life by basking in the ineffable light of the oneness of God, and at the same time let the richness of the "threeness" of God shed its own light upon us to enrich us with its own inestimable value. We must not allow the unending search for "the end of the tunnel" discourage us from continuing our voyage through it, because it is that continuing search that will enable us to grow into the very likeness of our creator as we travel through his light. The Trinity is not something we "cannot understand"; it is rather something we must continue to comprehend and absorb into eternity.

Shouldn't we be in communion with the pope and the church?

If a eucharistic minister doesn't believe or follow what the church and the pope teach, why do they give or receive Jesus in communion? My understanding is that the pope is Jesus' Vicar on earth, and if they don't believe his teaching, they must not believe the teachings of Jesus either. So why would they want to give Jesus to anyone?

■ *Answer*

Let me hastily answer your question. To give or receive communion properly and in keeping with its true meaning and purpose, we must be in communion (i.e., united) with the pope and the church.

You see, dear friend, the problem is that each of us can have (and properly so!) our own interpretation of what "being in communion with the pope and the church" really means. For instance, over the centuries many popes have said and done things that neither the church nor I would ever "believe in." Popes are very fallible human beings like the rest of us. Every one of them from St. Peter to the present has said and done things that were incorrect. The church has always known and believed that.

The doctrine of the papal infallibility has nothing to do with his personal opinions about doctrine or morality. Without going into a detailed explanation of infallibility, let me simply and succinctly restate here the basic concept of that doctrine. The pope enjoys the same infallibility enjoyed by the whole church! He exercises that infallibility only if and when he declares that he is teaching with the infallible authority of his office as head of the church and Vicar of Christ and that what he is teaching is part of "the faith of the church." Since the First Vatican Council defined papal infallibility in 1870, only one church doctrine has been enunciated infallibly, the assumption of the Blessed Virgin Mary in 1950. (The doctrine of the immaculate conception was enunciated in 1854, before the First Vatican Council defined infallibility.)

Let me hasten to add that it is *not* true to say that we can disregard or take lightly those teachings of the pope on faith and morals that are not given with infallible authority. As you indicate, he is indeed the head of the church and the Vicar of Christ on earth, and we as faithful Christians are bound to give his teachings grave consideration. We are free to dissent from them only if we have grave reason to do so. Also, if we are not well versed in theology, we should seek counsel from those who are well versed in it before making a judgment that is contrary to papal teaching. Finally, it is incumbent upon us who are in positions of authority in the church to beware lest we (even inadvertently) mislead others into thinking that they or we need not heed the voice of this Vicar of Christ.

Mary, Our Blessed Lady

Can you say something positive about Mary?

As we approach the celebration of Christmas, I wonder if you'd state something positive about devotion to the Blessed Virgin Mary, the rosary, her appearances to various people in the history of the church, and so forth. Almost everything I hear or read about her lately has been negative. Do you feel that way?

■ *Answer*

I do indeed have some positive thoughts and a strong faith in our dear Blessed Mother. I think every Christian of our day needs to see in Mary what St. John's account of the crucifixion scene makes her to be, the Mother of all Christians. We all recall the scene: Jesus looks down from the cross upon her and the beloved disciple and says, "Woman, there is your son" and "There is your mother." This passage should be a brightly shining symbol of exactly what the official church teaching about Mary has been from the very first days of its existence. She is the first of all Christians, since to be Christian means to be like Christ. Not only as another human being, but as his mother: his very physical makeup was formed out of her. Not only as a good person, but as his mother: she loved him more than any of us ever could. Not only as a faithful Jewish woman of her day, but as his mother: her faith in him and his mission as Savior was unquestioning. Not only as one of that group of his loyal female followers, but as his mother: she served his needs and the needs of his mission as none of us ever could.

Seeing her, therefore, not only as the mother of Jesus, but as *our* mother; seeing her not only as a great Christian saint, but the ultimate in what it means to be a Christian saint, each of us needs to make every effort to fashion ourselves after her. Each of us needs to see that our relationship and likeness to her grows constantly because thus we can be assured of a closer relationship and likeness to Jesus. Each of us needs to be devoted in our prayer to her, thus keeping her glowing image of Christianity before our consciousness. I like to think that John's account tells us she has to be "Mom" to us, with all that this endearing and meaningful term means in the intimacy of every family. It is similar, though not identical, to the concept that Jesus attempted to convey when he said we should call God our "Abba," an Aramaic term meaning "Father."

There have been hundreds of "alleged" appearances of Mary in the course of the twenty centuries since her death. In every authentic case the church has approved the devotions offered by the faithful in connection with the event. To the best of my knowledge the church has never officially declared or taught that such appearances actually took place (this is true even of the most famous, which perhaps are Lourdes and Fatima). What the church has approved are the devotions to Mary that center around the alleged appearances. For instance, I think the events at Lourdes over the last century have proven themselves to be of tremendous benefit to the faith of millions of people throughout the world, including my own (and many bishops and even popes). I remember with great fondness a visit I made to Lourdes some years ago, a visit that still today leaves its mark on my faith in and love for Mary as the Mother of us all.

On the other hand, there was much evidence of sensationalism, commercialization, and superstition in the town of Lourdes, which I think is out of place with the beautiful faith found in people at the shrine. It's these things that so often are the main emphasis whenever such claims of visions take place. When I am questioned about it, I don't hesitate to express the church's position on such matters. This in no way whatever lessens my love and devotion to Mary!

One more (unsolicited) thought: in the course of the history of the church, devotion to Mary grew very gradually from a very slight hint in the New Testament writings to its greatest height toward the middle of twentieth century when Pope Pius XII defined the assumption as an infallible dogma in 1950 and declared 1954 as "The Marian Year." By the time the Second Vatican Council convened in the early 1960s, many in the church were beginning to question whether Mary was being given a position above that of her Son. Thus, the Council saw fit to conclude its document on the church (*Lumen Gentium*) with an entire chapter on "Our Lady" (chapter 8), in the third section of which it clearly speaks of the danger and impropriety of placing Our Lady on a plane that is equal to or higher than that of her Son. This is the danger about which we must always be aware, since someone as attractive as Mary, beautiful in her universal motherhood, can so easily move us to unwittingly glorify her even beyond the glory of her Son. If we succumb to this, we do them both a great dishonor.

Is it OK to question Mary's virginity?

I've always believed in the perpetual virginity of Mary. At a recent Renew small group meeting, some members stated they believed that Jesus had brothers and sisters, and they quoted Mark 6:1–6 in support of their belief. I believe the Hebrew language had no explicit word to distinguish immediate blood brothers from cousins. Brothers (or sisters) are used in a more restricted sense today. Also Mark 3:31–35 seems to verify my beliefs. Who is right?

■ *Answer*

First let me state without any equivocation and as clearly as I possibly can: it is the official teaching of the church that Mary remained a virgin in the conception of Jesus and that she retained her virginity throughout her life. Second, I would like to profess openly, publicly, and as clearly as possible my full and unswerving faith in that teaching, without any doubts whatsoever. And so I beg all who question my loyalty to the magisterium of the church to reread those first two sentences before reading any more of what I have to say concerning the question asked.

Having stated the church's and my position on the matter, may I go on to express now my continuing agony in seeing the misuse of the Bible as a "proof" for historical facts or events, or as a "proof" for what we must or must not believe. But while not wanting or meaning to be offensive to many who use the Bible as a "proof book," I must say again that the Bible simply does not tell us or even try to tell us whether Mary remained a virgin throughout her life, nor does it try to establish as a fact that she remained a physical virgin even in the conception and birth of Jesus himself.

It is true that there are a number of passages in the Bible that would support the belief that Mary remained a virgin in the conception of Jesus. But the noted American scripture scholar Father Raymond Brown (who can hardly be considered "liberal" or "radical" in his views) has written extensively on this very topic, and his conclusion is that neither the Bible, nor church tradition, nor any historical evidence could prove Mary's virginal conception of

Jesus in a theological or scientific way. It is also his opinion that the gospels simply do not even touch on the matter of her continued virginity after the birth of Jesus. My understanding of his opinion is, therefore, that the church's teaching on the perpetual virginity of Mary (in which both he and I firmly believe) is based solely on the church's own authority to teach.

Volumes and volumes of words have been written concerning the passages you quote concerning the "brothers and sisters" of Jesus. Here again Father Brown points out quite clearly that it is possible that the evangelists were using the words "brother and sister" rather loosely as was often the case in Hebrew custom, as you seem to believe. But it is equally possible that the words were used in the strict sense of what we call a "brother" and a "sister." In this case, the gospel writers were very likely unaware of the question of Mary's continuing virginity. It is quite obvious in the passages to which you refer that the writers were not referring to the virginity, perpetual or otherwise, of Mary. That text of Scripture is simply not commenting on this matter at all.

Therefore no matter what we rightfully interpret those passages to mean and teach as the "word of God," on this we must agree: that they cannot be used to establish or deny as historical fact the perpetual virginity of Mary.

Getting back to the teaching of the church, I think it is extremely important that we emphasize the reality that our faith in the divinity of Jesus Christ in no way depends upon the factual history of his virginal conception and birth; much less on the perpetual virginity of his mother. He could have been born of a normal union of man and woman, and he could have had real brothers and sisters, and our faith in his divinity would remain very much intact. It is extremely important that we do not allow our faith in important teachings of the church about Mary to cast a negative shadow on the even more important truths about Christ himself. Otherwise we could find ourselves giving legitimate credence to the accusations of those Christian churches that criticize us for the exalted place of Mary in our church.

Can you prove Mary's burial and assumption?

On what does the church base the teaching of Mary's assumption?
I've heard that there are two places in the Holy Land that claim
proof of Mary's burial place. Did the apostles witness her death
and assumption?

■ *Answer*

To the best of my knowledge, the doctrine of the assumption is not
based on any reliable historical fact or direct biblical passage. It was
Pope Pius XII in 1950 who defined this teaching as a doctrine of
the church, but, while stating that this truth does have a scriptural
basis, Pius XII cited passages from Scripture that have no clear and
certainly no explicit reference to the assumption. Perhaps the most
significant passage used by Pius XII in this definition was the same
one used in the definition by Pope Pius IX in his definition of the
immaculate conception: "Hail, full of grace, the Lord is with you;
blessed are you among women."

Here is what the Catholic Encyclopedia says: "That fullness of
grace bestowed on the Blessed Virgin was, according to Pius XII,
only achieved by her Assumption."

As a matter of fact, then, the most solid basis for this teaching
of the church lies in sacred tradition rather than on biblical evidence. It is an almost incontrovertible fact that from the very early
centuries of the church's existence, there persisted the belief that
Mary was assumed into heaven "body and soul," and it was this
persistent faith of the people of God which, it seems, moved Pius
XII to declare it a doctrine of the church.

With regard to the supposed burial places of Mary, I can assure
you that there is and can be no proof that those are authentic, and
every possible historical criterion would declare them not to be so.
As a matter of fact, there has long been a sometimes rather bitter
controversy in the church as to whether Mary ever died at all. At
the present time, it is almost universally held that she indeed did
die. But if even that fact can be subject to doubt, how much more
so would any claim about a burial place?

Further, there is no way that we could know who might have or might not have witnessed the death of Mary, and there is certainly no evidence that there were any witnesses to what is now known as her assumption. Although belief in the assumption is of early origin in the church, there is no evidence whatsoever that any thought of it ever entered the mind of any of the apostles. Such a mysterious and miraculous event would certainly have found its way into the Scriptures had the evangelists or other New Testament authors been aware of it.

I would hope that all my readers will understand that none of the above is written to express or convey any doubt whatsoever in my own or any one else's faith in the doctrine of the assumption. After all, it is a defined doctrine of our faith, and as such I give it the full credence of my faith, as I hope would every Catholic Christian.

Did Mary retain her "physical" virginity?

I was somewhat taken aback by the statement by the pope that "Mary's virginity is not just symbolic, but physical," and that, Mary's "hymen...was not broken despite the fact that she became pregnant and gave birth." How remarkable it was that the bishops in Capua, Italy, in 392 were able to get hold of a photo of Mary's lower anatomy, which gave them the authority to make that public statement for the church to accept for centuries to come. Can you comment on this?

■ Answer

I, too, was somewhat "taken aback" by what the pope said there. I, like the pope and like the bishops at Capua in 392, have absolutely no historical evidence by which I can draw a logical conclusion about the historicity of the physical virginity of our Blessed Mother. But my real problem about all this is not whether their conclusions and resulting teachings can be reconciled with historical truth, but rather I can't for the life of me understand why our acceptance of this medical fact about her is so important to our faith in her as Jesus' Mom.

You see, dear friend, as I see it in faith, the virginity of the Mother of the Savior as expressed in the Scriptures and our tradition is very simply a means of emphasizing the great importance and unusual character of her motherhood, in the light of the person of the son whom she bore. Our ancient forebears who wrote our Scriptures and handed on our traditions were limited by their own languages, customs, cultures, and education as they sought to express the divine truths that they were inspired to pass on to all generations after them.

As we all know, the inspiration of the Holy Spirit, which by Christian doctrine was essential to God's revelation to us in the Scriptures and in sacred tradition, did not include the divine infusion of truth into the beings of the sacred writers and speakers. Nor did it include the infusion of an ability to express those truths in some sort of mystically acquired new language. These inspired people had to use their own natural (God-given, yes, but still only natural) abilities, and their language, storytelling, and intelligence skills to express what God wanted to reveal in their writings and teachings.

And I think it is clear that the doctrine of the virginity of Mary was not expressed in the Scriptures and in our tradition in order that we might know what a gynecological test would have revealed about Mary's anatomy before, during, or after the birth of Jesus. It was, I think, a matter of helping us see the importance, purpose, value, and dignity of her motherhood as the mother of the Christ, the Savior, the Son of Man, the Son of God. That, I think, is the point of this doctrine of the virginity of Mary, and an extremely important point it is!

Vatican II and Change

Why does the church put such emphasis on Vatican II?

For many years now, it seems that too much emphasis is being placed on the Second Vatican Council. I understand that it was important, but must everything the church has done in the last 2,000 years be forgotten?

■ *Answer*

Indeed it would be a gigantic tragedy if we did forget "everything the church has done in the last 2,000 years," but that is certainly *not* what the Second Vatican Council stands for. On the contrary, precisely the opposite is true. Vatican II explicitly sought to recapture or reinforce the rich tradition of the church over the last 2,000 years! And much of the work the Council did was to *restore* ancient traditions and hallmarks of the church.

You see, dear friend, for over 400 years church leaders strongly adhered to the tradition as it was understood and promulgated by the Council of Trent in the sixteenth century. In so doing, many more ancient traditions were lost. All this was in an admirable effort to counter the Protestant movement, which the church regarded for hundreds of years as her "public enemy #1."

What Vatican II did was to help the church take a deep look into herself to determine if "public enemy #1" might not well be within the church herself. Through Vatican II we learned that our fellow Christians—the Anglicans, Orthodox, and Protestants—weren't so awful after all. We found, in fact, they could be a tremendous help in our own efforts to live the Christian life more fully.

At the same time we discovered that in our 400-year effort to combat the Protestants we hadn't taken sufficient time or given sufficient effort to develop theologically and scripturally ourselves! Most were content to rely totally on the theological theories of past theologians and the doctrinal decrees of the Council of Trent and Trent's understanding of previous ecumenical councils.

In "opening the doors and windows" of the church, Vatican II gave a new breath of fresh air to the church, and all of us should open the "nostrils of our faith" to breathe it in ever more deeply. This breath of fresh air is not a condemnation of the past 2,000 years, nor even of the last 400 years (for where would we be without them?), but rather a chance to recapture ancient traditions and adapt them to the circumstances in which we live today, as Trent did for the church of its day and centuries thereafter.

You see, dear friend, our faith is not a dead faith in which there is no room for change or development. Our faith (and therefore our church) is very much alive, and everything that lives must move forward and grow or it will die. This, to me, is the great "revelation" of Vatican II. It made us aware that we needn't adhere slavishly to past interpretations of our faith. Rather we must look to those interpretations as the foundation for an ever-new understanding. This enables that faith to inspire us to new horizons of Christianity for today and the future.

No, my friend, Vatican II has not condemned the past! It has re-enlivened the past! In doing so it has not asked us to go backward to that past, but rather, like the resurrected Christ, it has shown us that past in an ever new light. It has helped us recapture the spirit of resurrected life and shown us again that this life is meant to be lived, not only in the next world, but even in this one.

(Author's Note: Please read the next two questions and answers for additional and somewhat different concepts about this matter. Thanks!)

Does anyone care about us pre-Vatican II Catholics?

I was already an adult during the years of Vatican II, and some of the changes in our church that resulted from that Council are very difficult and, in some cases, impossible for me to accept. Please know that I'm not alone in my feelings; I know of many once dedicated Catholics who feel left out because they cannot "unlearn" some of the things they learned long ago. The hurt these people experience is heartbreaking. Does anyone at all care about those of us in this situation?

■ *Answer*

Yes, I am fully confident that many, many people care about you and all such people. And we who do care about you, want very much to help you see that the church, that is, the *real* church, has not abandoned you, but is attempting to respond in many ways to your real needs. I hope I can shed some light on that here.

I am fully confident that just about everyone in the church has had at least some problem with some of the changes that have taken place in the church as a result of Vatican II. Many people cannot accept some of those changes as being for the good of themselves or of the church in general. I, like you, am one of those people who have had this experience. On the other hand, I have welcomed with open arms the very great majority of these changes as a giant step forward out of the crumbling past into the glorious future for our church. In other words, I have not allowed my disenchantment with some of the changes to blind me to the great positive influence for good that others have had. This, I think, is one way of coping with those changes that I struggle to accept.

Second, I think that many people suffer with the mistaken concept that they must "unlearn" what they learned in the past in order to accept the current teaching and practice of the church. I'm convinced this is not so at all. If we compare it to other learning experiences, I think we might understand it better. For instance, I learned to drive a car in a 1937 Ford. I bought a new car recently: if I hadn't learned new driving skills in keeping with the developments in automobile technology and driving customs and new traffic laws, I would long ago have been injured, killed, or jailed in the process of trying to drive my new car. Did I have to "unlearn" what I learned on that old 1937 Ford? Not at all! But I did have to add to, enhance, and develop my driving skills over the years.

Similarly, I learned to read when I was six years old. Once having learned that skill, had I insisted that I knew it all and refused to change, what would I do with words today like "television," and "astronaut," and "rocket booster," and "satellite" and so forth? Must I "unlearn" what I learned before? Hardly, but I sure had to learn more!

The same thing is true about our knowledge of the church, its teachings, and its practices. We do not have to "unlearn" anything! What we must do is be as open to learning new things about our faith and its practice as we are about learning new ways of doing the other things of life. For instance, one of the principal things we learned as children about our church was that it was an "unchanging" church; that the truths taught by our church were not going to change and that the ways we do things in the church were not going to change. That was definitely true when we were learning it (unfortunately I think, but it was a fact). That truth did not become false after Vatican II, so we don't have to go back and "unlearn" it. What we must do as a result of Vatican II is to realize that changes can and do take place in our teachings and practices. This adds to our understanding of the church. It doesn't negate the past.

Perhaps I can refer you to my dear departed mother, who was 72 years old when Vatican II ended. The changes that took place in her beloved church during the last 10 years of her life (She died at 83 in 1976.) were somewhat difficult for her to understand, and yet no one I ever knew accepted even the difficult ones more readily. Her love for the church moved her to see the good in what the Council did. Rather than spend her energy in resistance and anger, she spent it in accepting the reform of the church for the good that it was. Her own faith was strengthened in the process, and her life was thereby enriched. She not only avoided feeling hurt because of Vatican II, but found even deeper happiness. I hope it will eventually do the same for you and your dear friends.

(Author's Note: Please read the next question and answer for additional and somewhat different concepts about this matter. Thanks!)

Why does our young associate pastor dress, act, preach, and minister like priests did before Vatican II?

Thanks to a series of progressive pastors, we live in a parish brimming with enthusiasm about the progress we have made in implementing the teachings of the church since the Second Vatican Council. Our liturgies are outstanding examples of a "community at worship," with very active involvement and participation from all segments of the community. Our pastoral council, finance council, and their committees provide excellent leadership in all aspects of parish life, inspired by the spirit of Vatican II.

However, for several years now, many of us are rather dumbfounded by our young associate pastor, who seems to be a reincarnation of someone born 100 years ago; Whenever we see him he is always wearing a cassock or clerical suit and collar. He repeatedly tells us at every opportunity that we ought to return to the Latin liturgy of old, to kneeling at "altar rails" for communion, to being ministered to only by the ordained (priests and deacons), to banishing females from the sanctuary, and thus to basically turning the liturgy and the church back to what they were before Vatican II.

What's up with this guy? We ask our pastor, and he really doesn't seem to know what to say. Can you help?

■ *Answer*

Gee, I hope so! Believe me, I know exactly what you're talking about because your young associate pastor is not alone in this. There has been a concerted effort over the last twenty years or so, led by some rather "conservative" bishops and the staffs of a few seminaries in this country and others, to reverse much of the reforms and progress in the church since Vatican II. This "movement" (if we can properly call it that) seems to have some of its roots even in the Roman Curia (those who staff the highest positions in the church directly under the pope), and some progressive church leaders even think that our Holy Father, Pope John Paul II, has occasionally in his teachings, writings, and decisions shown a tendency to revert to some of the rigors of the past. It is also encouraged greatly by a well-known "Catholic" television network and its founder.

For us who lived for years through the sometimes comfortable rigor of the pre-Vatican II church (with most decisions "pre-made" for us), it was with much trepidation, doubt, and difficulty that we began slowly in the late 1960s and 1970s to allow ourselves to grasp first, then appreciate, and finally implement the teachings and reforms promulgated by the church as a result of Vatican II.

Having spent ourselves doing that, we now see our young people being urged by some church leaders to "back off" from the "new" church and to revert to the church that we needed to grow out of and that these young people have only heard or read about. It is not easy for us who have worked and ministered so strenuously to help our church (the people of God!) enter into the Third Millennium as a vigorous, growing, enlivened, worldwide community of renewed faith, to hear now, even from some church leaders in high places, that we have "walked too fast"; that, following the call of Pope John XXIII, we have "opened the windows and doors of the church" too widely and allowed too much of the "world out there" to get in, or too much of our "church world" to get out to the rest of the world.

Dear friend, I perhaps have said too much already in response to the plight in which you tell me you and your parish find yourself today. But let me add this: do not—please do not—denounce or judge too harshly this young man who is obviously struggling within himself to see the right path to the kingdom for himself and those whom he serves. Nor should you or I denounce or judge unfairly the older church leaders, be they religious, priests, bishops, cardinals, or even the pope when they seem to be going against what we see as the bounteous tide of grace brought to us as a result of Vatican II.

Somewhere deep within him, and all of them whom we cannot understand right now in the light of our own understanding of church, I think I can see myself some thirty-five or forty years ago. I, in my youthful priestly vigor and enthusiasm, heralded a "never failing and inerrant" church which was, is and always will be "One, holy, catholic and apostolic," but perhaps most of all: *"unchanging."* I can even remember as late as 1970 telling a slightly younger priest than I that I didn't see any need to further my education or development in the faith. After all, hadn't I been through eleven years of that in the seminary just a few (16) short years ago?

Yes, there was I just some 30 short years ago! Oh, how I thank God for the grace to grow out of that. *But I didn't do it because someone told me I was wrong!* I did it because of what I saw in those who were doing it before me; because they *invited me to join them* in the beauty and happiness of the "new life" they were experiencing within the renewed church. I did it because the lives of the people whom I served were "crying out loud" for what the renewed church had to offer. When I accepted that invitation and was "converted" (or perhaps "born again"?) into this newly enlivened church, there was and could be no turning back from this new "kingdom of God" on earth.

So let us not be condemning, as though they were *wrong* and we *right*, but let us be lovingly *inviting*, realizing that with God we can all be right. Let us not cast our new anathemas at them as Trent did of old (and *rightfully* so at, and for, that time), because they are no more anathema than we, but let us gently, kindly, lovingly, and "Christ-fully" *invite* and *encourage* them to walk *with us* through Pope John's open doors into the ever-new kingdom of God so that we might all share it unceasingly in the presence of God among us.

Why so much emphasis on the early church?

Why is there so much talk these days about how it was in the early years of the church? Why should we always be looking (and going) back to how the church was in the beginning, when the world today is so different?

■ *Answer*

I sincerely hope you are correct that there is "so much talk these days about how it was in the early years of the church." I think we, as the church, do need to think about and discuss the roots of our Christian faith and life. Pope John XXIII asked us to do this as part of the reforms launched at Vatican II.

Why is this so important? Because without keeping our roots and foundations constantly before us, we could easily lose sight of them and drift away to something that has no relationship whatsoever to what makes us Christian. Unless we know what it meant to be Christian to those upon whom our church was built, like St. Paul and St. Peter, for instance, then we can't be certain we are being faithful to the founding vision and mission.

We must not only consider what we read in the Bible, but also look at the history of those times and interpret the Bible in keeping with that history. We must try to establish how the principles of Christianity were applied to humanity as it was then, so that we can determine how those same principles, as they have been developed over the years, can properly be applied to humanity as it is today.

On the other hand, I think it is equally (and perhaps more) important that, in making ourselves more aware and knowledgeable of our roots, we do not make the frequent error of trying to "go back" to "the good old days." You are so right! The church today is indeed so different from what it was in the beginning; and so it should be! Every aspect of our world, our life, our relationships with the world around us and with God has developed, and therefore changed, dramatically over the last 2,000 years. If our faith and our faith-life or faith-community (the church) has not developed (changed) with us, then we would be living in an unrealistic world, an unrealistic life, an unrealistic church. In brief, we would be living in "make-believe."

There is indeed a tendency among some in our church not only to "think back" or "talk back," but also to "go back." Therein lies the great danger of looking at our roots. It's so easy to make this a simple nostalgic "trip." It's so easy for us to think that we should be doing the same things Jesus did; the apostles did; the early Christians did; the great saints of the Middle Ages did; the Council of Trent demanded; our great grandparents did; our parents did; we did some forty, or thirty, or even twenty years ago. If we read, think about, and pray over the Scriptures in a realistic way, I think they will cry out to us with a loud voice: *Be a people of today and tomorrow (not a people of the past).*

Build on the foundation of the past (yes!); but build for yourselves a humanity and church for today, a humanity and church for tomorrow, a humanity and church that are ever looking to the future as the only viable goal.

I think, for instance, that this is the message of that passage in the gospels wherein Jesus insists: "I have come not to abolish the law, but to fulfill it." We must ever be a fulfilling people, a developing people, a growing people; or, as Vatican II put it, "a pilgrim people." But unless we continually "look back" and "think back" to our beginnings, to our roots, and build that fulfillment, that development, that growth, and that pilgrimage upon the solid foundation of our beginnings, then I'm afraid we will grow or develop ourselves right out of Christianity itself.

That, I think, is what has happened to many "so called" Christians of today. By looking back to their roots only through their fundamentalist reading of the Bible, and then trying to "go back" to that, they have failed to keep the basic concepts of Christianity alive. We must look back, but we must go forward. There's a world of difference, and we must not fail to see it and make it real.

Heaven, Hell, and Purgatory

What does the church teach about purgatory?
I believe there is a heaven and a hell. I have trouble, though,

believing in purgatory. What is the official teaching of the church about this "holding" place?

■ *Answer*

The research that I've done on this matter, as well as recent theological articles that I've read, seems to indicate that the doctrine of purgatory is indeed an essential element in the belief of the Christian church. The core of the church's teaching on purgatory is that there is a purification of some sort for all who die truly penitent, but without having made full satisfaction for their sins.

Furthermore, it can well be established that the church's teaching is that prayers for the dead are "useful," although there is no clear definition of what that usefulness is.

The official teachings of the church do not impose any obligation upon us with regard to what purgatory is like. Is it a place of fire? Probably not. That notions seems to have arisen in our imagination from Dante's description in *The Inferno*. Is it a place with geographic dimensions, like our home town? No, the church has never taught that it was a place as such. Is it a state of existence in which certain people spend some time after death? No, because time is part of this world and does not, to the best of our knowledge, exist in the next world. Is it a means that God uses after death to purify us of the "temporal punishment due to sin"? That seems to be what the *Baltimore Catechism* said, but how is it possible that "temporal" punishment (punishment for a time) can take place in a state where there is no "time"?

Some theologians are saying today that purgatory is something that takes place at the instant of the actual and final moment of life as we know it. In that moment there takes place whatever "purification" is needed before the person can rise from the gate of death to the glory of eternity. I guess that makes about as much sense to me as anything I have ever heard about purgatory, but even that theory leaves some unanswered questions.

Am I skirting the issue? Well, in a way I am. You see, dear friend, I really don't think we should concern ourselves too much with the idea of purgatory right now. There are two reasons for this.

First, no human being alive knows about these things. We can point to it, as one points to the moon, but we cannot fully describe it. Second, we do believe in life-after-death because of Christ's resurrection. But exactly what life-after-death will be like has not been fully revealed to us, and nothing in our experience can teach us this. However, we can know from our own reason, and also from God's revelation, what we must be and what we must do *now* to be good human beings and good Christians. That's what we need to concentrate on right now: living up to our role as human beings and children of God in this world.

To the extent that we succeed in this endeavor, it seems to me we will have been through the purification known as purgatory, and perhaps have reached heaven by the time of our death, and, if that is so, there is nothing to worry about! To the extent that we fail, that failure could be our purgatorial suffering or purification in one way or another, and it may not be necessary for us to look forward to such purification after death.

Does this mean that we should not pray for the dead? Certainly not! Our prayers for the dead are very definitely "useful," even though the church does not teach us exactly what the usefulness is. But each of us knows within his or her own conscience how important it is to us in faith and within the "communion of saints" to include in our prayers, especially the great Christian prayer called the Mass, all members of that communion including the dead. For this reason, if for no other, let us indeed continue our prayers for the dead!

What happened to hell and the devil?

I've heard priests talk about "the OLD hellfire and brimstone." Do they mean to say that there is no hell, or that the devil has evaporated into thin air? Do they mean that there is really no reward for leading a good life and no punishment for the opposite? Was that all just a fabrication of medieval popes or moral theologians? Is there indeed a heaven and a hell, or were these things just made up by theologians to scare us into following the rules?

■ *Answer*

No, I don't think priests really mean to say all that by using the expression "the old hellfire and brimstone," but I'm happy you got that impression, since it gives me the opportunity to write a few words on the questions you do bring up.

By the "old hellfire and brimstone" we refer to that style of preaching and teaching that seems to envision God as a tyrannical taskmaster, ever keeping a strict accounting of our every minute thought, word, and action for the single purpose of not letting us get away with the slightest evil act without punishing us for it in the worst possible way. This style of preaching was intent on having us fear God, not in the true biblical sense of awe, respect, and love, but in the literal sense of being afraid of him.

I hope all of us have come away from that kind of religion. The very basic concept of Christianity is that God is the kind of loving, merciful Father depicted in the parable of the Prodigal Son. Rather than keeping an account of our evil deeds, God is depicted by Christ as reaching out with loving mercy and forgiveness to all of us sinners. Just read the gospel story about the woman at the well, the dinner Christ had with Zacchaeus, the woman caught in adultery, the Sermon on the Mount—and I could go on and on!

No, I don't think that heaven, hell, and the devil were fabricated or dreamed up by medieval popes or moral theologians to "whip us into place." On the other hand I do believe that the concepts of eternal reward and punishment, as well as the concepts of good and evil spirits, have been greatly over-emphasized in the teaching and preaching practices of the church, especially from the Middle Ages until after the Second Vatican Council. I am more thoroughly convinced than ever since Vatican II that our motivation for a Christian life should be based on love of God through our brothers and sisters, rather than on a desire for the reward of heaven or a fear of God's punishment in hell.

As for the "devil," I think the time has long passed when we have to be concerned at all about whether there is an evil spirit lurking at every corner trying to lead us into sin. The devil is, in my opinion, simply a means that the church and the biblical authors have used to personify the "forces of evil." In our age, we should know better than to literally attribute the evil that we do to the influence of someone or something outside of ourselves. When we sin, we cannot blame it on the devil, but rather we must accept the responsibility for our own actions. It would be much healthier, I think, for us to forget about the devil, and to think in terms of that tendency to sin in us humans that we now call original sin.

You see, dear friend, original sin is not something done by Adam and Eve in the Garden of Paradise upon the prompting of the devil. Original sin is rather that basic human tendency toward darkness and selfishness, the effects of which can still be found in all of us and throughout the world of humanity. True, Christ over-came and saved us from this tendency. But if his salvation is to be effective in us, we must see it for what it is and accept it as our own. We must give and totally commit ourselves to a life of love! Love of God, our Father, and love of our human brothers and sisters. If we fail, our lives will be "hellish"; we will be miserable. If we succeed, we will find "heavenly" happiness. Neither will be so much either a God-imposed punishment or reward for our actions; rather, we will simply live the result of our own lives.

Do heaven, hell, and the devil really exist? I'm sure they do, but I really don't think it would be wise for me or anyone to base our lives on their existence or the lack thereof. "Hellfire and brim-stone" should die a quiet death.

Why is the church focused on judgment, hell, and damnation?

As I write this, we're approaching the lenten season, when the Catholic religion emphasizes its already exaggerated focus on sin and brokenness instead of helping the people to see the goodness, love, joy, wholeness—the God within them. Why is the Catholic religion so focused on judgment, hell, and damnation?

■ *Answer*

First I think we need to make some distinctions. Our "religion" is the manner in which we live our lives in relationship with God and with the rest of creation. Our "church," on the other hand, is the group of people with whom we do that. "Church authority" or "the magisterium" is that group of people within the church who've been given the right and responsibility to teach, guide, and rule us within the bounds of our common faith. It's true (and quite proper at times) that we sometimes speak of the Catholic "religion" and the Catholic "church" as one and the same. Also, sometimes we use the word "church" to mean the "magisterium" (which is the pope and bishops of the church united with him) or even sometimes all clergy and religious, and this is OK, provided it's clear to us and to our hearers that this is precisely what we mean in this particular use of the word.

I make these distinctions because I don't think it is accurate to say that the Catholic "religion" is focused on sin, hell, and damnation. The Catholic religion is focused on the faith that we share in the revelation given to us in the person, life, teachings, death, and resurrection of Christ, and in the Catholic tradition that flows therefrom. Similarly, while the attention of our "church" (that is, the people who share our Catholic Christian faith) may at this time in history (and over the last few centuries for that matter) be focused on these negative things, I think that's because we've been guided by church authority over these same centuries to do so.

It's for this very reason that I, together with the entire world, breathed a sigh of relief when Pope John XXIII announced the convening of the Second Vatican Council in the early 1960s. This Council, we knew, would bring the church forward (*aggiornamento*, he called it). It would "open the windows and doors" of the church (the people, not the buildings) to let out some stale air. For centuries, the concentration was on gloom, doom, sin, damnation, and hell. Pope John and Vatican II, however, ushered in the fresh air of the love, peace, and joy that is our heritage as children of God and co-heirs with Christ in the Reign of our common Father.

This great Council, with the full authority of the magisterium, gave us the "documents of Vatican II" as the means by which we were to pry open those old doors and windows of the church. Document after document from Vatican II provides an optimistic, positive view of the Faith. Rather than condemning others, the Council sought to teach the truth of the Faith so clearly, and in such contemporary terms, that any who heard it would recognize its validity for their lives.

Today there are some who've chosen, either from the very beginning or of late, to remain closed to the reforms inaugurated by Vatican II. Included among these are some officials of the Vatican itself. Others, having welcomed the reforms at first, have chosen of late to return to the more negative values of the past. And it is these who continue the impression that we, the church, are focused on the negative values you mention. I feel this is most unfortunate, because, as you say, there is so much of positive value, so much warmth, joy, peace, and so many sources for true human happiness in the very fabric of our faith, and, because of the emphasis on the negative, many have never seen it or are losing sight of it again.

I think the gospel accounts of "the Christ event," and sound Christian tradition, give us ample evidence that you are correct in stating that we are to relate to God primarily and ultimately as a loving Father rather than as a harsh and demanding judge.

Is God to be thanked for good and blamed for evil?

In a recent "Dear Abby" column, Abby was asked why God was to be thanked for the good things that happen to us, but was not to be blamed for the bad things that happen to us. For instance, why should we thank God if someone escapes death or serious injury in an automobile accident, but not blame him if serious injury or death does occur?

Abby bypassed the question by saying that it was "an ancient unresolved theological question" that she was not qualified to answer. I think I know the answer, but I don't feel qualified to put it in words either. Can you help?

■ *Answer*

Dear friend, Abby was quite correct in stating that it is "an ancient unresolved theological question." The name that the question has been given in the history of theology is "the problem of evil." There have probably been as many attempts to solve that problem as there have been theologians in the history of the church, and to this date no one has come up with a solution that is acceptable to all, or even understandable by more than a few. In other words, the question is as yet still unsatisfactorily answered; the problem is still a problem!

On the other hand, we do know this: God is the creator of all that is good; God gives us our life, our abilities, our relationship with him and our fellow humans, our material possessions, and everything we are and have. Furthermore, as Creator, God must continually sustain us in existence.

It is in that sense that we must thank God for all the good things that happen to us. It is not as though he "goes out of his way" to save us from death under certain circumstances. If we are not killed in an automobile accident, we shouldn't think that God came down at that moment, worked a miracle to save us from death, and therefore should be thanked for that miraculous saving act. If we escaped death, it was simply that God continued to sustain in existence all of the things and forces that naturally resulted in such an escape. If we had been killed, it would likewise not have been because God came down and caused our death by a special act of his will. If we had died in that accident, it would have been because God continued to sustain in existence the things and forces that in that particular combination of circumstances resulted in our death. In neither case should God be thanked or blamed for the end result: namely, our continued life here on earth, or our entrance into the next life. He should be thanked in either case for his loving, and continuing sustenance of his entire creation on our behalf.

The philosophical or theological problem arises when we attribute to God the arrangement of the two sets of circumstances: namely, the set that results in death, and the set that results in continued life. While that is a legitimate (and very important) problem for philosophers and theologians, it need not be that great a practical problem for us. Let's just face the fact that God is good and that only good can come to us from him. We may not always understand the goodness of all of his gifts, but we can always be fully confident that it is only our understanding that is lacking, and not the goodness of his gifts.

Creation and Evolution

Is it possible for Catholics to believe in evolution?

Our pastor told us that it's possible to believe in evolution as a Catholic and that Adam and Eve in the Bible may mean humankind rather individual persons. Is that possible?

■ *Answer*

Dear friend, thanks for giving me an opportunity by your question to point out that creation and evolution are not necessarily opposing theories of how the human race came into being.

You see, dear friend, there is no doubt that God created us. Evolution is merely one of several possible ways of explaining "how" God creates us. Another possible process, I guess, would be for God simply to will something instantaneously into being with no connection whatsoever with any previous being. To the best of our scientific knowledge, it seems that God has chosen evolution as the process to be used in creating human life, plant and animal life, and the growth of our planet and solar system.

The two creation stories in the Bible (Genesis, chapters 1 and 2) are not meant to be *historical* accounts of God's creation. They're expressions of faith in God as the source of the entire universe including humanity. Actually there is much in those stories that would lead one to think that their author possessed at least some basic evolutionary concepts. For instance, the periods of time (days) elapsing between various stages of creation; humans being formed out of other already existing creatures ("man" from "clay" and "woman" from "man's rib"). Be that as it may, the Word of God proclaimed by these creation passages has absolutely nothing to do with the *how* of creation. God's Word there is simply telling us that God *is* the Creator of all, including us humans.

As for the identity of Adam and Eve as the first two individual human beings, Scripture scholars tell us that the Bible stories are not trying to say that Adam was actually the first historically real man, and that Eve was the first historically real woman. Adam and Eve are used, the scholars tell us, to represent the "beginnings of the human race." Now I suppose it may be possible that there were, indeed, two "first" human beings. But this story doesn't mean to imply that.

When speaking of creation, another very important aspect must be considered. We must not look upon creation as something that occurred in the past when the first creatures began to exist. You see, dear friend, the act of creation is going on today! The earth is still being formed—and so are we humans, all the time. This isn't accidental development. This continues to be part of God's creative activity.

If we remember that, we'll have no trouble accepting evolution as the process of creation. Through the millions of years that are required for each evolutionary step, God constantly, and without an instant of interruption, continues to create. Therefore, far from being opposed to creation, evolution is totally dependent on the continuing fact of God's loving creation.

If evolution is true, how did it get started?

In the enclosed article from a Catholic newspaper, I read that, at a recent seminar for religion teachers, the presenter said that "God always uses some preexisting material to call something into existence." Of course, we do accept evolution. But where does the first "preexisting material" come from? Was there ever any material that was not preexisting? Or, has the world been evolving from all eternity?

■ *Answer*

You see, dear friend, when what someone has said in a day-long seminar is quoted in a brief newspaper article, it is very difficult, if not impossible, to give the full context in which the quoted statement was made. I checked out the story and spoke to the presenter, and while he certainly did make the statement quoted in that newspaper article, he made it after a lengthy and detailed explanation of his own concepts about time, eternity, creation, and evolution. Unless we look deeply at each of these concepts, then any statement like the one he made could very easily lead us to believe that the statement implies that he would hold that some "matter" is (like God) eternal. Indeed he does not think that at all!

On the other hand, if we ask "when in the course of eternity" did God create the first matter, we are attributing (by the word "when") to eternity a characteristic that belongs only to time. There is no "when" in eternity, which philosophers can only weakly describe as "the ever-present now." Eternity is really a foreign concept to us "time-bound" humans. We can only think in "time-terms," and that is why we ask the question: what was there "before" (again a "time-word") creation.

We must see creation not as something that happened long ago, but something that—at least from God's eternal point of view—is happening right now. For God, there is no before or after. *Now* God creates the first matter (from nothing!); *Now* that first matter creatively evolves into further matter. For the creature, the first matter came before the second. For God, both come *now*!

Seeing it from that perspective, how should I answer your question: "Has the world been evolving 'from all eternity'"? Here again your question is a human, "time-bound" question. When we say "from all eternity" our human intellects think in terms of "billions and billions and billions of uncountable years or centuries." But, of course, there are no years or centuries in eternity. The world, therefore, has been evolving from the beginning of time, which in the eternity of God, is now. To us creatures, the first matter came into existence from God's creation billions of years ago (no one knows exactly how many). To God, it comes into existence now.

I feel that this is an important element in the history of our salvation. How often have we humans questioned why God waited "so long" to give us the great revelation of himself and our salvation in Jesus Christ? I think the answer to that question is that he didn't "wait" at all. Believe me, I don't pretend to understand all this, but I really think God (from his perspective) is now creating the world and us; is now being rejected by us (through sin); is now revealing himself to us in and through creation, tradition, Scripture, and Jesus Christ; is now redeeming us; is now expecting us to respond to the loving relationship of grace that he is constantly holding out to us, and so forth. It is "human" to think that God "waits" on the things we do and then reacts to them. But God is not a "human"; is not a creature; is not time-bound. As the Bible puts it in the story of Moses, God simply "*is.*"

So you see, dear friend, you have done us all a favor. By your question you have moved me to rethink and re-express my concepts on this important matter.

The Soul

Which book of the Bible mentions the soul and its separation from the body at death?

Could you tell me which book of the Bible mentions the soul? Also which book mentions the separation of the soul and body at death?

■ *Answer*

The word "soul" is used in just about every English translation of the first book of the Bible (Genesis), and in many of the other books also. In fact, the word appears more than 160 times in most translations. However, the word, as it is used in the Bible, does not mean the same thing we mean when we use the word "soul" today. In Scripture, the word is used primarily to designate one's entire being. Mary says in her Magnificat, "My soul magnifies the Lord...." She means to say that her whole being does that. And in the Old Testament, too, especially in the Psalms, the word suggests one's whole being. Read Psalm 25, "To you, Oh Lord, I lift up my soul...."

For St. Paul, who uses the word more than any other New Testament author, the word soul has a similar meaning: the whole human being.

Second, because the writers of the Bible did not look upon human beings as being "composed of body and soul," and did not see death as a "separation of the soul and body," there is no reference in the Bible to death as such a separation. The early writers of the Old Testament seem to have been unaware of any faith in a life-after-death, and therefore they spoke of death as the end of an individual's existence, with the exception that the "life" of the individual was considered to continue beyond death in the lives of descendants. Belief in life-after-death began to dawn on the Hebrew people only during the last two or three centuries before the coming of Christ.

Many modern theologians are moving away from the ancient Greek notion that we humans are essentially two parts, body and soul. To these theologians the ancient description of a body distinct from one's soul implies that we are actually two separate beings. Thus we have an improper separation of our inherent unity as humans. These modern theologians are moving toward a definition that is founded more on Scripture.

One rather technical expression of this new definition is that a human being is "an embodied spirit." For those who hold this theory, death is not so much a separation of the soul and body. Death is simply a transition or passing from one form of "embodiment" to another. To say that death is a separation of the body and the soul, with the soul continuing to live while only the body dies, is, to these theologians, almost a denial of the church's teaching that human beings die, since only half, or at best one part of the total human being, is what dies. I hasten to add, however, that the most common description of death even in today's church is that it is a separation of body and soul. Nevertheless, you would never find that description in the Bible.

How can we recognize the soul?

How can we recognize the soul in ourselves?

■ *Answer*

This is an excellent but very tough question, my friend. Philosophers and theologians have been debating this for centuries. Nonetheless, here goes!

We usually see the soul as the "spiritual" part of us. So first, let's look into the very concept of "spirit." What do we mean when we call something a spirit? Our philosophical concept of spirit originates in Greek thought as the expression of the active principle of perception or comprehension (Parmenides); or later, as the active principle or order in all things (Anaxagoras); and even later, the faculty that enables us to contemplate (Plato). But so much of our Christian philosophy is based on the thinking of Aristotle (because of the work of Thomas Aquinas). Spirit, to Aristotle, was the specific mode of human "self-realization" (or what later comes to be called "reason").

Following Aristotle's notion, early Western thought was dominated by the idea that spirit is *detached* from the "world" (space, time, movement). It is ordained only to "being," which is clearly distinguished from the physical or material world. Despite this strong tie to its Greek origin, the notion of spirit underwent a decisive change when it came into confrontation with the notion of spirit found in the Bible, and subsequently in Christianity. For St. Augustine, the spirit was the personal, dynamic point of contact and encounter between the human and God. In Thomas Aquinas, the spirit is spirit-soul. Aquinas also assigns the spirit to its place in the larger hierarchy of being and the Christian doctrine of creation. Being and spirit coincide for Aquinas, and actually do so in God. Thus God is sometimes looked upon as "pure spirit" or "pure being."

In a very real sense, then, our notion of the "spirit" dimension of human life develops at least partially from the biblical tradition that "we are created in the image and likeness of God."

What is recognizable as "spirit" in us then? Our ability to reason; our ability to be aware of ourselves; our ability, not only to be present to others, but also to be aware of that presence; our ability to be aware of our own experience; to have a history and historical perspective; our ability to have all of this independent of time, space, or movement; our ability to develop our skills consciously and deliberately, and to learn not only from our own experiences but from those who have gone before us. These are traits that obviously no other creatures around us share, and thus they distinguish us from the "rest of the world."

At the same time, we must not forget our utter and essential relationship with this same "rest of the world," which might well be called the "embodiment" of this spiritual element. Therefore, while distinct from the rest of creation in our spirituality, there is a bodily element in us that is absolutely essential to our humanity. If we were simply spirits, we would not be humans. Our spirituality then, recognizable as it is, must always be seen in the light of our embodiment; otherwise we aren't facing our totality as "human" beings.

Angels

Why are angels so little known and honored today?

Why are the angels so little known and honored today? I can recall when a prayer to St. Michael the Archangel was recited daily after Mass in all churches throughout the Catholic world. No more! Can you offer an explanation?

■ *Answer*

Unfortunately I'm afraid my response to your request for an explanation of the current "de-emphasis" on angels will not please you.
You see, dear friend, although you and I grew up and learned our
faith in an atmosphere and time when angels were emphasized as
an important element in our Catholic faith, it is obvious that,
especially since the Second Vatican Council, the church has not
continued this emphasis. One reason, I think, is that in Vatican II
the church expressed officially that the truths or dogmas of our
faith have a hierarchy, which means "an order of importance,"
and certainly the ones dealing with God, with Jesus Christ, with
the proper order of the relationship of humans to each other and
to God are far more important than those about "pure spirits" or
angels, of whom we really have no concrete experience at all.

The church is not telling us that angels do not exist anymore,
but I think the church is very definitely telling us that the existence of angels is not necessary to "protect" us from the powers of
evil. God, in his infinite goodness and love for us, has already
overcome evil for us, and we need rely only on him as we relate to
him in and through each other for the confidence that there are
no evil powers that can conquer us.

Furthermore, I don't think that we have "legions of evil spirits"
or devils all around us. If there is evil in this world (and there surely is!) we cannot be so irresponsible as to blame it on "the devil."
No, dear friend, we cannot truthfully say, "the devil made me do
it," just as we cannot give credit to "guardian angels" if we avoid
evil. The goodness and evil in our world is our doing. If we do
good, we can thank only God who has gifted us with an innate
tendency toward good and yet with the freedom to counteract
that tendency by making a free choice of evil. If we commit evil
we can only blame ourselves, not evil spirits or the "devils" as they
are sometimes called. To blame others for our own misdeeds gives
evidence of irresponsibility.

With regard to that prayer to St. Michael after Mass, I have
thanked God innumerable times that church authorities saw fit to

discontinue it as a requirement for public prayer after Mass. Those "prayers after Mass" or "prayers before Mass" (which many still promote rather vigorously) are counterproductive to the prayer that the Mass really is. In the Mass we are celebrating in prayer our victory over evil in the life, death, and continuing resurrected life of Jesus Christ. In Mass, we are also (if everyone there does his or her part well) integrating our prayerful celebration with every aspect of our lives; with everyone and everything that affects our lives from day to day. It's really not necessary to "say extra prayers" before or after Mass. If we feel a need for that, there is something lacking either in the celebration itself or in our own participation in it.

That is what we must look at and alter if needed, but let's not keep "adding on" to the Mass. We can only weaken it if we do.

Ecumenism

What is ecumenism all about?

What does "ecumenical" mean? I thought it had to do with the Catholic church, as in "ecumenical council." But now it looks like it has to do with Protestants.

■ *Answer*

There is more than one meaning for the term "ecumenical." It can mean "worldwide or general in extent," such as you suggest in your question. Vatican II was called as an ecumenical council, meaning a council of all the world's bishops. It can also mean "promoting or tending toward worldwide Christian unity or cooperation." Vatican II also used the term this way, and Pope John XXIII held this goal dear to his heart.

This latter ecumenical effort is a result of a dynamic and revolutionary stand taken by Vatican II in its *Decree on Ecumenism* wherein, for the first time, other Christian denominations (as we used to call them) were officially recognized as Christian "ecclesial communities." This is another way of saying that they are, indeed, truly "churches."

At the same time Vatican II encouraged positive efforts toward unity among Christian churches as well as cooperation with other faiths or religions of the world, such as Moslems, Buddhists, and Jews. It would be worth the time and effort of all of us to read and digest that document of Vatican II so that we could all pull ourselves out of that ancient (and really despicable) attitude whereby we look upon all who are not part of the "Catholic church" as being "unsaved" and in need of "conversion" or "salvation."

Thus I warmly commend those who have initiated, organized, sponsored, and promoted any type of ecumenical activity within their local church. I would encourage all Catholic people to participate in ecumenical efforts whenever they can. For too many hundreds of years we have rejected the valuable gifts of our fellow Christians of other faiths, and at the same time refused to share with them the gifts that are ours (unless, of course, they rejected their own church and were "converted" to and joined ours).

We surely can and must do better than that!

Must I believe that the unbaptized will not be saved?

In studying comparative religions, I have become more tolerant of other people's right to their beliefs, and I think an ethnocentric ("We're right; they're misguided") attitude is not conducive to seeing all as sons and daughters of one God, whatever one might call that God. So I see the belief of "no salvation" for those who are not baptized Catholic as very limiting. My question is this: can I continue to be a Catholic if I believe that those who are not baptized in the church will be saved?

■ *Answer*

This question concerning salvation outside the church has plagued our relations with our non-Catholic Christian brothers and sisters for centuries. Thankfully over the last forty years or so, and especially since Vatican II, this teaching of the church has been "softened" even in the official or magisterial teaching of the church to the point where it has almost (but not quite!) been obliterated.

In the late 1940s and early 1950s Father Leonard Feeney from Boston was reprimanded by Rome for persisting in his teaching that anyone who did not accept the Catholic faith and Catholic baptism *could not be saved* and would "go to hell." He was also strongly anti-Protestant and anti-Jewish. His approach was alienating and polarizing. He was dismissed from the Jesuits in 1949 and excommunicated for his activities in 1953.

In response to Leonard Feeney's activities, the church clarified this matter. This teaching on salvation, the church said, is meant to stress that the existence of the church in the world is the basis for all of salvation. This is even true for people who don't recognize it. Furthermore, salvation is dependent upon the acceptance (either explicitly or implicitly) of fundamental Christian truths. Therefore, since the Catholic church (in the view of its own teaching) is the continuing presence of these truths and the divinely appointed guardian and teacher of these truths in the world, anyone who accepts Christian truth is implicitly placing herself or himself "within the church."

The documents of Vatican II make it clear that we respect and love all people, whatever their beliefs. We don't think of those outside the Catholic church as evil or "unsaved." For the first time since the Protestant Reformation, in the documents of Vatican II the church officially speaks of other Christian denominations as "churches" and urges us all to reach out to them as "brothers and sisters" in the Lord. Since the Council, the church no longer calls them "heretics" or "schismatics." We now speak of them as "other Christians."

Similarly, at Vatican II, we examined our attitudes toward the Jewish people. They are God's chosen people, the Council declares, and God does not go back on a choice. They are *still* God's chosen people. Their ancient faith is seen in a new light as the source of our own Christian faith. It was, after all, the Jewish faith into which Mary, Joseph, Jesus, the apostles, and most early Christians were born. Even Moslems, Hindus, Buddhists, and peoples of other world religions are to be loved and respected, the Council tells us. All those in the Eastern churches are brothers and sisters with us in the Lord. Further, as a result of Vatican II, we are to respect and honor even those who believe in no God whatsoever, if they are good and true.

In other words, dear friend, within the latter part of the twentieth century our church has made a strong and bold move back to its roots. It sees itself no longer in isolation from other religions or the rest of the world, but rather as an open and welcoming organism demonstrating to the world the ever-present love of God for all his creatures, but especially for those whom he creates in his own image and likeness.

Despite what I feel is some official "backtracking" in the last few years, the church since Vatican II is a much more welcoming home. It is a sign of God's love, peace, and grace, reaching out to all of God's children of whatever faith (or of no faith). Our goal is not so much "to make them Catholics," but rather to love them. We love them, after all, not because *they* are Catholic but because *we* are.

Now please understand that neither the church nor I am saying that "one religion is as good as another." It is important that we remain faithful to our call to be Catholic Christians. And it is important that we announce the good news we ourselves have heard so that others can also meet Christ. But what I am saying is that failure to join the Catholic church does not lead to eternal damnation.

Are Episcopalians also Catholics?

A close friend of ours is Episcopalian and is very active in his church in our city. Whenever the subject of "church" comes up, my husband and I, who are Catholics, can't help but become both disturbed and amused inwardly, for he considers us Catholics (Roman) and himself Catholic (English).

We associate with others of his church who don't, and never wish to be, referred to as Catholics in any way. We don't consider him Catholic, but why does *he*? Have we missed something in the official teaching of the church, and how should we respond next time?

■ *Answer*

What surprises me in this situation is not that your friend considers himself an English or Anglican Catholic, but rather that the others of his faith with whom you associate do not want to be known as Catholics.

You see, dear friend, it is not uncommon at all for various branches of the Anglican church (of which the Episcopalian church is one) to consider themselves every bit as much Catholic as we are. You don't seem to recall this from your study of history, but King Henry VIII, who was responsible for the break of that church with Rome, prided himself in being known and declared a "Defender of the Faith," and also as head of the "Catholic" Church of England. The original separation did not include any basic doctrinal differences, but was simply a withdrawal from allegiance to the pope as head of the church. To this date, the Church of England officially maintains that it is a branch of the "Catholic" church, and they recognize us as a distinct (Roman) branch of the same "Catholic" church.

I would hardly consider it part of the "official teaching of the church" that these people do or do not have a right to the name "Catholic." If these good people want to be known as Catholics, I (and the church, I think) certainly have no objection to that. We simply must recognize some legitimate and definite distinctions and differences between their faith and ours, but the fact that we choose to use the same name is really no great problem. I suppose most of us grew up jealously guarding the "Catholic" name as our very own, and in most local circles, we tend to presume that when one uses the term "Catholic," a "Roman Catholic" is meant. But many Anglicans or Episcopalians feel they have every bit as much right to the term as we do, and far be it from me to deny them that right.

How should you respond next time? As gracefully and naturally as you would to one of his fellow Episcopalians or anyone else. Accept him for what he is in his own estimation: an Anglican or

English "Catholic." I'm sure you also want him to accept you for what you are in your own estimation: a Roman "Catholic."

Is the Catholic church still the one and only "true church"?

When I was a little girl in Catholic schools, I was told that the Catholic church was the "true church founded by Jesus Christ"; that the Protestant churches were founded by humans, and therefore were "false religions." Mixed marriages were frowned upon; going to Protestant services was a serious "no-no." Obviously all this has changed. I've heard that this is all because of ecumenism. What is ecumenism and how does it change our relationship to Protestants? What happened to the idea that the Catholic church was the only "true church" founded by Jesus Christ?

■ *Answer*

Yes, dear friend, all this has changed, and let us thank God and the Fathers of Vatican II for this long overdue change in our attitude toward our sisters and brothers of other faiths. It is indeed our church's call for ecumenism in Vatican II that began this important change in our attitude toward other churches, especially (though not exclusively) those of other Christian faiths. The opening words of the introduction to the *Decree on Ecumenism* of Vatican II are: "The restoration of unity among all Christians is one of the principal concerns of the Second Vatican Council." And then in Paragraph #4: "Today, in many parts of the world, under the influence of the grace of the Holy Spirit, many efforts are being made in prayer, word, and action to attain that fullness of unity which Jesus Christ desires. The sacred Council exhorts, therefore, all the Catholic faithful to recognize the signs of the times and to take an active and intelligent part in the work of ecumenism."

Since this document was promulgated in the mid-1960s, a tremendous amount of progress has been made to break down the ancient barriers and misunderstandings that led to the teachings and laws that you mentioned in your question. For instance the following is only a partial list of documents that have come from Rome on ecumenical matters:

1. *Instruction on Mixed Marriages*: March 18, 1966
2. *The Joint Declaration on Cooperation* (between Anglicans and Roman Catholics): March 22, 1966
3. *Marriages between Roman Catholics and Orthodox Catholics*: February 22, 1967
4. *Directory Concerning Ecumenical Matters: Part One*: May 14, 1967
5. *Directory Concerning Ecumenical Matters: Part Two*: April 16,1970

(Note: It was in these last two documents that the church officially relaxed many of the "rules" mentioned in your question).

6. *Declaration on the Position of the Catholic Church on the Celebration of the Eucharist in Common by Christians of Different Confessions*: January 17, 1970
7. *Apostolic Letter on Mixed Marriages*: January 7, 1970
8. *Joint Declaration on Unity* (Armenians and Roman Catholics): May 12,1970
9. *Reflections and Suggestions Concerning Ecumenical Dialogue*: August 15, 1970
10. *On Admitting Other Christians to Eucharistic Communion in the Catholic Church*: June 1, 1972
11. *Note Interpreting the Document of June 1, 1972*: October 17, 1973

I would urge you and all good Catholics to read all these documents, which would give you clear (and official) answers to the questions you have in this matter. The documents can be found together in an inexpensive book entitled: *Vatican Council II, The Conciliar and Post Conciliar Documents*, edited by Austin Flannery, O.P., and published by Costello Publishing Company. Other very significant documents have been published as well, some very recently. All of these are also available in English on the Internet.

When you read these documents, I think you will find that the church no longer views Protestant churches as "false religions," and that taking part in the services of Protestant churches is not improper. Our church does indeed still consider itself the true church founded by Jesus Christ, but she no longer automatically excludes from membership and unity within this true church those people whose faith differs somewhat from ours.

Pope John XXIII longed for an opening of the "windows of the church" in and through the Second Vatican Council. In our efforts at ecumenism, those windows are being opened, and a breath of fresh air keeps flowing into our church precisely from those good people from whose influence our "rules" were previously "protecting" us.

Is Martin Luther still "bad" or is he back in the church?

When I was growing up in Catholic schools, we were told that Martin Luther was a bad fellow, possibly in hell for splitting up the Catholic church. Is it true that Luther is now back in the church? Luther stated that "faith and faith alone" would gain salvation, not good works. Recently I read in a Catholic publication that Catholic theology was off base too during the time of Luther; that we don't really earn salvation by good works. Please help clear up all this.

■ *Answer*

Surely you must realize, dear friend, that it would take a few books and a tremendous amount of talent and divine assistance to answer your question adequately. I hope I can at least steer you and other readers in the right direction concerning these questions.

First of all, if indeed you were taught those horrid things about Martin Luther in the Catholic school you attended, that school has by now, I hope, been updated sufficiently to realize that we have no right to be so judgmental about anyone. Although there have been bishops, priests, religious, and other Catholics in teaching positions who have had such unkind thoughts and words concerning Martin Luther (and others), the church has never officially taught that any human being has been sent to hell. Gratefully, we leave that to God's mercy and judgment.

Furthermore, excommunication from the church has absolutely nothing to do with whether we "go to heaven or hell." It is simply an official act or declaration of the church whereby a person is declared to have lost membership in the church.

The age-old controversy about whether faith alone or faith together with good works will bring about our "salvation" or entrance into heaven is important and interesting. A recent agreement between the Lutheran church and the Roman Catholic church has shed some new light on it. We now agree with one another, and whatever divided us in the sixteenth century has been resolved to everyone's benefit.

True faith in God, the statement says in short, will always lead to good works or a good life, if you will. A true and living faith in God that is accompanied by "evil" works (or a totally sinful life) is, in my view, an absolutely impossible combination. In this, both Luther and the Catholic church were right. It isn't one or the other. It's both.

Was Catholic theology "off base" in the time of Luther? Oh, I'm confident that much of it was. However, I don't think that the reform movement instituted by Luther was initially meant to attack bad theology so much as the corruption that indeed did exist in so many areas of church life, especially among the clergy and hierarchy of the church. Luther very rightly saw this corruption as degrading to the church, and he was determined to wipe it out by whatever means he could. One can seriously question whether his methods were proper or not, but that a reformation of church life and practice was needed at that time cannot be denied.

What is the church's official attitude toward Luther today? Since Vatican II tremendous strides have been made in bridging the gap between our church and the Lutheran church. I think you would have to look long and hard to find any Catholic teacher "worth his or her salt" who would speak of Luther or Lutherans in the terms that you indicate were used at the Catholic school of your childhood.

I see our church today not so much as "defending" itself against those who disagree with us, but rather as a beacon of light and love warmly welcoming anyone who might want to share this light and the warmth of her love. If by our lives we make our church what it is meant to be, the divisions that began in the time of Martin Luther will be readily dissolved.

God be praised for that!

Can a non-Catholic have a church funeral and burial?

My husband and I are quite elderly (both in our eighties), and he is very ill now. Although I hate to even think about it, I have to ask this question before he dies. He is not a Catholic, and there is no church or minister of his religion (Lutheran) here. He really hasn't had much connection with them since we were married over 50 years ago. Throughout our married life, he's attended Mass with me every Sunday, but he just never felt comfortable about officially giving up the religion of his parents. He's told me he'd like to be buried from our own Catholic church, and that he'd like our parish priest to officiate at the funeral. Under these circumstances, is it possible for our pastor to grant this request? And also, can we have it at Mass? (I would ask my pastor, but I wouldn't want him to be embarrassed in case the answer is no.)

■ *Answer*

Thanks so much for your question, the answer to which may lay to rest the fears of many good people who are in the same or a similar situation.

It certainly would be within the rights of your pastor according to the law of the church to conduct this funeral with the full rites of the church, unless the local bishop judges otherwise. Under such circumstances, Canons 1183 through 1185 of the Code of Canon Law make it quite clear that your husband could not only be granted Christian burial in the Catholic church, but that this could be done within a Mass, which is always permissible (and strongly recommended) at all funeral rites conducted in the Catholic church.

I think it pertinent to note here that cremation is no longer forbidden by the church (Canon 1176, 3 specifically refers to this.) provided, of course, that it is not chosen "for reasons which are contrary to Christian teaching." (Such reasons would be to defy or deny the church's teaching on resurrection or an "afterlife.") Many feel that as our human population continues to grow and available burial places become scarcer, the practice of cremation may well become the common and ordinary replacement for burial.

So we can readily be assured that even in official church law, the right to a Christian burial within our church is very much protected. That is as it should be, and I hope all of us who must make decisions about Christian burial will always remember this.

PART FIVE

Marriage, Divorce, Annulments

General Questions

What did Jesus mean when he spoke of celibacy and divorce?

In the nineteenth chapter of Matthew's gospel we read that "Jesus said, 'Because of your stubbornness Moses let you divorce your wives, but at the beginning it was not that way. I now say to you, whoever divorces his wife (lewd conduct is a separate case) and marries another commits adultery, and the man who marries a divorced woman commits adultery.'

"His disciples said to him, 'If that is the case between man and wife, it is better not to marry.' He said, 'Not everyone can accept this teaching, only those to whom it is given to do so. Some men are incapable of sexual activity from birth; some there are who have freely renounced sex for the sake of God's reign. Let him accept this teaching who can.'"

Is the Lord Jesus making an exception when he says, "lewd conduct is a separate case" and when he says, "Not everyone can accept this teaching, only those to whom it is given"? Also, in view of the above quotation, can a priest erase the holy sacrament of matrimony?

■ *Answer*

In response to your first question, the particular passages you use in your question (although offered in the gospel narrative very close to one another) really refer to two entirely different matters: the first passage refers to the stability or indissolubility of marriage, and the second refers to the advisability of celibacy for individuals. Accordingly I will have to treat those as two separate questions.

Was Jesus "making an exception" to the indissolubility of marriage in the first passage? It certainly would seem so, but Scripture scholars and theologians have labored over this passage for centuries and are still unable to agree as to what that exception is or even whether it is an exception at all.

Whenever you read a passage in the gospels you must remember that the author was writing to a first-century audience and was responding to that culture and people. For us to know what the gospel demands requires us to apply this to our times and culture. That's not always an easy task! It prevents us, though, from ever reading a passage literally.

As Pope John XXIII said so eloquently, "All that the gospels demand of us is not yet fully understood." We must never rest from exploring the gospel's meaning and direction for us. It isn't that the gospel changes, but that we do and our understanding of the gospel grows ever deeper and more profound.

In this case, we have the development of the *Jewish* theology of marriage in the first-century Middle East. Later this would be transformed into a developing Christian understanding. Jesus represents and amends the Jewish teaching and offers us a guide for doing the same in today's world.

We depend upon the guidance of the church through the ages to know what this means. We also look to the development over the ages of Christian religious experience and culture, to our own prayerful reflection on this biblical passage, and to the matter itself. We simply cannot pull that single little passage out of the text and treat it as the be-all and end-all of our theology and law about marriage. To do so would be doing Jesus and the gospels a grave injustice.

So there are simply no easy answers to this delicate and important question. The church labors over the best way to treat divorce, remarriage, and the people whose lives are at stake.

Now let's turn to the question of celibacy that you raised. Here too, the passage you quote seems to recommend it for certain people, and that almost by way of exception. Again we must not read and interpret this passage too literally. The very same approach to Scripture that I outlined above must also be applied here. I really don't know what Jesus himself would say about celibacy if he appeared again in human form in today's world. I do know that this passage does not mean that there is something "less holy" about marriage than celibacy. It's obvious from our makeup as humans that the most normal and sacred way of life for a human being is to live within the context of marriage and family life. For this reason, I'm confident that this passage is not telling us that Jesus felt otherwise. After all, he called the God who made us this way "Abba." In his love for that God could he possibly have held that our creation as human beings was a mistake? Hardly!

Now to turn to your last question. No, a priest cannot "erase" the sacrament of matrimony, nor can he "erase" a marriage that is not sacramental. I think you are somewhat confused about the process in the church that is known as a "declaration of nullity" or getting an annulment. A declaration of nullity does not dissolve or "erase" a previously existing marriage. It simply declares that in the opinion of the marriage tribunal (court) that is judging the case, no real marriage ever existed between these two people because of some unknown impediment.

This is a rather serious oversimplification of the work of the marriage tribunal in the church, but please read the next few answers for a more thorough treatment of this matter.

Shouldn't the church enforce its laws on marriage and morality?

I've been contemplating an issue for quite a few months now. I don't know how to get help. The pope's statement in January 1991 on "easy annulments" and polygamy prompted me to ask you to share your views on the subject.

My husband, an alcoholic, is involved with another woman whose husband died a few years ago. Because of my strong convictions about the permanence and sacredness of marriage, I don't feel that it would be right for me to leave my husband and get a divorce. So my husband keeps coming home after his drinking escapades with this woman.

What I feel strongly about is that I will never give him a divorce, because I firmly believe that when one says, "for better or worse" and "until death do us part," we have an agreement in which God is a part. To get an annulment from the church after 46 years would hurt my children emotionally, although all of this is really destructive for them and for us.

Are extramarital affairs morally acceptable to the church, and does the faithful party in such circumstances have a right to divorce? Then, how can the church promote family life and marriage as a sacrament but still tolerate annulments? Why doesn't the church address the psychological issues involving divorce, remarriage, or just plain lust that destroy family life? How can the church control the morality of people?

■ Answer

No, the church does not consider extramarital affairs to be morally acceptable. The church holds strongly to the unity and indissolubility (permanence) of what she has come over the centuries to call sacramental marriage, and considers marital fidelity to be morally inviolable. To the best of my knowledge, this has been the steadfast position of the church from its very inception to the present day.

Because of her strong stand on the unity and indissolubility of sacramental marriage, the church teaches that even such morally unacceptable conduct as extramarital affairs does not qualify as an adequate reason for divorce. By divorce here the church means the actual termination of the first marriage, which prevents a person from marrying again.

I hasten to add, therefore, that in such cases, and especially under circumstances as described in your letter to me, the church does certainly recognize the right of such abused parties in a marriage to seek the protection of the law through whatever civil action may be available, including a civil legal separation and a civil divorce. Thus, while the church does not consider the marriage ended by these civil actions, and therefore does not recognize the right to remarriage (as does civil law in the U.S.), she very definitely does not impose upon her people the obligation to continue living in impossible circumstances such as those you described in your letter.

Now, having said this, I'm also happy to report that there are those in the church today, and among them prominent members of the hierarchy, who are doing some healthy soul-searching, study, and prayer over this extremely sensitive issue. Why? Because they feel that there is a real possibility, well within the teachings of sacred Scripture, sacred tradition, and sound Catholic theology, that there could be such a thing as the "death" of the sacramental marriage bond, even before the death of one of the parties. I doubt this development in theology will be generally accepted by the church or affect the church law in the very near future (and certainly not in time to resolve your current problem). But I mention it here because I firmly believe that the church must ever be looking to *grow* in finding the means to meet all human needs. And certainly there is a need here.

Your statement about "annulments" gives evidence that you share the misapprehension of a majority of Catholics. The word "annulment" is a misleading description for what should really be called a "declaration of nullity." You see, dear friend, a "declaration of nullity" does not nullify or end a marriage; it's simply a declaration or statement by competent church authority that, after due consideration of all circumstances, the church has come to the conclusion that no marriage ever existed in this case.

To some, perhaps to most, this "declaration of nullity" process seems the same as divorce. I know some church officials who agree, at least privately. But the fact of the matter is that the decision rendered in such cases is not that a first marriage "no longer exists," but that that first marriage "never existed."

Thank God I am able to say that since Vatican Council II the church has increasingly placed much greater weight on the "psychological" issues of marriage, divorce, and remarriage. Before Vatican II within the church, human psychology was given precious little consideration in the theology of marriage, marriage preparation, the marriage ceremony, marriage counseling, marriage laws, and marriage tribunals as they considered the millions of cases that came before them through the years.

Today (again, thank God!) human psychology plays a major role in the church's handling of all of these areas. The result is that people are finally beginning to see the loving touch of the Lord in how church officials speak and act in treating marital matters and concerns.

The 1983 Code of Canon Law gives ample evidence of the church's official recognition of the major role that basic human psychology plays in every aspect of human life. Also, the procedures used in the marriage tribunal are replete with dependence upon the psychological professions as sources of evidence and evaluations in handling marital difficulties.

For my part, I feel very strongly that all our theology, ritual, law, and procedures must be deeply rooted in what we humans are. That must include due emphasis on our physical and psychological aspects, as well as the spiritual aspects. And please note that I did not say our physical, psychological, and spiritual "lives," but rather these "aspects" of the one life each of us has.

Let me respond to your remark about the church's ability to "control the morality of her people." It's quite obvious, I think, after almost twenty centuries of existence, the church has been distinctly *unable* to "control" the morality of anyone. Not that she hasn't tried in myriad ways, through hundreds of laws, programs, and what not. But they've never worked! God has given us free will and no law can change that.

Actually, if we look deeply at the history of humanity, it's quite obvious that even God has not "controlled" the morality of people. For God, though, it's not because of a divine failure but because God has simply never tried! Oh, don't get me wrong. God has given us very powerful directives through creation, revelation, the Scriptures, and our sacred tradition. God has made every effort through divine love to teach us how to live a moral life. But God has never taken away the great gift of free will.

You see, dear friend, it's not "control" over the morality of the people through authoritative laws that the church needs. Rather, as Pope John said in his opening speech at Vatican II, we must demonstrate the validity of our teachings rather than imposing them on anyone or condemning others. The church must inspire her own people and the peoples of the world toward the kind of moral behavior that God wants. She needs to impress upon humanity the immense likeness of human nature to God's own nature. She needs to encourage the building up of this understanding so that humans continue to grow increasingly into the image of God—which is how we are created to live!

To the extent that she has succeeded in this effort, good morality has resulted. To the extent that she has failed, immorality continues to flourish even among her very own.

Can the church do anything about the immorality in today's world? You bet she can—and should! But that will not happen by "control." It will happen by the loving and inspirational leadership that is the only successful means of improving the lot of humanity.

Annulment and Divorce

How does one go about getting an annulment?

How can the church allow an annulment after a fifteen-year marriage with several children, after a divorce, a second civil marriage, and just a year's waiting period in the annulment process? If an annulment declares null and void a fifteen-year-old Catholic ceremony, then anyone can laugh at misdeeds (such as adultery), then get married (at Mass, no less), as was done here two weeks ago.

■ *Answer*

Let me begin with a clear definition of what an annulment is. The proper name for what is commonly known as a church annulment is a "declaration of nullity." I think a proper understanding of this definition is very important, because the name "annulment" can give the impression that something that was previously a real, valid marriage is now being "annulled" or made invalid. But a declaration of nullity does not (and cannot) make invalid something that was previously valid. The declaration of nullity by a church tribunal is a declaration that, after a very thorough investigation of all aspects and requirements for a valid marriage between two particular individuals, the tribunal discovered and made the judgment that something essential was lacking to make this union a true and valid Christian marriage *from the very beginning.* Such a declaration is not taken lightly by the church, and there are very stringent regulations and procedures that must be followed before such a declaration can be made.

The problem that you bring up in your question arises from a misunderstanding of the nature of the proceedings whereby the declaration of nullity is made. You see, dear friend, neither the misdeeds of either party before or after the original wedding, nor the length of time after the separation, divorce, or civil remarriage are of any consequence to the work of the tribunal in such a case. Certainly the church does not approve of these misdeeds, and we must do everything possible to help these persons see the wrong of such actions. But if the original "marriage" was indeed improperly contracted, no number of misdeeds (or good deeds for that matter) done thereafter can correct that situation.

If indeed the parties did not covenant a valid marriage in the beginning, they must either "do it over" properly with each other and thus enter a valid union, or they must accept the fact that they are living in an invalid marriage, or get a declaration of nullity, which leaves them both free in the eyes of the church to enter into a valid Christian marriage for the first time.

Thus, rather than weakening the church's stand on the permanence of valid Christian marriage, a declaration of nullity actually upholds that position. If the church would agree to declare a previously valid marriage as no longer valid and binding, then this would be granting a divorce and declaring that a previously valid Christian marriage has ended. As of this date, the church has steadfastly refused to do this, although there are a growing number of solid Catholic theologians who are urging the church to reconsider her position in this important matter, because they feel that the Christian ideal of a permanent lifelong marriage sometimes fails, and that the church is simply failing to recognize this factual situation and to deal with it with true pastoral care.

As indicated above, I feel that the very strict and careful procedural rules by which diocesan tribunals must operate would tend to uphold, rather than weaken, the stand of the church on the permanence of a valid Christian marriage. I think the same holds true of the church's position on the sacramentality of Christian marriage. If, in fact, an apparent marriage was never a real and valid sacramental marriage, then I think that, as soon as this becomes obvious to the church through sworn testimony and in accord with the usual and accepted standards for valid evidence, then the church has not only a right, but an obligation to declare that apparent union null and void. Not to do so would be to continue to publicly declare through silence that the union is valid when in fact it is known by the church to be invalid.

With regard to the question of some requests being granted and others not, with no regard for actual evidence in the individual cases: I really have seen no evidence of this. Where I must admit some element of unfairness and perhaps lack of justice is when we priests (and I must admit my personal guilt of this in the past) hesitate to assist couples with their cases for fear that it will entail too much additional difficult work on our part. This has sometimes caused considerable unnecessary delay in the processing of these either to a positive or negative solution. On the other hand, I have known many priests, especially those who serve on the tribunal, who work long and hard hours on these cases in order to help find a solution to the serious problems being faced by one or both good parties to the original apparent union.

Thank God there are more priests of the latter type than the former.

Does the church offer guidance to the divorced?

After a marriage of 26 years between two Catholic partners has failed, despite a hard struggle to keep it together for five children and despite a problem with a drinking husband, please tell me what a good woman is supposed to do with the rest of her life. She needs someone to love her and to be loved by her in return. Yet, according to the laws of the Catholic church, she cannot divorce and remarry. Does she have to accept living alone and never having someone to share the rest of her life with?

■ Answer

Yours is a very deep and very difficult human problem for which neither the church nor I have come up with a satisfactory solution. If I could assume that you were as much at fault as was your husband for the failure of the marriage, it would be a lot easier to answer. But I can't assume that because to do so would simply be a "cop-out" and thus a refusal to face the real problem. I must assume that you are totally innocent because, even if you would not be, there are certainly thousands (or should I say millions) of good women (and men) in that very situation who indeed are totally innocent. So what can I say to you? What does the church, what do I have to offer to someone like you who is so desperately searching for new meaning in life?

Having admitted the church's and my failure to provide an adequate answer to your problem, may I simply offer you my own love and sympathy with the hope that the Christian community in which you live (which is the real church to you and to all of us) helps you to feel that you are loved, needed, wanted, and cared for. I guess for me trying to answer this question is like trying to find the right words or the right thing to do to comfort the loved ones of someone who has just died. There really are no right words; no right things to do or say. All we can do at a moment like that is let such hurting people know that, despite their loss, they are not now and never will be alone or without love. Either literally or symbolically we must throw our arms around them and let them feel the warmth of our love, for it is only the warmth of human love that can ease such pain.

Since the official teaching authority of the church has decided that a validly covenanted and consummated marriage between two Catholics can be ended only by death, we, the people who make up that church, must do everything in our power to overcome whatever pain and suffering may result from compliance with that decision. And the only thing I can think of that might accomplish any positive and helpful results in this regard would be for the church to embrace you warmly in full compassionate love in compensation for the problem that this official decision is causing in your life.

Now let me rush to say that I do also understand that friendship and companionship are not the same as a loving, sexual, romantic, and spousal relationship. Your own hunger for "more" is healthy and human. But at the moment, the church offers no more than this.

Please understand, dear friend, that I am not saying that this is all that should be done! On the contrary, I think that our theologians and bishops must apply themselves diligently to find a solution to this problem. It is not enough to throw up our hands and say we don't know the answer to such a heart-rending problem. We cannot stop death from occurring; that is an obvious fact. But it is far from obvious that it would be impossible for this teaching of the church about marriage to be developed or changed. It is far from obvious also that there is no solution to this great human dilemma, for if ever the church that Christ founded fails to deal straightforwardly with such deep human problems, she will have failed to carry out her purpose in this world: she will have failed to be the beacon of God's loving concern and the proclamation of the Reign of God on earth.

And so, my dear friend, please know that my heart and my thoughts and my theological efforts are and will be with you! Please know that your church has not abandoned you! Please know that there is still a strong need for the warmth of your goodness and love within this Christian community! Please don't give up hope! May God bless you with the peace that you so obviously deserve.

Can divorced and remarried persons receive holy communion?

I've heard that a divorced and remarried man has been given permission by a priest to receive communion, even though his first marriage has never been annulled. Is that possible? I'm in that same situation, and every priest I've talked to has refused to give me such permission. Why?

■ Answer

First let me clarify the basic issue. No priest has a right to give "permission" to anyone to receive the sacraments when that person is not allowed by church law to receive them, just as no priest can refuse the sacraments to anyone who legitimately requests them. If indeed the man to whom you refer was in a valid Catholic marriage at one time; if he has attempted a second (civil) marriage since then; if the first marriage was never declared null by the church; then, *unless there are some circumstances of which we are not aware*, the law of the church would say he may not receive holy communion. If all these circumstances are true, then *no one* (not even the pope) could legitimately (by law) give him permission to break the law.

On the other hand, that clause in the previous paragraph that I put in italics is of vital importance here. What a priest (or any other knowledgeable person) can do in this case is simply help this person determine whether the particular circumstances of his case might not change the application of the law to his case. In other words, the priest might well be able to help this person see that this law does not necessarily apply to him. If, after talking to the priest, the man himself (*not* the priest) decided that the law did not apply to him, *he* could very properly decide to receive the sacraments. Thus the priest is not giving permission, but only advice. This is a very important distinction, which should never be forgotten.

Often in giving such advice, the priest might find it necessary (unfortunately) to point out that, because members of the community in which he lives might misinterpret his actions (as you may have in this case), it might be well if he chose another place (where the circumstances of his marriage are not publicly known) to receive the sacraments. This is sometimes known as acting in the "internal forum" or "privately," as opposed to the "external forum" or "publicly." I say this is unfortunate because it is necessary only because of the basic human weakness that prompted your question in the first place.

It seems to me that all of us would be so much better off if we simply rejoiced with someone who joins us in holy communion, especially if we had reason to believe that he or she should not have done so! Instead of judging that the person in question did something improper, why could we not assume that we simply don't know all the facts (which are really none of our business) and simply open our arms in joyous welcome toward this seemingly unfortunate brother or sister? Why are we so intent on seeing to it that everyone else follows the law? Why not leave that up to them, and simply assume that they are doing so?

You see, dear friend, if you are divorced and remarried, then you must make a judgment about yourself. No priest (or anyone else) can make it for you. Get whatever advice you can and then make your decision. If you decide that you have a right to join us again in holy communion: welcome home!

What are my rights to an annulment as a convert after marriage?

I was married some time ago in the Catholic Church. At that time I was Protestant, and my husband was Catholic. Now I have since become a Catholic also. If we became divorced now, would I be the one to seek an annulment? Since I've never been married as a Catholic, it seems to me that I'm entitled to another Catholic wedding to someone else who is also Catholic, provided he is legally free to marry, without my having to pursue the annulment. Am I correct?

■ *Answer*

Obviously, dear friend, you have a slight misunderstanding as to what an annulment is all about, and I think a clarification of that would in itself answer your question. I state here again: what is commonly called "seeking an annulment" is actually asking someone (either the civil or religious court) to declare that what you and everyone else thought was a valid marriage from its beginning was actually no marriage at all because of some defect either in the consent that either party gave, or some other circumstance that made it impossible for the two parties to enter a valid marriage with each other at the time the wedding took place.

In your case, for instance, when you (as a Protestant) married your Catholic husband, a pre-marital investigation should have taken place to determine if both of you were free to marry each other. Also, unless this marriage took place within the last few years, the Catholic priest who was handling your case would have had to obtain from the diocese a "dispensation" to allow your Catholic husband to marry someone who was not a Catholic, and your husband would have had to promise that he would do everything within his power to see to it that any children born of the marriage would be baptized and raised as Catholics. Furthermore, both you and he would have had to have the intention of a life-long union, and neither of you could have had the intention of never having children. These, plus a great number of other perhaps less "glaring" requirements had to be fulfilled for you to enter properly into a valid marriage.

To seek an "annulment" means that you or your husband would be contending that one or more of these necessary conditions for a valid marriage was not fulfilled when you got married, and therefore you are asking the court to declare that the marriage never really existed as a true marriage. That is why the more correct name for this process is to seek a "declaration of nullity" rather than "an annulment." In other words, a so-called "annulment" does not "break up" a previously existing marriage. It simply says that what was thought to be a valid and true marriage never really was one at all.

So you can see that it really wouldn't matter who would seek the annulment. If either one of you ever came to the conclusion that your marriage was not valid, and you wanted that officially stated by the civil or religious court, you would both be free to make that request. The fact that you later became a Catholic has absolutely no bearing on the validity of your first marriage, and neither you nor your husband is free by church law to enter another marriage unless and until the church tribunal would declare that your first marriage was not valid. In other words, according to church law one party to a marriage cannot be more entitled to another marriage than the other party. As long as their marriage has not been declared null by the church, neither one is free to marry someone else. If the marriage is declared null, then both are equally free to marry a new partner.

You see, dear friend, although you were not a Catholic at the time that your wedding took place, that was a Catholic marriage. And presuming that you were a validly baptized Protestant, in your wedding and marriage you and your husband celebrated and participated in the Catholic sacrament of matrimony. In other words, according to the laws of the Catholic church, both before and after you became a Catholic, there was and is absolutely no difference whatsoever between your marriage and that of any other Catholic couple. You are presumed to be living in a valid Catholic sacramental marriage, and until someone can prove that not to have been true from the very beginning, church law does not allow either of you to marry again.

Don't annulments bring ridicule on Catholics?

Before Vatican II, my parents were separated and divorced. Naturally they were excommunicated from the church. My mother remarried civilly to retain her civil rights. But she was never allowed her rights in the church. She went to church anyway and even kept up with her church support—which was not refused—but could not receive the sacrament of the Eucharist, and had she died in that state, she would have been refused Christian burial. She knew this, yet she instructed us that when she died we should not call a priest and lie, because she would not renounce her new husband on her deathbed in order to receive the last sacrament. She was taught that Extreme Unction gives life to the soul and sometimes to the body, and if she lived she would have to be living a lie.

Now Vatican II steps in with annulments. I think that is a big mistake. We Catholics are now a mockery. We are being laughed at and ridiculed by non-Catholics. I've looked up the word "annul," and it means "to bring to nothing, to do away with, nullify, cancel." Vatican II also says that you can annul a marriage that has not been consummated, which means to bring to completion, finish, to make marriage actual by sexual intercourse.

Vatican II says annulment is acceptable. Vatican II needs to look over this mistake, and go back to the old *Baltimore Catechism*. Of course I am only a mere human, without the power to make decisions like Vatican II, but if there are to be any changes made, it should start with the church. We, the people constitute the church, remember. Catholics should be granted a divorce and retain all their rights as Catholics. Annulments are being granted too freely to some, sometimes more than once to the same party, and even allowing them the rights of the sacraments. Humans (Vatican II) shouldn't be able to change the laws of God. Humans do make mistakes; not God.

Now that I've given my honest opinion about Vatican II, I do hope that you don't tell me I've had some problems with priests or the church. You'll probably sympathize with me and offer me your prayers and blessings.

■ *Answer*

Indeed I do sympathize with you and offer you my prayers and blessings, as I think all of us should do for each other when we see each other suffering in any way whatsoever. However, I won't tell you that you "have had some problems with priests or the church," because your entire letter said just that much more eloquently than I could have. You see, dear friend, when we speak about Vatican II we are talking about a gathering of all the Roman Catholic bishops of the world, along with observers from the Orthodox, Anglican, and Protestant churches of the world! And therefore since you obviously have problems with what Vatican II did, your problems are indeed with priests and the church.

I printed most of your letter here (rather than just your questions) because I felt it was important for my readers to know the full extent of your dissatisfaction with the changes in the church since the Second Vatican Council. I know for a fact that you are not at all alone in this, and the very publication of your opinions might enable others to see that their problems with the church are not unique. It is my intention to deal with all of your questions and observations with the hope that all who feel as you do might be somewhat relieved of this troubling anxiety.

First, I think that it is important for all of us to be aware that the so-called "annulment" procedure in our church was not a result of Vatican II. That process has been in place for hundreds of years now. May I remind those who are somewhat familiar with church and English history that the Church of England was founded by King Henry VIII precisely because the church refused to grant his request that his first marriage be declared null and void so that he could marry again, and that was more than 400 years ago. Put simply, he asked for an annulment and was refused.

However, what the church did do in Vatican II was to give us a much clearer picture of what truly Christian marriage was all about, and thus theologians and canon lawyers were able to develop new procedures and bases for the declaring the validity or invalidity of marriages. Once this was done and given approval by the church, our individual diocesan matrimonial tribunals were given responsibilities and rights with regard to making judgments on cases presented to them, and these cases could now be judged on the bases of the newly developed theology and law of marriage. As I saw all of this over the years since the Council, the process whereby cases have been handled, conclusions reached, and declarations of validity or of nullity made has been greatly simplified, and the time element very greatly reduced.

I realize that just about everyone in our society (including myself) usually uses the word "annulment" to describe what should more properly be called a "declaration of nullity." But, if you have not already done so, please read my response to the other questions in this chapter, and I think you will see that, though your dictionary is obviously quite correct in defining the word "annulment," that is not what our matrimonial tribunals do. Briefly put, a declaration of nullity does not end a marriage, it simply declares that the marriage in question never really existed.

Next I would first like to stress that "Vatican II" was not some separate entity outside of the church that allowed or demanded certain changes in the church. The teachings and declarations of Vatican II are the official teachings and declarations of the church. I very strongly agree with my good questioner that it is the teaching of our church (very beautifully clarified and strengthened in Vatican II) that we, the people, are the church. But in any and all human groups, organizations, or communities, someone must be designated to be in authority, and for us it is our bishops who have been so designated, and it is they who spoke out authoritatively in and through the Second Vatican Council.

I hope that this treatment of the matters that you, dear friend, have brought before me will be of some service to those who find them rather difficult to understand. I personally have many misgivings about the manner in which the official church has and still does handle the entire matter of marriage in its teachings and laws. Let us hope and pray that we will all help each other to move forward and inspire our leaders to develop the church's teachings and laws on marriage to the point that the concerns and questions addressed here might be resolved in the best interests of all Christians.

I have been divorced: will I go to hell?

What's really necessary for a Catholic marriage to be annulled? For 28 years I lived in a marriage in which only I professed my faith. My husband never went to Mass or lived up in any way to the Catholic faith. He set a bad example for our children, and left all responsibility for the children up to me. Eventually we separated and were divorced. I met another man, fell in love with him, and was forced (by church law) to choose the only alternative under the circumstances, a civil marriage.

I know that I love God, Jesus, and Mary and that I'm loved in return by them; of that I'm certain. But is hell all I have to look forward to in the next life? Is that what I am supposed to believe if I'm to be a good Catholic?

■ *Answer*

First let me hasten to assure you that, in order to be a faithful Catholic, you definitely do not have to believe you are going to hell when you die, no matter what you may have done. The church does not teach that anyone at all, even Judas or Hitler, has gone to hell for their actions. We leave the final judgment up to the mercy of God, as we should. We don't declare certain of the dead to be "devils" as we do certain others to be "saints."

And second, let me assure you that living in true love is the most important choice we make as humans. I don't know your full situation from your letter but it seems to me you have chosen for love, not against it. If that is indeed true, how could you be judged harshly? It sounds as though you've followed your conscience quite carefully, which is a blessing for you, not a curse.

Please understand that I don't blame you for thinking that church teaching indicates you're destined for hell because you're living in a marriage that is not considered valid by the church. Believe me, I grew up with the same impression. And that impression, unfortunately, was not erased by my seminary training. On the contrary, that training (almost 50 years ago) only made that impression stronger. Now I strike my breast in agonizing sorrow when I realize that, even as a priest, I held that opinion and even taught it as the truth.

Thank God I've been able to grow in his grace and a better knowledge of who and what God is, what it means to be church, and what human relationships are. With God's grace and the help of some wonderful people, I've come to realize that I was wrong, and I thank you for the opportunity you have given me through your question to express this conversion publicly, and to teach the real truth. I hope it isn't too late for me to help good people like yourself.

In response to your direct question may I simply state that I feel you need to visit with a priest to discuss with him the possibility of bringing the case of your first marriage before the diocesan tribunal. It may well be that there was some defect in what you and everyone else at the time thought was a valid marriage, and if that can be proven, it is possible that your first marriage could be declared null. In that event, of course, your desire to be married in the church to your current husband would then become a real possibility.

But even if that isn't possible, I'm confident from the way you expressed yourself in your letter that you are indeed living in close union with God; in his love; and therefore in union and love with his people, the church. So even if a declaration of nullity isn't possible from the church, you may live with a clear conscience in knowing that you've chosen the way of love.

Please know that my prayers are with you.

Sin, Morality, and Church Law

Morality

My nephew is having an affair. What is his sin? What is hers?

My nephew is separated from his wife and is having an affair with his first cousin, who is a widow. His wife asked me what sin they were committing. I said he was committing adultery, but I don't know what his cousin's sin would be. Could you please clarify this?

Also, my daughter and her fiancé are engaged to be married next June. She's told me they've been having occasional sex. They believe there's no reason to confess this before going to communion. I say they should. Please advise.

■ *Answer*

In response to your first question, I must admit that I cannot clarify that issue. You see, I don't have any idea whether your nephew and his first cousin are sinning or not, much less what sin they might be committing. I don't even know them, and certainly cannot judge them.

As you state it, it would seem that what your nephew and his cousin are doing is improper in view of the consistent position of the church against extramarital sex. If, however, you or I jump to the conclusion from this that your nephew and his cousin are guilty of a particular sin, then you and I would really be "playing God," and setting ourselves up as judges for fellow human beings.

If you feel that the relationship between your nephew and his cousin is improper (as it would seem to be), then it does neither of them any good whatever to simply identify their sin and accuse them of it. What you should be doing is letting them know that no matter what they do, God still loves them, and so do you! Let them see love in you, rather than accusation. Let them look at you and see God's loving forgiveness reaching out to them in your arms. What sin (or sins) they may have committed is not really important. God's loving forgiveness, and yours, are the important things.

Your second question is similar to the first, since again you are asking me to help you judge whether someone is sinning or not. If they are doing something seriously wrong, know that it is wrong, are totally free in their decision to do wrong, then they indeed sinned seriously and should, according to church law, repent of their sin and celebrate that repentance in the sacrament of reconciliation before receiving communion. But, my dear friend, they and only they can make that judgment!

Here, too, our concern should not be to judge whether they've sinned or have a right to receive communion or not. We are to be concerned about their total welfare: is the life they're living good for them? Does the celebration of the Eucharist within the Christian community fit into the lifestyle that sees "occasional sex" as proper?

These are the questions we have to try to help these young people answer for themselves. Then once they've made their own judgments and decisions, they'll know how to act in the future to ensure for themselves a life of committed happiness within the Christian community, of which they wish to be a part.

Can my dear friend and I receive communion?

I'm 73 years old, and have been a widow for 11 years. I have a man friend, 78 years old, who's been a widower for four years. We have an arrangement whereby I cook for him at my home; he cleans the yard and helps me with other chores around the house. He takes me out to eat, to dances, bingo parties, and to church. We're both Catholics and receive communion every Sunday.

Is it all right to receive communion when we aren't married? As you probably have guessed, we're just about living together, although he goes to his house every night! I was raised by very strict parents, and at that time it was very wrong to do what I'm doing.

■ *Answer*

What a magnificently delightful couple you and your friend must be! Both of you obviously need each other's help (which is so willingly given!). You serve as a delightful barrier for each other against the loneliness of old age. You obviously enjoy one another's company tremendously and support each other in ways that most elderly people must go to a retirement home to accomplish. May God bless both of you for all of this.

I really see no reason whatsoever, from what you describe in your letter, why you and your friend should not continue to receive holy communion. Actually this could be a very fitting celebration of the friendship you share with each other, and obviously with many others. Very often in the "old days" our parents were taught, and then taught us, to judge every situation according to some rigid standards, always presuming the worst possible result of every relationship between a man and a woman who were not married. I'm not blaming them or their teachers for this. It was the way things were done then. Everything had to be judged in advance as to whether or not it was sinful. Sin usually got the benefit of the doubt!

Please don't get me wrong! I'm not saying that sins are no longer committed! On the contrary, all of us are sinners, and our sins are those things we do that are contrary to the norms that govern our conduct and relationships with others. The point is, though, that we should not judge one another. Each of us is individually responsible to live according to our own conscience. No one can make that decision for anyone else, not even a priest.

So getting back to your situation. If you believe that there is something improper about your relationship with this man you might decide not to receive holy communion. If you have doubts about the matter, I suggest that you discuss this confidentially with one of your local priests or someone else in whom you have much confidence. But the decision is yours; not mine or anyone else's.

May God continue to bless you, your friend, and your beautiful friendship.

How can we teach our children to judge the gravity of sin?

I'm a new religious education teacher, and my class was studying the sacrament of reconciliation. I told them that if they were in serious sin they must go to confession before receiving holy communion. One of my young people asked, "How serious is serious?" I told them about turning away from God, but I don't know what sins indicate such a turning away! I've pondered this, and frankly about this time I'm wishing for the cut-and-dried approach of the old *Baltimore Catechism*.

So my question is this: how serious is serious when it comes to sin? Which sins require the sacrament of reconciliation before communion?

■ *Answer*

This is a problem that has baffled me throughout my life (and every one of us, I think!). Every human being seems to want someone else to make these judgments for us, and thus relieve ourselves of our innate responsibility as children of God, human beings, and members of human society, to live a morally good and balanced life. It is certainly true that we adults must, under the guidance of the church, assist our young people in forming sound consciences by helping them from our own education and experience to better distinguish good from evil, and to establish within themselves a scale or hierarchy of moral values. But there is absolutely no legitimate way whereby we can judge whether an individual act of another human being was sinful, nor can we judge the degree of that sinfulness. It is only I as an individual who can properly judge the morality of an act that I have done, and if I judge it to be sinful, it is only I, again, who can judge the seriousness or severity of my sin.

This is an ancient teaching of the church, not something new that just came about from Vatican II or any other modern source. The old *Baltimore Catechism* insisted that in order for something to be seriously sinful, the sinner himself or herself must *believe it to be so and do it with full freedom.*

Yes, the church does have a law that requires those who judge themselves guilty of "serious" sin (the type we used to call mortal) to submit that sin to the mercy of the church and celebrate its forgiveness by God and the church in the sacrament. For this reason we have to weigh each and every situation in the light of a good and well-informed conscience, and in keeping with our own status in life, our education, our faith, and our position in the community. For instance, the murder of one human being by another would certainly be considered a very serious matter. On the other hand, breaking the arm of another human being would, it seems to me, still be a serious matter, but certainly not as serious as murder.

Speaking unkindly or falsely about another human being would also be morally improper, but this would not have nearly the serious nature of murder or physical injury. Or would it? Think about it! Suppose I tell a friend the untruth that his wife was having an adulterous affair with another man, and as a result of my lie, my friend is so infuriated that he immediately leaves his wife, gets a divorce, and thus breaks up the family. In such a case my "little" lie has caused much more serious damage to my friend, to his wife, and to his family than a broken arm would.

So you see, dear friend, we cannot necessarily tell our students whether any specific act of theirs is a serious or mortal sin. We can only teach them the principles by which they can judge the morality of their actions. And we must always respect their right, and their responsibility, to make those judgments.

Am I committing a sin every time I smoke?

In his book *Ministry*, Father Richard McBrien states that the use of tobacco is "morally evil in itself...given all that is now known about its physically harmful effects on users and innocent bystanders alike." As a smoker, I find this labeling of my moral character to be quite insulting. Does the Catholic church agree with Father McBrien? Am I committing a sin every time I light up? What about the many priests, brothers, and sisters who smoke?

■ *Answer*

I knew it had to come! Ever since I quit smoking in July 1981, I've dreaded having to face the eventual and inevitable question about the morality of smoking because I felt that any negative position I would take might well be interpreted by smokers as evidence of the "reformed smoker syndrome." On the other hand, if I failed to brand smoking as immoral, then the nonsmokers would probably denounce my insensitivity to their rights. At any rate, I thank you, dear questioner, for giving me some time to prepare and to buffer myself from the pending barrage of disagreements.

First, I must state that I know of absolutely no specific teaching of the magisterium, or of any group of moral theologians, on the morality of smoking or other use of tobacco products. The only mention of it I can recall in any books on moral theology was a caution against "excessive" smoking, much like a caution against excessive eating or drinking. I agree there are a great number of theologians, bishops, priests, religious brothers, and, if you say so, even sisters (I don't think I know any!) who smoke. And I also agree the chances are rather slim that we will ever hear any kind of strong condemnation of smoking from a major part of the teaching force within our church, or even from the magisterium. On those grounds, therefore, I think avid smokers can relax.

Judging from the brief quote you mention in your question, I think Fr. McBrien's opinion is soundly based on an ancient and fundamental moral principle. I'm certain most moral theologians through the ages have accepted this principle and consider it valid today. The principle is that no one has a moral right to take one's own life (suicide), or do anything that might be harmful to one's health. This is especially true if the action would even indirectly bring about an earlier death than would otherwise occur. This same principle applies to the unnecessary endangering of the life or health of another.

I think, therefore, given the abundance of medical data about smoking communicated over the last thirty years, each of us who smokes or is considering smoking, must give serious consideration to the effect that smoking has on our health or the health of others. Second, before we can legitimately choose to smoke, we must come to a reasonably deduced conclusion that the benefits we acquire from smoking sufficiently outweigh the dangers to health and life (our own and others) that will result.

So do you commit a sin "every time you light up"? I'll say again: only you can answer such a question properly or adequately. To make that decision you must determine—through the process mentioned in the previous paragraph—what "lighting up" means or is doing to you, and you must do this with all due consideration and care for your own well-being, and just as importantly, for the well-being of others.

Does God love sinners too?

I'm a seventy-year-old man with little formal education, whose training in the Catholic faith developed in me only a fear of God so awesome that it distorted my understanding of who God is and who we are as humans. This distorted view has really plagued me all my life, until I recently came across a little book by Father John Powell, who writes that the admonition of Christ that we must "be perfect as our heavenly Father is perfect" is really a mistranslation.

He says that Jesus is really just challenging us to love our enemies and to be worthy children of a heavenly Father, who "causes his sun to rise on bad men as well as good, and his rain to fall on the honest and the dishonest alike."

Thus the challenge he extends is not to be "perfect," which is impossible for us mistake-makers, but to be as lenient and loving and forgiving as our heavenly Father is! After reading this, I felt that a great burden had been lifted from my shoulders, and I breathed a great sigh of relief that God was not really asking the impossible (perfection) of me, but rather that I be patient, tolerant of the weaknesses in myself and others, and willing to share my life with him and all my brothers and sisters in the Lord.

Am I on the right track at last?

■ *Answer*

My Catholic upbringing also led me more to fear an angry God than to embrace God as a loving Father. That training resulted from the heresy of Jansenism, with which much of our church was infected when we were growing up: it still prevails today among some Catholics. Jansenism sees God only as the Almighty Ruler who is (excuse the expression) "hell bent" on punishing all of us worthless humans unless we meticulously "toe the line," which is clearly and boldly marked out by his commandments and the laws of his church. Humans, in Jansenism, have no value other than as the slaves of God's law.

Upon reaching a more mature faith, I found that the Jansenist view of God doesn't fit our theology very well, starting with the very first chapter of the first book of the Bible (Genesis). There it is revealed to us that we're created by a loving God in the divine image and likeness. Not only that, this same God also brings us and everything else into being. God then looks upon creation and finds it all to be very *good*!

Furthermore, repeatedly throughout the Old Testament humans are grappling with this very problem, and inevitably find it resolved in the image of a God who is more loving than demanding.

Then Jesus comes in the New Testament, where we find an

image of God that is unflinchingly loving and caring. It's true that Christ says: "Be you perfect as your heavenly Father is perfect." We often misunderstand this saying of Jesus. It is a call to continual growth, to ongoing improvement, to ever-greater love. It directs us toward our eventual life when we are, indeed, a full and complete "image and likeness of God."

The problem so many of us have faced over the years is that, because of our warped Jansenist view of our own humanity (believing we are only sinful and worthless), it seemed that Jesus, in asking us to be perfect like this, was asking the impossible of us. In fact, however, Jesus was only asking us to be what our loving God has created us to be: our own most selves; true, honest, and full persons; in short, images of God who is perfect love.

Dear friend, you are indeed on the right track when you recognize that God "causes the sun [and divine love!] to rise on the bad as well as the good, and the rain [and divine love!] to fall on the honest and the dishonest alike." In other words, by asking us to be perfect "as our heavenly Father is perfect," he is simply asking us to love as God loves; to be forgiving as God is forgiving. Jesus is telling us that God's perfection should be expressed to others by our love for each other in the Lord. In so doing, he is telling us, we are "becoming perfect" despite our own human mistakes and imperfections.

Yes, dear friend, you are on the right track!

May I vote for a political candidate who is for abortion?

Some tell me that I shouldn't vote based on a single issue, but may I as a Catholic vote for a political candidate who's for abortion?

■ *Answer*

Let me quickly assure all that I am unalterably opposed to abortion. Despite that expressed conviction, I am fully aware that I will incur the wrath of many a right-to-lifer among my readers when I candidly admit that I am in agreement with those who have advised you not to base your vote in the presidential election on this single issue.

In my decision to vote, I would certainly consider a pro-abortion stand "a strike against" any candidate. On the other hand, I must also look at each candidate's position on other issues, as well as all aspects of each one's character, philosophy, integrity, and voting record. Then I must compare these positions with those of the opponents as well as all aspects of their characters.

Let's presume that a thorough investigation revealed that the opponents of our candidate are "right-to-life champions" in connection with the abortion issue. This would certainly make me favor them over others on this particular issue. But what if those same opponents were found to be proponents of such things as a build-up of nuclear weapons, or the oppression of minorities, or disregard for many issues of social justice, or the oppression of the poor? What if the opponents degraded religious values or showed no respect for religious values in their way of life? What if the opponents favored wiping out our enemies through the use of nuclear weapons? What if the opponents proposed euthanasia as a solution to lengthy terminal illness? What if the opponents were openly living a way of life that the church considers immoral? What if the opponents were guilty of fraudulent tax evasion or other flagrant offenses against honesty, integrity, or morality?

Do you get the point? If I see any of these extremely negative issues in the record or character of the opponents of our fictitious pro-choice candidate and, and if I were constrained in conscience (or by church law) not to vote for anyone who was "guilty" of anything wrong, my only choice would be not to vote at all! But it is a civil right and, more important, a civic responsibility.

No, dear friend, the decision on my vote in any election cannot be made on the basis of a single issue alone. The single issue you mention (abortion) is indeed extremely important; but it is not the only issue. No, I must look at the entire picture. I must look at and responsibly weigh each and every issue. I must vote with total integrity. I must vote for the candidate whom I am convinced will serve the best interests of all the people of our country and of humanity as a whole.

"Single issue voting" can be the most dangerous (and immoral) way of all!

Is birth control always more sinful than other options?

Several years ago Pope John Paul II said he and the church were against any type of birth control method except the rhythm method. My question is, wouldn't it be a greater sin to bear more children than one can afford to feed, clothe, and care for? We're a family of four, soon to be five, and sometimes we wonder how we're going to pull through these hard times. I feel there are hundreds of women who have this question on their minds about birth control.

■ *Answer*

Obviously, you're putting it very mildly when you say that there are hundreds of women who have this question on their minds, because if we think beyond the people we know personally, this question poses a very serious problem to hundreds of millions of people, both men and women, throughout the world. For instance, a study at Princeton University recently concluded that at least 70 percent of American Catholic women are using some form of birth regulation that is condemned by the church. Another poll indicates that approximately 30 percent of American priests consider artificial birth control to be immoral in itself and only 26 percent indicated that they would deny absolution to those who practice artificial birth control.

The above facts were taken from a talk by Archbishop John Quinn, former Archbishop of San Francisco, and former President of the National Conference of Catholic Bishops, before the International Synod of Bishops in Rome in September, 1980. In that talk Archbishop Quinn stated that it was the clear teaching of the church, as enunciated by Pope Paul VI in his 1968 encyclical *Humanae Vitae*, that artificial contraception of any kind whatsoever is contrary to the moral law.

In view of the almost universal rejection of this teaching by Catholics in the United States, and in view of the very widespread rejection of the same teaching by many well-respected moral theologians throughout the church, Archbishop Quinn told the synod of bishops that he felt that the church could no longer fail to face this "profound theological and pastoral problem for the church." Archbishop Quinn made it quite clear that a simple authoritarian restatement of this teaching would in no way solve the problem. He called, therefore, for the creation of a "new context" in which this whole matter would be dealt with, including "an elaboration and greater emphasis on the church's teaching on the responsible transmission of life," and a positive expression of the church's teachings on human sexuality, with its proper biblical foundations. Most important, Archbishop Quinn called for a "widespread and formal dialogue with Catholic theologians throughout the world on the problems raised by this dissent from the teachings of *Humanae Vitae*."

So you can see, dear friend, that you are not alone in your problem, and that it is shared by many concerned and responsible people. It might be of interest to some to hear again what Pope Paul VI himself said only two weeks after he issued the encyclical *Humanae Vitae*: "This encyclical clarifies a fundamental chapter in the personal, married, family, and social life of man, but it is not a complete treatment regarding man in this sphere of marriage, of the family and of moral probity. This is an immense field to which the magisterium [the teaching authority] of the church could and perhaps should return with a fuller, more organic and more synthetic exposition." Obviously, Pope Paul VI was not "closing the door," as some would seem to indicate at times.

In the meantime, every couple must face this situation within their own life. The sinfulness of each couple's action cannot be judged by a pope, a bishop, a priest, or anyone other than the couple itself. All the church can rightly do is provide theological reflection regarding this matter and give us needed guidance (sometimes through laws) so that we can live our faith as God wants. But the church cannot tell any couple that they have actually committed a sin by following their own consciences.

Therefore, dear friend, it is really up to you to consider all the circumstances of your life: the condition of your family, the moral and social consciousness that you share with your husband, and the present and future needs of your family and of the entire community. Only then can you determine whether or not it would be sinful for you and your husband to express your marital love for each other through a sexual act that is not open to procreation.

Dear friend, you very obviously are what you signed your letter: "A concerned and devoted Catholic." Therefore, I have no doubt whatsoever that you are in a much better position to judge your own actions than I am, and I find it impossible to tell you whether it would be "a greater sin to have more children." But as long as you are a truly concerned and devoted Catholic, and as long as you do nothing that is contrary to the obviously strong and loving relationship that you currently have with your husband, with your family, with your fellow Christians (the church), and with God, you need not fear that you are sinning. Should you ever make the mistake of acting against these loving relationships, and thereby committing sin, please be assured that those whom you have loved throughout your life, from God "on down," will overwhelm you with their loving forgiveness.

Why don't priests tell us more about "Natural Family Planning"?

I'm a young mother with three children. After being uninformed and misdirected before I had these children, I discovered N.F.P. (Natural Family Planning) as a good, safe birth control method. I didn't want to go against my church, but through ignorance I did for five years. I'm disturbed by the great number of women using birth control methods condemned by our pope and church. And I see these same young women receiving the sacraments after having their tubes tied or using the Pill or an IUD. If the church forbids these methods, then isn't it wrong to receive communion while practicing them?

Yet I never hear priests mention this safe, Christian method of family planning in their sermons. Shouldn't priests address this subject once in a while to inform our young people?

■ *Answer*

First let me state that to the best of my knowledge there are three or four methods of contraception that fall under the general title of natural family planning. However, the one with which I am most familiar is the Billings Method of natural family planning.

I've discussed the Billings Method of natural family planning with a considerable number of people who have studied it and used it. A great number of them are quite enthusiastic about it, as you seem to be. Many, many couples have found in that method the answer to a problem that has plagued them for many years. On the other hand, some other couples who have used this method of family planning have indicated to me that they find it somewhat distasteful, emotionally disturbing, and often very impractical. These latter couples hardly see it as the long-sought answer to this problem.

There is some evidence in your question that you have a tendency to judge other people, and perhaps to condemn them for what you judge to be improper conduct. It is true that the church does not approve the use of contraceptive pills or intrauterine devices (IUDs). It is also true that the church teaches that those who are in serious sin should not receive holy communion. But it's not up to you or me to judge whether individual men or women are guilty of serious sin because they've used some method of birth control that isn't approved by the church. Only they, in their own consciences, can make such a judgment.

Your experience of never hearing priests mention this method of family planning in their sermons or homilies does not surprise me. I'm really not so sure that the homily is the right time or place for this kind of information to be dispensed. I do know that many priests (including me) have brought this method to the attention of couples, and have recommended that they participate in the programs of instruction scheduled by the family ministry offices of the church.

I really feel that couples must come to grips with this situation within their marriage. Unless they can face it squarely as a loving couple, neither this method, nor any other method of birth control, is going to be the answer to this challenge.

What is the church's stand on "scientific conception"?

What does the church teach about "scientific conception"? The church denounces the deliberate, human decision to end life outside life's natural course; that is murder or abortion. But what is the church's stand on the deliberate, human decision to create a life outside of what would be life's natural inception? We cannot usurp God's right to take life (murder, abortion) but are we allowed to usurp God's right to create it?

■ *Answer*

The church began making its views on this known with a 1949 statement of Pope Pius XII concerning artificial insemination, and another by the same pope in 1956 concerning *in vitro fertilization* (the official name for what you call "scientific conception"). This continued to be the "official line" of the more conservative Catholic theologians in the years since then. It has been the clear teaching that *in vitro fertilization*, even when using the sperm and ovum of a validly married couple, is contrary to the official moral stand of the church. On the other hand, a number of well-known and highly respected Catholic theologians question this stance, and some even heartily endorse *in vitro fertilization*.

I found it almost unbelievable, however, when I read an article on this matter in the quite conservative monthly publication *Ethics & Medics* (Nov. 84) by Rev. Albert S. Moraczewski, O.R., of the Pope John Center. In this article, Fr. Moraczewski, while strongly discouraging the practice and indicating every possible negative moral aspect in its regard, falls far short of declaring the practice immoral. His conclusion is: "far too little time has passed to make a valid assessment of what the impact of these alternative ways of human procreation will have on the well-being of those involved, as well as on the social structures which, to the present, have given a degree of stability to human society. But this writer proposes that in time this technology will be questioned seriously as to its worth for the true well-being of society. . . . The proliferation of methods to bring about a new human individual after IVF for a married couple was successfully accomplished, and also shows how difficult it is for human beings to restrict by any certain requirements the use of any discovery of new knowledge or technology."

Now let me add my own comment. Whenever I'm asked a question like this one, or even follow the line of reasoning your question implies, I always conclude that such a line of reasoning depicts God as someone who "sits on a throne in heaven" like a mighty emperor of the universe, initiating each individual event in the lives of each human being as though we were "puppets on the end of a string." Your question seems to imply that the normal method of human conception does not involve a human decision or cooperation as does "scientific conception." Your question also seems to imply that when someone dies of "natural causes" it happens by a direct act of God who takes that human life. Your question also seems to imply that when death does occur as a result of an unjustified human act (as in murder or abortion), God "plays no part" in that death but that the murderer or abortionist, rather than God, "takes away" that person.

God's creative power certainly is intimately and essentially involved in every moment of the existence of every creature of the universe. Thus, as the *Baltimore Catechism* put it, God is everywhere. Therefore, God is no more or less involved in the creation of new life when that new life is generated by "normal" human intercourse, or when it is generated by *in vitro fertilization*. Both methods require both a divine as well as a human "involvement" and decision. Similarly, God is no more or less involved in a death from cancer than in a death by murder. In neither case then, as I see it, should we speak as though we're making decisions that are God's personal prerogative. After all, it is God who creates us in the divine "image and likeness": giving us an intellect and free will. We are free to use this free will as we wish, be it for good or for evil.

Having said all this, I must add that, given the proper circumstances, and assuming that all proper technical and ethical safeguards were carefully attended to by all concerned, I would have an extremely difficult time advising a faithfully married couple that, all else failing, it would be immoral for them to use this method to enable them to procreate a child "of their own."

Suicide

What are church teachings about suicide?

Someone in our family recently committed suicide, and some of the relatives are having a very hard time because of the church's old teaching on the subject. What are the church's current teachings on suicide?

■ *Answer*

I presume that by the "old teaching" of the church you are referring to the law (rather than the teaching) of the church by which those who were known as "public sinners" were not given Christian burial. (By the way, I would agree with your relatives that it was and is a bad law). If that is the case, I think that you and your relatives can rest at ease, since that law would never be applied to a suicide if properly interpreted. The application of this law to suicides in the past was based on the moral principle that no one has a right to deprive anyone of life, including oneself. To do so was considered a moral evil, and since the fact of suicide was usually publicly known, some church authorities often presumed (very improperly I hasten to add) that the person who had committed suicide was a "public sinner," and therefore unworthy of Christian burial.

Modern psychology, philosophy, and moral theology tell us rather clearly that the person who commits suicide cannot be judged guilty of moral evil. Suicide presupposes some sort of mental disorder that would eliminate or diminish moral responsibility. In other words, a person who commits suicide is incapable at that moment of acting in a fully responsible way, since otherwise he or she would certainly not do this thing at all. No act for which we are not fully responsible can be properly judged to be sinful. Thus no one who commits suicide can properly be judged to have committed sin, much less to be a public sinner.

To the best of my knowledge and experience in my many years as a priest, no one has ever been denied Christian burial on the basis of suicide. I have known priests who have hesitated briefly before making a decision, but in every case that I have ever known, the decision has always been in favor of the deceased, and Christian burial has not been denied.

I sincerely hope that the stigma that this law of the church and especially its improper application to suicides has placed on so many hurting people (those left behind by the suicide) will be forever removed for the future. The death of a loved one from any cause is difficult enough to take without that burden being made worse by such legislation.

Conscience and Law

Could you explain the Ten Commandments?
I think we Catholics need to have a clearer understanding of the Ten Commandments of God and how they affect us. Could you give that to us?

■ *Answer*

I think the Ten Commandments are and always have been an excellent code of ethics for human society, and they became the "Ten Commandments of God" by being included in the Bible as part of God's inspired word. You will recall that Christ, when questioned by the leaders of the Jews, said that the two great commandments were: "You shall love the Lord your God, with your whole heart, your whole soul, your whole mind and all your strength; and, you shall love your neighbor as yourself." Then he added (most important): "In these two commandments are contained the entire law and the prophets!"

Then in the Sermon on the Mount he gave us the Beatitudes: Blessed are the poor in spirit, for theirs is the kingdom of heaven. Blessed are the peacemakers, those who hunger and thirst for justice, the ones society rejects.... In this sermon, Jesus went far beyond the commandments as given to Moses. "You were taught," he said, "Thou shalt not kill." *But* (and this is a *big* "but") I tell you, he continued, it isn't right even to harbor hate in your heart for another person. Jesus, you see, takes us beyond the commandments. He takes us into the arena of love.

Then when a young man asked him: "What must I do to gain eternal life?" Jesus quoted the Ten Commandments to him, and then said, "If you wish to be perfect, go sell what you have, give it to the poor, and come, follow me." Again, do you see how Jesus takes us beyond the Ten Commandments?

If we consider these three events in the gospels along with the entire life of Jesus as it is portrayed there, I think we'll naturally come to the conclusion that Jesus is saying to us: "Surely you should obey the Ten Commandments, but please don't stop there. If you are to follow me, the Ten Commandments should be so ingrained in your everyday life that you don't even have to think of them any more. You, my beloved followers, should be far beyond that minimum code of ethics. You should be more concerned about how you can best give your life totally to God.

Love my Father, Jesus said in essence, love our brothers and our sisters. Really love them and you need not worry because all that was taught by the commandments and the prophets of old will come naturally to you. You will obey those commandments and follow those teachings and you will do more: you will feed the hungry, clothe the naked, and shelter the homeless. You will make blessed the poor in spirit, and those who hunger, and those who thirst, and those who are persecuted for my sake.

Am I saying that the Ten Commandments aren't important any more? Certainly not! They are just as important and essential to our Christian code of ethics as they ever were; perhaps more so. As a matter of fact, they are so important that we cannot begin to become real Christians until we have already mastered the Ten Commandments in our personal lives, and then gone beyond them.

But, you might ask, how can we master them unless we know everything they command and everything they forbid? I think Jesus' response to that is, "Love God; love your neighbor; and you will obey the commandments." The specifically Christian "secret," then, is to ask ourselves constantly if our life and our individual actions are manifesting our deep love for God, and for our brothers and sisters in Christ. If we are honest and sincere with ourselves and with God, we will know the answer to that question, and thus we will know whether we are "keeping the commandments." However, if we are trying to "get by" with the minimum needed to "stay out of hell," we will probably fail as Christians and as humans and keep neither the Ten Commandments, nor Christ's two Great Commandments, nor his Beatitudes, nor his Counsels.

I suppose, then, my response to those who feel so burdened by a long list of possible sins against these commandments is this: Christ, by his life-giving death and resurrection has won new life for us. Let us live this new life in the spirit of freedom and Christian love for God and for our brothers and sisters; let us live this new life "with the freedom by which Christ has made us free." If we do, I assure you that we will live it in the peace and joy that we all seek in this life.

And in the process, we will obey the Ten Commandments, whether we know it or not!

Is shopping on Sundays sinful?

A couple of years ago, our pastor asked us not to patronize business places that stayed open on Sundays. What is the church's teaching now regarding shopping on Sundays?

■ *Answer*

For hundreds of years the church has discouraged us from shopping on Sundays, and has insisted that we should not do unnecessary work on Sundays as part of our observance of Sunday as "the Lord's day."

The basic problem with shopping on Sundays, as far as church law is concerned, is not the shopper but the person who must work in the shop on Sundays. But here, too, if one is required by his or her employer to work on Sundays, then the law allows for that.

So then the question becomes: is it lawful, according to the church, for the shop owner to open his shop on Sundays; or to work in it; or to require the employees to work in it? Well, basically the law says no, unless there is a sufficient need in the community for the availability of the services or goods for sale in the shop. Also, if the owner must open his shop on Sunday to have sufficient income to support his or her family, he or she may certainly open the shop, work in it, and require employees to work as well.

Basically, what it comes down to is that the church cannot make a general policy about shopping on Sundays, or on the morality of working in shops, or opening a shop on Sunday. Circumstances are all important here, and each person must conscientiously determine what constitutes "necessary" work on Sundays.

To give you a few examples: It may be an absolutely essential service to a given community that a drug store be open on Sunday to provide needed medicine for the ill. It may be necessary for our "corner grocery" to open on Sundays to provide the owner's family with sufficient income to make ends meet. Since Sundays are very often used for family outings and recreation, our society would require certain businesses to be open on Sunday to provide for family "rest and recreation." The list goes on and on!

About the best the church can do is present the ideal to our people by teaching that Sunday is indeed still "the Lord's day" in our faith if not in our culture. We should make every effort on Sundays to refrain from doing anything that will detract from dedicating our lives on this day to things that promote a better relationship among ourselves and God. The church teaches that one way to do this is to avoid unnecessary work on Sundays, and thus allow ourselves more time to strengthen our relationships with family and friends, which in turn will strengthen our relationship with God.

How do "conscience" and "informed conscience" differ?

Would you please explain for me the Catholic teaching on the two terms "conscience" and "informed conscience"? In reading Catholic books today I find that these terms are used incorrectly.

■ *Answer*

In *An Encyclopedia of Theology* edited by Fr. Karl Rahner, a German theologian by the name of Rudolph Hofmann describes conscience well. In his own language (which suffers from a lack of gender inclusivity because it predates our sensitivity to that) he says, "in conscience man has a direct experience in the depths of his personality of the moral quality of a concrete personal decision or act as a call of duty on him, through his awareness of its significance for the ultimate fulfillment of his personal being."

Please note that he doesn't speak of the traditional "little voice," nor of any effort on the part of an individual to evade compliance with the law, nor of the long list of typical cautions about conscience. He speaks, rather, of an "experience," an experience that speaks to the individual regarding the moral quality of a particular decision or act. He even speaks of it as a "call of duty" and says that this call comes through one's "awareness" of the significance of this particular act or decision for the ultimate fulfillment of one's being.

In order for one's conscience to do its job well, then, it needs to be well "informed" so that it can discern its options and help a person decide and act as a true call of duty. It needs to be informed to make a person truly aware (and consistently aware) of the significance of each decision toward one's ultimate goal. So an informed conscience is one that has been equipped by its "owner" to perform the function for which it was created as an essential element in human nature. If a conscience is not well informed, it will certainly lead a person into decisions that are not conducive to the ultimate fulfillment of its being, but rather to arbitrary decisions that could well lead to the moral destruction of the person.

Later in the same article, Hofmann very clearly demonstrates that the judgment of one's conscience is the ultimate norm by which the morality of an act or a decision is determined. This does not mean, he clearly states, that this judgment of an individual's conscience thus becomes a "general" norm for other people faced with the same decision. It's not necessarily even a norm for that same individual's moral decisions of the future. It's only a determination about the morality of this particular decision for this particular individual.

Furthermore, information and experience garnered after the particular act or decision in question could well move that same person to make a different decision in the future. In both cases one's act would be morally good, because in each case one would have been acting in keeping with the judgment of his or her conscience.

So you see, dear friend, when we speak of an "informed" conscience we are indeed speaking in a relative way. All consciences are informed to one degree or another. Each conscience is constantly in need of being newly informed by the knowledge and experiences of each day. An uninformed conscience is really an impossibility.

How do informed Catholics deal with church law?

You recently called a former law of the church (prohibiting Christian burial for public sinners) a "bad law." This raised some questions for me. Any institution is capable of error that may result in the promulgation of a "bad law," and the church does not seem to be an exception. How does a Catholic—one who wishes to be truly loyal to Christ through the church—deal with a law that he or she considers to be "bad"?

■ *Answer*

Many thanks for your question! The answer, however, will probably leave me dangling precariously from the high-wire between being a hero (for those who agree) and the devil (for those who disagree).

First let me express my agreement that the church is capable of error in disciplinary matters and has admitted (though sometimes belatedly and begrudgingly) many such errors in the course of its two thousand years of existence. Let me hasten to add, though, that this capability of error on the part of the church does not give its members the right to "pick and choose" the laws with which we will or will not comply. We must presume that the laws have been established for the individual and common good of the people of God, and there will be times when the "individual good" will clash with the "common good." We must also realize that until the official church retracts what may be an admittedly bad law, we are still bound to comply with it. These are general principles of law and morality that must be kept in mind no matter what resolution of your question might be reached.

Actually you have asked two questions: first, how does one deal with the bad law itself, and second, how does one deal with the real-life situation that has developed as a result of the bad law. Perhaps the first question is the most difficult in that there is no easy or immediate way to deal with such a law. The reason for this is that the right thing to do with a bad law is to do what one can to get it repealed. In our church this process has often taken years, sometimes decades, and really in some cases centuries. Our church does not work quickly, and the processes by which her laws are made, promulgated, altered, or repealed is probably the slowest process of all. For a law to be repealed there must first develop a conviction on the part of a significant number of responsible people that the law is indeed bad. They, in turn (and in time!), must bring it to the attention of church officials (priests, bishops, canon lawyers, and theologians) who, after being similarly convinced, must eventually send it "up" to those who are responsible and have the authority to make changes in the universal church law (the pope and the sacred Roman congregations). There are reasons for this lengthy process, and some of them are excellent. But good reasons or not, it makes the problem of dealing with a bad law almost intolerable for those most affected by the bad law.

Your second question, especially as you have worded it, is almost an answer unto itself: if indeed someone's conscience is "well-informed, well-formed, and loving" in the best sense of these terms, such a person will know whether the letter or spirit of the law is really binding on a particular individual or situation. I believe (and here is where I become the hero or villain!) that in the end, a person *must follow the dictates of his or her own conscience,* even if that is not in keeping with church law. In carrying out such a decision of conscience one is bound to make every effort to diminish public knowledge of the act in question, and thus public disapproval and scandal. And there always remains the danger that one could come under the public disapproval of the church.

Be that as it may, our conscience must be the ultimate decisive factor in the actual moral good or evil, virtue or vice, gracefulness or sinfulness of our acts. The words of Scripture are the light for our path, alongside the good counsel of others and our own willingness to place our cares at the foot of the Cross. In the end, the law of the church is also a beacon of light for us. Let us pray that we will be guided toward good, virtue, and a grace-full life.

What's the difference between the law of the church and natural law?

I recently heard a priest make a distinction between natural law and church law. I didn't understand what he meant. Can you help me?

■ *Answer*

You've asked an important question and one that points to an area of confusion for many people. To resolve this confusion, it's important for us to make distinctions between *laws* that are made by the church, and the *teachings* of the church about the law of God and about what is known as "natural" law. The law of God (sometimes called "divine" law) might be defined as those laws specifically revealed to us by God either in the Bible, in our Christian tradition, or in creation. The natural law is very similar to that: it is the law that can be reasoned from the very nature of things. If God specifically reveals a natural law, it becomes thereby also a divine law. If the church decides to include that same law among its own laws, the law also becomes church law.

An example of divine law would be what we commonly call the Third Commandment: "Remember to keep holy the Lord's Day." We know this law only through the direct revelation of God in the Ten Commandments. An example of natural law would be the Fifth Commandment: "Thou shalt not commit murder." We can know this law from the very nature of human beings and their interrelationship with each other and God, even without God's specific revelation. Thus both divine law and the natural law were here long before the Catholic church ever came into being, but the church does have the right and responsibility to assist us in becoming aware of these laws, and to teach us that we're obliged to obey them. The laws made by the Catholic church (church law) are contained and summarized in what is known as *The Code of Canon Law*. Specific individual items in this law are sometimes referred to as "canons."

The importance of this distinction between various types of "religious" laws can be seen when we realize that both divine and natural law bind all human beings. In other words, if I'm a human being, I'm bound by all divine and natural laws of which I am aware. I am likewise bound to do everything in my power to become aware of those of which I am presently unaware. The laws of the church, on the other hand, bind only those who are members of the church. Thus if I am not a Catholic I am in no way bound to obey any of the laws of the church (unless, of course, the same laws are contained in the divine and natural law).

Because the natural law is based upon deductions by human reason from their understanding of God's creation, natural laws can and do change as humanity comes to a better understanding of that creation. In the not too distant past, much of humanity would have considered surgery, even in a medical setting, contrary to the natural law against mutilation of the body. Today our understanding of the human body makes surgery an important part of self-preservation. Only God can change divine law, since it is God who establishes and promulgates it in revelation.

The ancient Hebrew laws, however, revealed in the first five books of the Bible, are no longer binding to us in the New Testament. Church laws (unless they are also divine or natural laws) can be changed by the church as she sees the need to do so. The church no longer requires us to abstain from meat on Fridays, for example, and allows cremation. Both of these were strictly forbidden by church law in the not-too-distant past.

The prohibition of abortion is not really a *law* of the church, but rather a *teaching* by the church that abortion is against the natural law: the church teaches that a new and separate human life begins at conception, and therefore anyone who knowingly and willfully does anything to destroy that life has murdered another human being, and thus has broken the natural law, which prohibits such murder. No responsible person would ever argue that murder is acceptable. But those who disagree with the church's position on abortion often argue that it is simply not murder because they believe that a new human life does not begin immediately upon conception but later in the growth of the fetus. Thus the disagreement is not really about the law, but rather about the facts: everyone agrees that the law against murder is a just law; not everyone agrees that in abortion one is killing an already existing and distinct human being.

Somewhat similarly the teaching of the church against artificial contraception (often erroneously called "birth control") is not really a law of the church. The church here is simply expressing itself on what it holds to be a natural law. That teaching (not law) of the church states that a married couple may not place some artificial barrier in the way of the normal process of sexual intercourse. This assumes that the primary end of sexual intercourse is procreation. Thus one who chooses to practice artificial contraception is not breaking a law of the church, but rather is choosing not to abide by this teaching. The morality of that choice is where conscience comes in.

Now allow me, dear friend, to comment on the question of whether we should follow our conscience or the law when we are faced with a decision. The proper answer is that they each have a distinct and important part to play in such decisions. Consciences don't make laws; nor do they overrule them. Laws don't make consciences; nor can they overrule them. The conscience is the process whereby an individual judges whether it would be right or wrong (and how seriously so) for that individual to perform a certain act or to refrain from doing so; conscience tells the individual not whether something is right or wrong within itself, but whether she or he is innocent or guilty of the proposed act.

To put it in extremely simple terms and to use an example from civil law: I am bound by law not to drive through a red light. But what if I'm rushing my dying child to the hospital when the traffic light turns red. I look in both directions and see no cars coming. My conscience tells me it's against the civil law if I disregard the light. My conscience also tells me that my child's life is more important than the law. It tells me that, provided I don't risk hurting myself or anyone else, I would not be guilty of wrongdoing by driving through the light. I decide to go ahead and run the light. Am I guilty of wrongdoing? No, I don't think so! Does my conscientious decision make it "right" to break that law? No, it doesn't. It only affects my guilt or innocence in breaking the law that one particular time.

In other words, I was not declaring by my action that running a red light is OK. I was only following my conscientious decision that—at this time, for me, and under these circumstances—I was not guilty of any wrongdoing by disobeying that particular law.

It's a very fine line. I realize that. But it's an essential one to good moral decision making.

Homosexuality

Is homosexuality right or wrong?

I'd appreciate having this question answered once and for all from the church: is homosexuality right or wrong? In an article I read recently Pope John Paul II said during his United States visit that the homosexual condition is not evil. Did Pope John Paul actually say that? I have a son who is a homosexual. Have I been wrong in telling him this is evil?

■ *Answer*

May I say first that I think we are asking for the impossible when we request an answer "once and for all" on a matter like this. Religion and morality are not "yes and no" matters. There are always many "gray" areas that we must also face and cope with. Certainly the whole question of homosexuality has not been given final definitive treatment by the official magisterium of the church, and I'm afraid I am not in a position to do that either.

The article you quoted was correct in reporting what Pope John Paul II said on this matter. He was complimenting the bishops of our country for the pastoral letter they issued in 1976 entitled *To Live in Christ Jesus* (USCC, Nov. 11, 1976). The pope actually quoted from that pastoral letter when he said, "Homosexual activity, however, as distinguished from homosexual orientation, is morally wrong." The pope commended our bishops for exemplifying in this teaching "the real charity of Christ." He continued: "By your witness to the truth of humanity in God's plan, you effectively manifested fraternal love, upholding the true human dignity of those who look to Christ's church for the guidance which comes from the light of God's word."

I think it's extremely important that we always make a distinction in our judgment between issues and human acts. This seems to be what the bishops and pope are saying when they make the statement that the homosexual condition is not evil but that homosexual activity or acts are morally wrong. This should be of some comfort to you in your relationship with your son. Realizing that his homosexuality itself is not evil, and therefore does not make him evil, you can continue to give him your loving support in his struggles with life. Furthermore, even if he does engage in some homosexual activities, you certainly should not judge him to be guilty of sin or to be an evil person; just as heterosexuals should not be judged by us to be guilty of sin, even when we know they have done something that we consider to be morally wrong. His guilt or lack thereof is something that he must resolve between himself and his God.

Furthermore, dear friend, even if the homosexual condition were evil, and even if your son were guilty of homosexual acts, God would certainly continue to love him just as much. I realize that this problem causes great difficulty for you and many other people, but it is a fact that we must face in a loving way, and with all the sympathy and understanding that we can muster within ourselves. Jesus taught us that God is a loving, forgiving Father. He also taught us, just as effectively, that we must be like our Father, ever offering each other that kind of loving forgiveness.

Please know that you are not alone in facing the pain this problem is causing you. Certainly you are in my prayers and, I hope, in those of all who may read this response. May God grant you the grace to face it in love, and may your pain be lightened by that love.

Will all homosexuals be cast into the fires of hell?

I know that the Bible states that homosexuals will be cast into the fires of hell. I believe what I read, but in my heart I don't feel like God will cast us homosexuals out. What do you think?

■ Answer

As you undoubtedly know from firsthand experience, the question you ask is a sensitive one. Therefore I approach it with extreme care and with all possible sensitivity to you and other gay or lesbian people living among us. I'm also aware of those whose attitudes toward homosexuals are unsympathetic or even openly hostile. I must also be true to the teachings of the church as well as to all my own convictions. This is a tough assignment with many things to keep in balance.

First let me assure you that I do not think a proper reading of the Bible would indicate that homosexuals will be "cast into the fires of hell." With you I am totally convinced that God would not be so unloving or unmerciful. We have ample evidence for that in the Bible, in Christian tradition, and even in the official teachings of the church. Whatever you may have heard preached "at" you by fundamentalist preachers (either Catholic or otherwise) it is a total misunderstanding of Scripture to give the impression that, as a homosexual, you are automatically condemned to hell. Such a position is contrary to the love of God for humanity as faithfully taught by Christ and the church and ever more joyously emphasized in today's teaching and theology.

With no hesitation and without any fear of significant contradiction I can state unequivocally that God loves you with the same infinite love with which he loves his own Son, Jesus Christ. God will never cut you off from that love no matter what you might do either as a heterosexual or a homosexual. God's love for us is unflinching, unlimited, unconditional, and absolute.

Further, our purpose as human beings is to be living and visible examples of God's love in this world. This should move all of us away from the prevalent attitude in society that limits the objects of our love to certain people who conform to our own concept of what is right and good. In other words, if we are to be true to our purpose as human beings, each of us, no matter what we think of your homosexuality, must offer you our love. That's it, period. That's our call and our destiny or nothing is!

Unfortunately, many of us have failed in this mission. We have not offered the love we ourselves received from God to our sisters and brothers who are gay or lesbian.

Having insisted on these basic Christian principles, emotions, and convictions, may I now make it clear to you and all my readers that none of the above is meant either to condone or condemn any immoral sexual act, be it heterosexual or homosexual. You did not ask me to do so (and I thank you for that). I am simply trying to reach out to you as a fellow human being as I know Christ would want me to: with love!

Does the church approve discrimination against homosexuals?

Many people are upset about the statement released in 1992 by the Vatican concerning discrimination against homosexuals. "There are areas in which it is not unjust discrimination to take sexual orientation into account," it says, "for example in the consignment of children to adoption or foster care, in employment of teachers or athletic coaches, and in military recruitment."

Even leaving aside the gospel considerations, it is the hypocrisy of this statement that hits many people. It is well known that many priests are homosexual, and that bishops continue to accept many homosexual seminarians. How, then, can the church dare to say that homosexuals should not be accepted into professions like the military? As if anyone is going to believe the military is a more sensitive area than the priesthood!

American Catholics have to be shocked at hearing something like this preached by a church that so blatantly practices the opposite. Such statements drive people further away from a church (at least from its hierarchy) whose teaching authority they can no longer respect.

What do you think?

■ Answer

What I think is that you are very angry right now. From letters I've seen in both the secular and Catholic press, I realize that a great number of people are likewise angry. My initial reaction upon hearing the statement was similar. So I waited until I felt I was in better control of that initial angry emotion to respond to your question with faith-filled reason and composure.

My initial angry reaction to the statement stemmed from this: the statement was intended as an instruction to the U. S. bishops, telling them they should *oppose* any civil legislation that might recognize or protect the rights of homosexuals. The Vatican reasoning is based on the church's conviction that homosexuality is a human "disorder." Therefore, homosexuals can be discriminated against and can be denied specific rights that need the protection of civil law.

I find that stance quite difficult to understand, not to mention support. But what I find so inconsistent about this is that, by very pertinent contrast, the statement does not urge our bishops to examine church law and practices with regard to homosexuality. Nor does it even address the anomaly wherein our own church leadership, while standing in public opposition to homosexuality—and even condemning it and encouraging outright civil and social discrimination against homosexuals—is seen by many, as you point out, to be "blatantly practicing the opposite," especially in its process of accepting candidates for the priesthood.

I have given this all much scriptural and theological research and prayer and engaged in hours of discussion with friends and acquaintances, both gay and straight. I have come to the conclusion that I must confront this matter from a much broader perspective than simply the question of the church's teaching on homosexuality.

In the study edition of his book *Catholicism* (published in 1981), Father Richard McBrien (after pointing out that the tradition of the church consistently declares homosexuality to be a human "disorder" and homosexual acts objectively immoral) states on page 1030: "Notwithstanding the clear and unequivocal teaching of the hierarchical magisterium on this important moral issue, *new questions are arising* in light of new developments and scientific research in medicine, psychiatry, and psychology" (emphasis added).

Please note the four words in this statement to which I have added the emphasis of *italics*. In my opinion, this is the absolute crux of the matter. Indeed new questions are *forever* arising. This is true of everything in the church and the world, no matter how sacred or important or dogmatically taught throughout our tradition. These new questions arise out of the development and evolution of human intelligence, spirituality, experience, and scientific research. They deserve thorough consideration from the hierarchy of the church. The church must be open to development of its own understanding and doctrine.

When we look for answers to today's new questions, we can start by simply repeating the dogmas and teachings and moral dictums of our forebears in the faith. Our heritage and history are the teachers of life. But this, by itself, is far from adequate in addressing today's social life. Looking only to the past for pat answers to new questions can only lead to a growing disregard for the authority of the church, and to unbridled disrespect and disregard for the faith values that those pat old answers attempt to uphold.

For generations now in differing and ever developing forms, all humanity has been screaming out new questions about human existence itself, but particularly about human sexuality and the evolving moral implications. And as I see it, our official church has been adamant in refusing to give these new questions informed, thorough, and truly evaluative consideration. It continues to recount the same old formulas, trying to *con*-form today's thinking to the old answers, rather than trying to *in*-form those old truths with the light of today's thinking.

Evidence of this is in this very question of homosexuality, and very clearly, in my opinion, in the question of continuing discrimination against women in the church, in the question of the position of the church on just about every aspect of sexual ethics, in the prohibition of *discussion* about the ordination of women, in the whole question of mandatory celibacy for priests in the Western church, in the question of total authoritative control of the church by this celibate male clergy. And this is only my short list!

Please understand, dear friends all, I am not here calling for a reversal by the church in her teaching on any of these questions. But they are real questions in the minds and hearts *and lives* of millions of people who are unswervingly dedicated to the church and her mission. So, what I am calling for is a proper recognition, serious reconsideration, and continuing review of all these questions, and, most importantly, an openness to change.

In keeping with the above, I now challenge the magisterium of the church to give in-depth attention to the following questions. As Pope John said upon opening Vatican II, the world is waiting for us to act and expects us to be both pastoral and real.

1. What is human sexuality, and what are its innate moral implications in human behavior?

2. Are sexuality and sexual orientation of the essence of our nature as humans, or are they simply incidental to it?

3. Is homosexuality necessarily a "DIS-order" or could it possibly be *"another"* order of human sexuality?

4. Are our human sexuality and sexual orientation only expressed in genital sexual acts (wherein our tradition and culture has exclusively embodied our sexuality) or do they apply as well to the rest of life? If the latter, do we think that non-genital acts of love in a loving gay or lesbian relationship have the same moral implications as genital sexual activity between them?

5. In its *Pastoral Constitution on the Church in the Modern World*, Vatican II does not continue the traditional distinction between the primary (procreation) and secondary (mutual love) ends of marriage. Prior to the Council, procreation was always the more important and absolutely essential end; mutual love was the less important and nonessential end. Could the purpose of genital sexual acts be likewise redefined to give them the equally important purpose of mutual love and procreation? If so, when the fulfillment of procreation as one of these ends is impossible, as is true, for instance, in the genital sexual relations of married, elderly couples, could the other purpose of mutual love possibly give validity or positive purpose, rather than disorder and sin, to such acts even outside of marriage when done between persons lovingly and permanently committed to each other?

By raising the above questions, I do not intend thereby to take a position on them. My current position on all these matters is the same as that of the church, even if my reasoned opinion sometimes differs. On the other hand, the remainder of this response will indeed be an expression of my opinion on the Vatican instruction to our bishops on homosexuality and civil discrimination against homosexuals.

A thorough and open-minded reading of the text leads me to *commend* its authors for at least this paragraph: "It is deplorable that homosexual persons have been and are the object of violent malice in speech or in action. Such treatment deserves condemnation from the church's pastors wherever it occurs. It reveals a kind of disregard for others that endangers the most fundamental principles of a healthy society. The intrinsic dignity of each person must always be respected in word, in action, and in law."

Bravo! Especially for this last sentence, which calls for application in all areas of society and the church. This is an important instruction because it is so often woefully disregarded in our still-rather-sexist culture and church. The document carries other positive and commendable points to which I think most would adhere, even most gay or lesbian people.

Having noted that, it is nonetheless my opinion that this instruction was ill advised in that, while it is in keeping with the traditional teaching of the church on homosexuality, there is no evidence that any effort was made to apply to that traditional teaching "new developments in scientific research, medicine, psychiatry, and psychology." (See paragraph 54 of Vatican II's *Pastoral Constitution on the Church in the Modern World* for more on this.) Further, this document instructs our bishops to oppose only proposed civil legislation that might grant protection to homosexuals from discrimination. It even urges such discrimination "in the placement of children for adoption, in employment of teachers or athletic coaches, and in military recruitment." But in the face of public knowledge that many priests are homosexual (though, presumably, celibate), the bishops are not instructed that it would be just to discriminate against homosexuals who seek to be candidates to the priesthood.

If indeed we must accept the teaching that homosexuality is incontrovertibly, inevitably, and ever unchangeably a human "disorder," then we must assume from the practice of the church that it is perfectly legitimate and in "order" for many such "disordered" humans to be priests. Further we must assume that, despite this "disorder," it is perfectly in "order" for them to teach, coach, and chaplain our military services, not to mention preach, preside at liturgy, and do the myriad other things that are part of the ministry of priesthood.

Note well: by these statements I do *not* imply that homosexuals should be barred from the priesthood. I'm simply saying that we have a rather glaring inconsistency, which some deem grossly hypocritical.

I am not homosexual. I have friends and acquaintances who are. They respect me as a heterosexual and I respect them as homosexuals. Our presumption is that each lives according to his or her state in life. This trust and respect, unless betrayed, is the only sound basis for a universal and mutually satisfactory living and working relationship throughout a society. The fact is that we live together, heterosexuals and homosexuals alike.

God creates us "in the divine image and likeness." All of us are created that way. No exceptions. Equipped with this likeness, and with this in-dwelling divine presence, we can trust and love one another. Indeed we must! Otherwise justice will never prevail, and humanity will always be at odds.

PART SEVEN

Prayer and Spirituality

Prayer in our Lives

Does lack of time endanger our spiritual health?
Until about three or four years ago, my wife and I were very conscientious about making retreats at least every couple of years, regularly reading spiritual books, and doing all those special things that were recommended in Catholic school, in homilies, and in books for the betterment of our spiritual lives. Now that our four children are teenagers and our family business requires more and more of our time, we find it increasingly difficult to spend time doing the "extra things" to improve our spiritual life. If we have to give some of it up, will we be endangering our spiritual health?

■ *Answer*
Thanks for an excellent question with which I also have grappled many times over the years of my adult life. I presume this has been a problem for others who, like you and me, were educated within the venerable culture and tradition of our church. Before

getting to my response let me hasten to state in advance that I will always value that culture and tradition (and my education in it) as a very important foundation for what I've become as an adult, Catholic, Christian human being.

In my reflection over the years on this question, I have come to the conclusion that the basis for the problem is the very concept or expression: "spiritual" life. The separation in our language and culture of our life into "spiritual" life and "physical" life is a very natural result of the traditional definition of us human beings as "creatures composed of body and soul." The impression was given that the body had its own "physical" life, and the soul had its own separate "spiritual" life, and since the latter would never die, it was by far the most important.

But we do not have two such lives; each of us has a *single* life, which, if we believe in resurrection, will never end. Our faith in an afterlife implies that what we call death is really not the end of a human life, but rather the end of a part or phase of human life. But this portion of our life, which is perceivable by others (as the next portion is not), is not a separate or distinct life; it is one and the same as that which we believe continues to exist after death.

We run into a similar problem, I think, when we speak about such things as our "married" life, or "family" life, or "sex" life, or "school" life, or, for some, our "vocational" or "priestly" life. This terminology tends, I think, to split what we would all admit is essentially just one life into many separate and often seemingly independent ones. Certainly no one is deliberately saying that all these "lives" are separate and distinct entities, but it is so very easy to get caught up in this terminology and begin looking upon them and dealing with them as though they were not firmly united.

What these are, of course, are various "aspects" of our lives, and not really different "lives" at all. I am firmly convinced that if any of these various aspects of our lives is not healthy, it invariably is detrimental to the others. Each of these aspects of our lives is interrelated with the others, and therefore the care or attention that we give each or any of them will have a very definite and distinct effect on our lives as a whole. If we're doing something that is detrimental to the "physical" aspect of our life, it is also detrimental to the "spiritual" aspect of our life.

If our "family life" requires more of our time or financial resources than our attendance at a regular annual retreat would allow, then fulfilling those family responsibilities is what our one life is in need of and that in itself is beneficial to our "spiritual life," as a retreat under those circumstances would not be.

The time and effort you consciously and conscientiously devote to reflection, reading, study, discussion, and carrying out your responsibilities as total human persons, as a husband and wife, as a mother and father, as business woman and man, as citizens of the community, state or country, as members of various social and/or religious groups, as participants in wholesome recreational activity, etc., will invariably contribute to the well being of your lives in all their aspects, including the spiritual. In other words, you must realize that everything mentioned in the previous sentence is and must be part of and contribute to the health of your "spiritual" life. It is not just the "religious" things we do that have a spiritual aspect or impact.

No, you need not fear for your "spiritual" health; not as long as your life as a whole continues on a balanced and healthy path. In a very real sense, there is no distinct spiritual life. There is only life, and may you continue to care for it in every way, and live and develop it to its fullest potential. This will serve your health in all its aspects.

Why is it that God is not helping me now?

I've been a loyal and devoted Catholic all my life and have a deep devotion to Our Mother of Perpetual Help. I've been attending that novena weekly for over 30 years, and have received many favors from her. Why is it, then, that despite my sincere devotion to my religion, I still feel that I'm not being helped by Almighty God? I live with my family in a "foreign country" under very substandard conditions. I'm unemployed and my family must rely on the income of my wife as a dressmaker. Furthermore, I've been praying all these years for a chance to go and live in the United States, but I'm still here. Why aren't my prayers answered?

■ *Answer*

Obviously you have a somewhat different view of prayer from mine; otherwise your question would be worded somewhat differently. It would seem that your prayer is primarily directed toward the obtaining of "favors" from the Lord (prayers of petition), and that you consider only those prayers "answered" which result in your obtaining the requested favor. But really, I don't think that is what prayer is all about. It isn't, or shouldn't be, simply a request for some miraculous or magical resolution of some problem or need.

Rather, prayer is a human attempt to communicate with God and to express to God the intimacy of our relationship with him, our innermost feelings of love and devotion, as well as every possible need that we might have. In doing so, however, we go to God not so much for a solution to these needs and problems, but rather to fill a personal need on our part to "unload" them. God is one in whom we can have unbridled and unlimited confidence. God's response (or "answer") to us, then, will be in the form of an assuring confidence that God indeed does share our innermost thoughts, emotions, and needs; that God is with us; that God is on our side; that we can lean on the divine heart. The solution to our immediate need, or the granting of our specific request will come not as a direct result of special or miraculous action on God's part, but rather these will be born of a combination of interrelated and interactive natural circumstances and events that involve not only God, but also ourselves, other human beings, and really all of creation.

In other words, dear friend, while it is perfectly proper and commendable for you to bring your need for employment, your living conditions, your desire to live in another country, and any other needs to God in prayer, you should not be expecting that, in response to that prayer, God will miraculously provide you with a job opportunity, good living conditions, both in this country rather than your own, and all the other needs that you may bring to your prayer. All of this will come only if you, as well as those people and things having a direct bearing on your life and that of your family, provide the proper circumstances for these changes to occur in your life. God will certainly support your efforts toward a better life, as well as those of others who are trying to help you. But God will do it through the normal or natural means by which his continuing universal and active presence supports us all.

Just think of this: it is possible that a job for yourself, better living conditions, or a move to another country may very well not bring you any more real happiness than you have right now. Don't get me wrong! I pray with you for a solution to all these problems, and I would be more than happy and eager to do whatever I can to assist you in solving them. But I assure you there will be other problems to take their place once these are solved. Real happiness in this life will only come with the full assurance that you are living a meaningful life and thus fulfilling to the best of your ability your God-given purpose in life as a human being (and therefore child of God), a husband, a father, and a member of your immediate broader civic and religious community.

Prayer can help us toward that assurance, but the miraculous granting of favors by God will not.

So you see, dear friend, neither God nor our Blessed Mother has abandoned or forsaken you. Continue your prayer; it is being heard and answered. Just be open to the answers being given, and I hope you will find the happiness you seek.

Does the church approve of "chain prayers"?

The following prayer/instruction keeps appearing in our local paper: "Holy Spirit, you who solve all problems, who light all roads so that I can attain my goal. You who give me the divine gift to forgive and to forget all evil against me, and that in all instances of my life you are with me. I want in this short prayer to thank you for all things and to confirm once again that I never want to be separated from you. I wish to be with you in eternal Glory. Thank you for your mercy toward me and mine.

"The person must say this prayer for three consecutive days. After three days the favor requested will be granted even if it may appear difficult. This prayer must be published immediately after the favor is granted without mentioning the favor, only your initials should appear at the bottom."

What are your thoughts about it?

■ *Answer*

How long, oh how long will it take us to overcome the ravages of superstition in organized religion? Dear friend, what you have there is nothing more than a chain letter or "chain prayer," which has no true religious value or contents whatsoever.

Our God, the God of our parents, the God of our church, the God of Jesus Christ, the God of our sacred tradition, is not one who will count the number of times we say a prayer or the number of words or even what words we might use in prayer. Second, God is not one who would make such ridiculous stipulations like publishing a prayer in the paper if we get what we ask for in prayer.

The gospels portray Christ as specifically condemning such "prayer" when, before teaching us the "Our Father," he says, "In your prayer do not rattle on like the pagans. They think they will win a hearing by the sheer multiplication of words. Do not imitate them. Your Father knows what you need before you ask him" (Matthew 6:7–8). Does that sound like someone who would make such requirements as that published "prayer" indicates? Hardly!

Such chain prayers, like chain letters, should not only be disregarded, but if you have any knowledge whatsoever as to who is spreading such garbage, you should do everything in your power to see that an end is put to it. All such things do is lend an air of credence to those who oppose organized religion, especially our church, on the grounds that we support such foolishness. Just last week among the "trash mail," I received a large poster condemning our church from every possible angle, including an alleged promotion of superstition such as this. While none of those accusations were really valid, there is much in the religious practice of many in our church, and even much that is promoted by both clergy and laity and has become habitual religious practice in our church, that lays a valid foundation for such conclusions.

For instance, while novenas are officially not meant to give value to "numbers" of prayers, they do, by their very name, specify "nine" as a somehow especially valuable number and urge the participants to carry out this specific number of prayers or services. While there is certainly nothing wrong with praying nine times, there is just as certainly nothing particularly valuable about praying or doing anything else nine times. But in our promotion of novenas we cannot avoid the practical consequences implied by the very concept: people will draw the conclusion that we are giving to the "nine times" some particular value, and thereby they logically conclude that our church promotes such superstitious practices. That is unfortunate, because in many cases the prayerful content of some of these novenas is quite good. There have been novenas of masses, novenas of rosaries, and novenas of scriptural prayer. The Mass is a wonderful prayer, the rosary is a good prayer, scriptural prayer is good prayer; it is tying these good prayers into numbers that I find dangerous in its possible consequences.

Our prayer should not be a "numbers game." It should be an expression of faith.

Is there any value in praying for other people?

I'm a teacher in a Catholic high school and am currently on the topic of prayer. Having studied theology under some excellent theologians at Loyola University, I'm of the opinion that prayer causes a change in ourselves rather than in God, and this is what I'm teaching my students, who seem to accept it quite readily. If that is so, however, I and my students would like to know what value there is in praying for the sick and for people other than oneself. Can you help us?

■ *Answer*

To me, prayer is much more a matter of *listening* than talking. It is an effort on our part to allow God to speak to us through the generous revelation he offers us in the ongoing creation of which we're a part. God speaks through those around me, through Scripture, historical and current events, and even through my own intuitions. Prayer is much more a response on our part to that revelation. In other words, we "hear" God by recognizing what God is saying to us in revelation, and we "speak" to him by the way we allow this revelation to affect our thinking, our speaking, our actions, and our very lives. If that indeed is the essence of prayer, I think it is abundantly clear that you are correct in believing that any change caused by prayer would be in us rather than in God.

But note that in my description of prayer there is no mention of praying *for* anyone or anything. And I really don't think that this aspect of prayer is very important at all. But it must be addressed, because it is certainly a major element in the minds of most people when thinking about prayer. Prayers of petition (that is, when we pray for someone or something, or ask a "favor" of God for ourselves) is beneficial to us because it is really born out of our response to his revelation.

Let's look at it this way: having been involved in the kind of "essential" prayer mentioned above, we have allowed the Lord to speak to us through his revelation. What we hear in that prayer is that each of us needs to love ourselves and all our sisters and brothers, and that out of that love must flow a response to needs. When we know the need of another, by expressing our concern for that need in the intimacy of our relationship with God (that is in prayer), we will make the one in need aware that we are "reaching out" to him or her with the warmth of God's own love.

I also think that when we do pray for someone, that prayer will go a long way toward helping *us* to realize and actually moving *us* to do what we can in a practical way to help resolve the problem for which we are asking God for a solution. For instance, we are praying for the healing of an illness with which a friend is afflicted. Our prayer might very well move us to seek some medical help for the person or advise the person as to how he or she might be able to find medical help. We might also be moved to actually contribute our time or money to assist in the research and development of a treatment for the ailment our friend is suffering. All of this is what I would call the "answer" to the prayer, which answer does indeed come from God through us.

I do not think, however, that God answers our prayerful petitions by allowing those petitions to move him or "change his mind" about how he is going to relate to the needs of the person being prayed for. In other words, the prayers will not produce a miraculous intervention into the life of the petitioner; God will not "zap" a miracle in response to our prayers. He will respond to them in the very same way that he speaks to us every day in his ongoing revelation: in and through the created world and people around us. In other words, God already has in motion the answer to all our prayers for ourselves and others. What we must do is be open to that by being open to each other and to the entire world around us.

What is the true meaning of prayer?

I'm not a Catholic. I'd like you to discuss a subject that has come up recently with my Catholic friends and family. I've been told that if one buries a small statue of St. Joseph and prays and believes for a certain thing to happen, then it will happen. I believe that prayers and believing are all that is necessary. I'd really appreciate your sharing your views on this.

■ *Answer*

The thing about burying a statue of St. Joseph is only another example of pure superstition working its way into Christian prayer. For an understanding of what real Christian prayer is, I suggest that we might all read, study, and pray over a little book called *A New Look at Prayer*, by Bill Huebsch (Twenty-Third Publications, 1991).

I'm afraid that many of us have a rather warped sense of what prayer is all about. Many of us think of it solely in terms of words that we speak to God or to a saint, usually including a request for a favor, and we consider the prayer answered or not answered depending upon whether the requested favor is granted. Further, when we address the prayer-words to God, we usually look up as though somehow God or our saintly friend is up in the sky somewhere, or that the heaven in which they dwell is distantly "up there," beyond what we have come to know as outer space.

What Bill Huebsch does so beautifully for us in this little book is to give us a new insight into the true meaning of prayer. He clearly articulates the constant faith of our church that our God, like the God of Jesus, is not a distant God to be found or spoken to "out there somewhere." Huebsch points out that the God of our Christian faith is a God who dwells right here within us, and that therefore to contact that God we must look inward: that is, directly within ourselves as the bearers of the God who is creating us.

Prayer in this context, then, would be simply recognizing and being conscious of that very intimate presence of God within us. Prayer, further, would be the conscious and willful growth within ourselves of this realization that God is right here with us; right here within us; not "out there"; not distant; not in a distant heaven, but in the heaven of God's kingdom on earth, which Christ came into the world to reveal to us and within us.

Then, of course, there is the matter of words. Are they really necessary to prayer? I don't think so. Mr. Huebsch puts it so well. Oh, not that words cannot be part of prayer. On the contrary, they usually are. Most activities of the human mind and heart involve words. But it isn't the words that are the prayer, but rather it is this intimate presence of God to us, combined with the intimate presence *of us* to God, which constitutes the essence of prayer. Then, whatever we think or say or do in the context of this intimate state of presence becomes an integral part of that prayer.

This is why it can properly be said that prayer can be and really should be an integral part of every moment of our lives, so that whether it be in words addressed to God, or to a saint, or to a friend, or to an enemy; whether it be at work or at play or even in sleep; whether it be a physical, mental, or spiritual act. In other words, no matter what, we can be "at prayer" at all times as long as we enter each moment aware that we are joined with God in this bond of loving creative presence.

Not that prayers of petition are out of place or improper, but petitions are not of the essence of prayer; they are not required in prayer.

The value of prayer lies precisely in sharing with the God who lives in the kingdom within us, the innermost and strongest desires of our beings. It's very much like a loving, but wordless, hug and kiss of a reunited husband and wife after a long absence. Does this require words to be properly expressive of the emotion of the moment? Of course not! Can words bearing a request be inserted there meaningfully? Most certainly! But it is not the words or the request that express that emotion. It is the wordless hug and kiss. That is the essence of it all. And so it is with prayer.

Again I say: read *A New Look at Prayer*; and then pray that way!

What is the value of the Charismatic Movement?

What's the meaning and value of the Charismatic Movement in the church? Some seem to think it's the best thing to ever hit the church, and others think it's just a bunch of fanatics. What do you think?

■ *Answer*

Neither! I really think you are hearing only the two extreme positions on this matter, rather than the truth, which lies somewhere in the middle. Let's see if we can get there.

First, let's put the entire matter in perspective. The Charismatic Movement (with capital letters) is a relatively recently organized movement in the Catholic church. My research indicates that it became formally organized in the early 1960s, about the same time that Vatican II was in session, or shortly thereafter. On the other hand, the charismatic movement (with small letters) is something that has been going on in the church (for that matter in the human race) from the very beginning of its existence. My point is that as an "organized" movement, it is very recent. As a phenomenon or "happening" in the church, it has been here all along.

This is a very important and even vital distinction in any discussion of this matter, and, therefore, to emphasize this distinction, I will use capital letters (Charismatic Movement) when speaking of the recently organized movement, and small letters (charismatic movement) when speaking of the underlying and basic movement that has been with the church from the very beginning.

To understand any of this, we first look into the basic meaning of the word "charismatic" or "charism." A charism is a gift from which flows some action, which by its very nature gives emphatic and visible witness to the faith or interior ideals of a person, a people, or a nation. The gift itself or the action flowing from it does not have to be miraculous or even unusual in nature. A mother's strong love for her child can be a charism from which flows a heart-warming caress for the child, giving charismatic witness to what "mothering" or "motherhood" is. The patriotism of a soldier can be a charism from which flows an act of heroism in defense of his country, thus giving living charismatic witness to what patriotism is.

Charisms are part and parcel of our everyday lives. They have been part and parcel of the life of the church from its very beginning. The charismatic movement in the church is that series of charisms and resulting charismatic acts whereby its members (all of us) have manifested or given witness to our own personal faith, and thereby to the faith of the church. In other words, our charismatic acts have given witness or demonstrated in an emphatic, visible way the presence of Christ in us, and therefore in the church; and it is this "presence of Christ" whom we know as the Holy Spirit.

That is why it is said, and rightly so, that charismatic acts and the charismatic movement in the church are manifestations or acts of the Holy Spirit in our midst. It is also the reason why people who belong to the Charismatic Movement profess strong devotion to the Holy Spirit and make every effort to be aware of the "action of the Spirit" in our lives.

Charisms, charismatic actions, and therefore some sort of charismatic movement have been a part of the life of the church from its very beginning. They have also been part of human beings or humanity from the very beginning of our existence. In our secular history we have such outstandingly charismatic figures as King Tut, Helen of Troy, Alexander the Great, Julius Caesar, Cleopatra, Charlemagne, Henry VIII, Queen Elizabeth I, Napoleon Bonaparte, George Washington, Thomas Jefferson, Abraham Lincoln, and even a man like Adolph Hitler. Each in his or her own way had what is known as "charisma" through which each was able to be a living symbol and inspiration to others of the ideals by which each lived or wanted others to live, even if their ideals are evil.

Then there were the charismatics of the Hebrew Scriptures or Old Testament. These were such men and women as Noah, Abraham and Sarah, Isaac, Jacob, Rachel, Joseph, Moses and Miriam, the Egyptian Pharaoh of the Exodus, David, Solomon, Ruth, Esther, Isaiah, Jeremiah, and other great prophets. Were it not for the charismatic characteristics of each of these people and many others, there is no way that anyone would have been moved to remember them in the first place, or to adopt their ideals as part of a people's heritage, or even less to put these into writing as the inspired word of God. The charismatic movement was indeed quite alive throughout the Old Testament, and it burst forth into the New Testament with the coming of the extremely charismatic figure of John the Baptist who announced the coming of the ultimate charismatic figure, Jesus Christ.

Evidence of the prevalence of the charismatic movement in the church comes from Scripture itself and from every page of our history. St. Paul and many of the early Christians about whom he writes in his epistles were outstanding charismatics, and therefore could be called the initiators of the charismatic movement in the church.

The most obvious charismatics in the church are those whom we know as saints: people like the Blessed Mother, St. Peter, St. Paul, St. Augustine, St. Benedict, St. Francis of Assisi, St. Thomas Aquinas, St. Catherine of Siena, St. Dominic, St. Joan of Arc, St. Ignatius, St. Francis Xavier, St. Therese of Lisieux, St. John Vianney (the Curé d'Ars), Mother Cabrini, to name just a tiny number.

From the charisms of these people and millions like them flowed actions that showed to the world in a most emphatic way that the Spirit of the Lord (his presence in our lives) was indeed active and alive in every moment of our Christian history and in every corner of our world.

This is why it is of the highest importance that we do not allow ourselves to think that the charismatic movement in the church is no older than the Charismatic Movement. As I stated above, the latter is only a generation or so old, and it would hardly be fair to the Lord and his Spirit to think that they had abandoned us for all these centuries. But if that is so, why was the Charismatic Movement organized; what is its purpose; what role does it have in the Christian life; how vital is that role?

Well, I pointed out above the many heroes and famous people in our history who were charismatics. I hasten to add here, however, that we don't have to be heroes or famous to be charismatic. Each one of us Christians, for instance, is and must be part of the charismatic movement in the church; each of us has our own charismatic moments. As we live our lives from day to day, and thereby give emphatic and obvious witness to our faith and that of the church, our own charisms become effective—and this is essential to the effectiveness of the church in her mission in the world.

The noted Jesuit theologian Karl Rahner says in an article he wrote for the *Encyclopedia of Theology* (Seabury Press, 1975): "The charismatic dimension is therefore as necessary and permanent a part of the life of the church as are offices and sacraments." Father Rahner speaks in that same article not about the recently organized Charismatic Movement, but rather about the charismatic acts of all of God's people and of the charismatic movement in the church from its very beginning. He describes these as the "action of God's sacramental grace," without which, he says, even the sacraments cannot sanctify (i.e., make us holy). Quite a strong statement, no?

Then why the "organized" Charismatic Movement? I think the principal purpose and function of the Charismatic Movement in the church over the last few decades has been to draw attention to, and to help us recognize in a conscious way, the importance and even necessity of charisms, charismatic acts, and therefore the charismatic movement that already existed. The founders of the current Charismatic Movement felt the need to call to the attention of the world that the charisms were indeed still there; that charismatic action was still prevalent but not being recognized; that there is still a need for charisma in our theology and liturgy. To the extent that the Movement has succeeded in doing this (and it has!), I think it has done a great service to the church, and I hope this will continue!

Unfortunately some over-zealous people within that Movement sometimes seem to have the attitude and conviction that members of the Charismatic Movement are the only charismatics in the church; that this Movement has "brought the Holy Spirit back" to the church; that being a member of the Charismatic Movement is essential to salvation or renewal in the church; that one cannot be a complete Christian without being part of the Charismatic Movement. These are serious errors (and recognized as such by the "solid" leaders in that Movement), and although they are not the official position of the Charismatic Movement, these errors on the part of some have led many to denounce the Charismatic Movement (incorrectly) as a "Better-Than-Thou" organization, or as you put it in your question, "a bunch of fanatics."

You see, dear friend, like every other good movement or program in the long history of the church, the Charismatic Movement is a very good thing that has its proper place within the broader framework of Christian life. But also like most other good movements or programs, there are some individuals who have abused it and tried to make of it what it was never intended to be. We can avoid that with the Charismatic Movement if we always remember that we can be quite charismatic without being a member of the Charismatic Movement.

Furthermore, being charismatic outside of the meetings and liturgies of the Charismatic Movement is much more important than being so in those meetings and liturgies. We must witness to the presence of Christ (the Holy Spirit) not only among ourselves, but even more so in the world and to the world.

That's why the charismatic movement is essential to the church;

and the Charismatic Movement can help it achieve that lofty position.

Can the cross of "Down Syndrome" also be a blessing?

I've occasionally read explanations of why God allows bad things to happen to people, and I can accept most of what I read about that. But I recently gave birth to a baby with Down Syndrome, and I can't help but wonder why this cross was given to us. Is it because my free will said "yes" to another pregnancy?

My husband and I have had a wonderful life, and we've often wondered aloud why we've been blessed with so few "crosses"; and we've been so thankful. While I hate to think of this child as a cross because he is a joyful child and loved dearly, this situation is a cross because it does really hurt. At the same time, I know it could be so much worse, and after some of the handicapped children I've seen in recent months, I'll take Down Syndrome any day. But if I had chosen not to have another child, would my cross have come at a later time and in another form?

Perhaps I'm asking for an impossible answer in these questions. Perhaps the Lord is the only one who can answer them. But I guess the human side of us always wants to know "why!?" I truly believe the Lord will make us what he wants us to be.

■ *Answer*

Thanks ever so much for sharing with me and my readers the incomparable and almost incomprehensible beauty, warmth, and love of a mother's heart as she suffers with her child who is "differently abled" from the rest of us. Even when something like this occurs to someone near and dear to us, it is easy for us (especially for us celibates) to become almost smug and even cold in the face of such heartrending situations, especially after the initial shock of the matter subsides. We have a tendency, I think, to "chalk it up" as another statistic, rather than reach out continually with loving concern to the parents who are living every day with a challenge.

While the answers to your questions are indeed difficult, I don't think they are impossible, or that only God can answer them. I have little confidence that the words I write here will provide an adequate answer either, but I'm fully confident that, searching together, we will come to understand all this more deeply.

We must constantly use the gifts with which God has endowed us in our human nature and in the world around us. Just think, had God not endowed us with the capacity to reproduce ourselves through procreation, you would never have known the boundless gift of a mother's love. In the case of this child, something went awry by an accident of nature, not by God's specific design for you and your husband. This particular child, the result and object of the beauty of your married love, came forth with an abnormality, Down Syndrome. But the child is nonetheless a gift.

Indeed it is a cross, but do not look upon it as mysteriously "sent by God." I think it's more proper that we look upon the beautiful wonder of this new human being as God's gift, and the abnormality as an unavoidable accident for which no one (and certainly not you and your husband!) can be held responsible. Yes, this child will help you to grow in a way that no normal child could. That, I think, gives him added (be it imperceptible at times) grace.

I do not think, by the way, that this "cross" would have come in another way or at any other time, if not now. I just don't believe God works that way with us. Human life is not perfect, but God doesn't sit in heaven dreaming up ways to test and challenge us. God isn't the source of pain. Jesus didn't roam the backroads of Galilee inflicting illness and suffering on people. He offered them healing love, divine strength, and holy peace.

As I grow older I see more and more clearly that the important thing in life isn't what we have or wear; it isn't what our home looks like or how fit our bodies are. The important thing in life is the *quality of our love*. When we die, that's what we take with us. That and nothing more. Perhaps this child will help you focus on that, on pure and steady love in your home.

Here is where the Paschal Mystery of Christ informs our own

lives so fully. The cross, you see, is always at once both a blessing and a painful thing to bear. Why? We don't know. It's part and parcel of human life. The point is that we must look beyond the cross to the end of the story, to the joy and happiness that comes without measure, to the peace and love that God showers on us.

Thank you for sharing your blessing with us!

Is a parent's blessing for their child just as powerful as a priest's?

Is the blessing of a father or mother for their own child as powerful as that of a priest? In their God-given power of giving life, the parents, in a manner, share in the creativity of God. I've heard people make both claims, that a priest has more power, and that parents do. But I haven't had an adequate answer. Personally, I believe that God would favor the parent. Do you agree?

■ *Answer*

I really can't say that I disagree or agree! My problem is not with the answer to this question, but with the question itself, which I have heard raised on a number of occasions. I don't know if I can adequately deal with it here, but I will present a few thoughts for your consideration. By the way, what I have to say is in full keeping with the official teachings of the church.

You see, dear friend, blessing is not an exercise of "power." Therefore, I don't consider the blessing of a priest an exercise of "power" derived from the priesthood. To me a blessing is a prayer, prayed on behalf of whatever or whoever is being blessed. When you or I pray a blessing over our meals at home, our prayer is to thank God for making this meal possible for us and to ask that this meal will benefit all who share it. The prayer or blessing is not made more powerful because of the one who prays it. Priests have no more power to bless a meal than anyone else.

Now to get to the point of your question: it seems to me that a blessing given to me by my father or mother could very well be more beneficial to me than that of a priest, especially when I'm old enough to recognize my parents for what they are to me. I don't think this results from my parents having more "power" than a priest. Rather, having the blessing come from my parents rather than from a priest could be (for me) a continuation of the life-giving that began at my conception. They teach me to love God. They provide me with a home. They love me on a daily basis. Their blessing goes on and on and on.

On the other hand, in the right situation, a priest's blessing also expresses a powerful and loving divine presence. He represents the entire Christian family, expressing thereby the entire Christian world's interest, love, and involvement in my life. Here again, though, it's not because ordination has given more "power" to the priest's blessing, but rather because of what ordination has singled him out to be and represent in the community.

I guess, when you come right down to it, I would prefer not to make a choice between the blessing of my parents and that of a priest. I feel a strong need for both. Neither, in my opinion, is more "powerful" before God; both are extremely powerful and important to me. And in the end, it's not a question of power at all, is it? It's a question of love.

Miracles and Apparitions

Wouldn't it be great if the Shroud of Turin were proven true?

I've been following very closely and am very excited about the recent news about the Shroud of Turin! Wouldn't it be just a tremendous boost to our faith in the resurrection of Jesus if it were proven to be what is claimed?

■ *Answer*

Dear friend, I really don't want to disappoint you, but I'm afraid I can't share your enthusiasm for the Shroud of Turin, nor do I look upon it as a "faith-booster." For me, and I think for the church, there is no connection between the Shroud of Turin and our faith in the resurrection of Jesus. Nothing, absolutely nothing, about the history of that piece of cloth can help anyone's faith, because faith is a free gift of God, and thus does not come to us through proving historical facts. Furthermore, our faith is not in historical events themselves, but rather our faith is in God who reveals himself in the events. The more what-we-believe-in can be proven scientifically or historically, the less faith it takes to believe it; and once it is proven to be a historical or scientific fact, no faith is needed at all!

What I have a hard time understanding is all the "fuss" made over this piece of cloth. Don't get me wrong: archaeological and historical facts and artifacts are extremely important, and if the Shroud of Turin can be proven to be one of these it indeed would have great historical value. But let's suppose that the Shroud could be proven to be the actual cloth that wrapped the dead body of Jesus in the tomb. How much value would that have in comparison to the actual living and resurrected person of Jesus Christ whom our faith tells us is with us all the time? What is it about something that touched the dead body of Jesus about 2,000 years ago that makes it more valuable or sensational than the things or people the living Jesus Christ touches every day in our own time?

Again, supposing that it were "real," why is there so much excitement about *it* and so little about our everyday faith? Christ is indeed living and truly present *in our own day* in the Scriptures, in the people of God, his church, and especially in the Eucharist. When was the last time you saw a headline in any newspaper, religious or secular, saying that "The Living Jesus Christ is Present in Our Town Today"? Yet our faith says he is here every day, eating and drinking with us, working with us, playing with us, praying with us, and sleeping with us. If we really want to strengthen our faith in a resurrected Jesus Christ, let's not depend on things like the Shroud of Turin, but rather let's start "shouting from the housetops" (through our lives): "Jesus Christ is risen! He lives among us!" and then make him live in our communities by being him to one another.

Religious devotion to the Shroud of Turin or faith in its authenticity certainly does not deserve and should not have a major place in our lives as Christians. It is the living Christ of today, proclaimed in the loving and caring lives of all true Christians, that must be the source, the summit, and the goal of our faith. When some people asked Jesus for a miracle or sign of his power, Jesus told them that "an evil and unfaithful age is eager for a sign!" (Mt 12:39). Let us not come under that condemnation.

Do we have to believe in apparitions?

After reading an ad in a popular Catholic magazine, I ordered some free scapulars from a group in California. They arrived along with all kinds of stuff about apparitions that I never heard of, like one about a Sr. Faustina in Poland who was told by Jesus in apparitions from 1930 to 1938 how displeased he was with all of us. Also enclosed was a card on how to say the rosary and all kinds of warnings about "fearing" God. Does the Catholic church "endorse" such nonsense, as I see it? What should my attitude be?

■ Answer

Until a few months before her canonization on April 23, 2000, other than for very brief glimpses on the EWTN TV network, your letter was only the second bit of information I had ever seen concerning Sr. Faustina or the appearances she is alleged to have experienced. While I still have no idea whether the particular devotions promoted by the literature you sent have the approval of the church, I do know that the church has never required that we believe in such "apparitions" (even after the canonization of the recipient of the "apparitions"). But I am certain that none of this is essential to our Christian life and much of it deserves the name you gave it: nonsense.

I find it totally confusing and incomprehensible that so many people get so excited by these claims of apparitions and conversations with Jesus and Mary. Most of them seem to have Jesus and Mary constantly suffering and in tears. It seems to me that, if our faith tells us that Jesus and Mary are already enjoying the fulfillment and happiness of resurrected life, their time of suffering and tears has long ago ended. Furthermore, the church has long ago assured us that we in no way need these so-called private revelations to reassure us in our faith. The rosary is a fine prayer for those who like to pray that way, but I will never believe that either Jesus or Mary is telling anybody that we have to say the rosary "or else." Nor will I ever believe that Jesus or Mary is telling anybody that we have to say any other particular prayer or perform any other particular action to assure ourselves of "salvation." In my opinion, faith in such "nonsense" is a denial of some of the basic teachings of Christ and the church.

It is Christ, in and through his people (the church), who is the source of our salvation today. It is the church (the people of God) that is the extension of Christ's life, teaching, and salvation to our day. No sudden alleged apparitions or private revelations can ever alter that truth of faith or add one single bit of truth to what we all can learn from the general and normal sources of revelation: Scripture, tradition, creation, and the day-to-day relationships that we have with one another and with everything else in the world. In my opinion it is time for the official teaching authority of the church to restate this article of our faith in a clear, concise, and readily understandable fashion. Too many people are being led astray by having so much confidence in and "hanging" their faith on such sensational things as alleged private visions and revelations.

Are pilgrimages to shrines important to Catholic life?

Would you please comment on this excerpt from a Catholic newspaper of April 22, 1987: "In his homily…the Pope praised popular religiosity, especially pilgrimages to Marian shrines. Mass attendance is low in Argentina, while hundreds of thousands of people participate in organized pilgrimages to local and national shrines to the Blessed Virgin. 'The pilgrimage of the church and of every Christian toward the house of the Father is manifested and realized, in a manner pleasing to God, in the pilgrimages of Christians to Marian shrines,' he [the Pope] added."

Do you agree that such pilgrimages (like those to Medjugorje) are important to Catholic life?

■ *Answer*

First, may I state that I'm not so sure that the pope would consider Medjugorje a "Marian shrine," since the local church authorities in Yugoslavia duly appointed by him have repeatedly insisted that they have grave misgivings about the happenings at Medjugorje, and both the local bishop and the national conference of bishops have requested that no pilgrimages be made to Medjugorje.

It is true that "Mass attendance is low in Argentina, while hundreds of thousands of people participate in organized pilgrimages to local and national shrines to the Blessed Virgin." This is an indication that, despite the brave efforts of Vatican II to stem the tide of what had become a grave overemphasis on the role of Mary in theology and practice of the church, and to return the emphasis in our liturgy and sacramental celebrations more properly to Jesus Christ, there are millions in our church who still look to Mariology as the source and end of their "religiosity" (to use the pope's word). Apparently for many Catholics in Argentina, devotion to Mary is more important than devotion to Christ. Pilgrimages to Marian shrines are more important than participation in the celebration of the Mass. Doesn't it seem that something is wrong with this picture?

Were I speaking to the Catholics of Argentina, I, with the pope, would certainly not want to dampen the spirit of devotion the people have to our Blessed Mother, but at the same time I would feel the responsibility to help these people realize the much greater treasure that is the presence of Christ in their very midst.

You see, dear friend, I would not accuse the people of Argentina of doing wrong in their overemphasis on Marian devotion. I would want to help them to realize that in this overemphasis on Marian devotion they are missing out on a much greater marvel of our faith; I would want to help them to know and appreciate a wealth and beauty that resides within them as the Christian community, a wealth and beauty that far surpasses even the fabulous beauty and wonder of the Blessed Mother.

In fact this beauty of the Christian community, which is Christ present in today's world, is really the source of her beauty, since it is our firm belief as Catholic Christians that Mary derives her place in the Christian community and "religiosity" solely from her relationship to her son, Jesus, who is the Christ. Therefore, if we could strengthen our faith in the presence of Christ in our midst and the celebration of that presence in the sacraments and liturgy, and if we could by the way we live our lives make him even more forcefully present among us, we would be doing far more to strengthen our devotion to Mary than by going off on pilgrimages, especially pilgrimages to places where the best theological evidence indicates a questionable connection with Mary in the first place.

It is for this reason that it saddens me to see all this "fuss" about Medjugorje. There is absolutely nothing there (even if it could be proven without a doubt that the Blessed Mother did appear there) that we don't have in even greater measure right here within our midst. I am fully confident that, if we feel the need to please our Blessed Mother, the best thing we could possibly do would be to stay here at home; right here at home with her Son, who lives right here among us.

Epilogue

At the time of my retirement from active ministry in the priesthood in July, 1998, I had been a priest for forty-four years, of which some 21 were spent in parish ministry, and about 27 in various ministries in diocesan administration (including four when I was also a pastor). In the homily at the Mass that the diocesan community (with most of my family and many friends) celebrated to mark my retirement, I thanked God, all those present, and all of God's people for allowing me to be the vehicle through whom Christ's priesthood was exercised among them over those 44 years. Then I expressed as best I could what I saw as the thrust of the rest of my life. Here is the conclusion of that homily, which I hope forms a suitable epilogue for my active ministry and for this book:

Since hearing of my pending retirement, many have asked what I would be doing in those retirement years. In response to some I said that during my active ministry I had to live out my *responsibilities* as a priest, pastor, and diocesan official; in my retirement, those responsibilities are no longer with me, so I can now live out my *dreams*. Well, that's what I'm going to do!

And what are my dreams? My dreams, my dear people, are for a church announced by Pope John XXIII; a church with open windows and open doors; a church not shackled by sometimes oppressive people like me; not shackled by such rules and regulations and such hard and fast doctrine that we cannot see and share the love of people who don't share the same beliefs; a church that is synonymous with humanity: that doesn't draw lines; a church that is open to all people; a church that could even give Jews communion at the Last Supper; a church that could appoint one who denies Christ as the first pope and head of the church; a church that welcomes sinners with the love of God: all kinds of sinners; any kind of sinner; people of all faiths, all beliefs; a church that is open to the Spirit of God, so that never, never, *ever* will a human being feel unwanted, no matter where she or he might be; a church where we will have scorn for none, and we will have heart for everyone.

I dream still, and will dream still more in the future, about a church that is open to all, and is willing to look into the gifts of all, discern those gifts, and choose the people with the greatest gifts to place in the proper roles within the church, whatever they may be—pope on down—to choose the people that have been best gifted by God to carry out the roles that God has designed for his kingdom. And I will continue to dream this, because I think that it is the key whereby the Holy Spirit will open up the windows and the doors of our church to all of humanity. It is the key whereby the wind will come in and out; yes, *in and out!*! We need *them*, folks; we need the people out there; we need the people of India; we need the people of China; we need the people of the African countries; we need the people of Israel; we need the people of the Arab countries; we need the people of all countries, all races, all faiths; we need the people of both genders; we need the young and the old. We need *all* people to be *our* people because they are all God's people!

In the first of the Prefaces for Sundays in ordinary time, the presiding priest proclaims us a "holy people" of God; a "priestly people" of God; but then he says, "a people set apart." I don't like the "set apart" description, because I don't think we are set apart. We are set apart only if we cut others off. We need not set ourselves apart because even the most evil person out there is part of the priestly people of God.

And I think Jesus told us that at the Last Supper when he said (embracing all God's holy people): "*This* is my Body!" What I think he was saying is: Not just, or so much that bread and wine, but "*This, the people of God,* is my Body!"; "*This, the people of God,* is my Blood!" The Body of Christ and the Blood of Christ, which is the people of God, is how he carries on his ministry to the ages: his ministry of life, his ministry of love.

As you know St. Paul tells us there is to be no distinction between Jew and Greek, man and woman in this Body of the church. But I think that, for reasons other than those Paul had in mind, there does need to be a distinction or at least a recognition of the gifted differences between Jew and Greek, between woman and man, between French and American, and Chinese and Japanese, and so forth, because we need every one of our races and nationalities; we need every one of both genders because everyone has something unique to contribute to this Body of Christ. And we can't all do it the same way. We need our women to do what only women can; we need our men to do what only men can; we need our boys to do what only boys can; we need our girls to do what only girls can. We need all peoples of all races, all colors, all nationalities, and all genders to make up and extend this Body of Christ.

And rather than comparing one part of the Body of Christ to his head and another part to his heart, and so forth, I'd rather compare us all to the Blood—that we are the Blood of Christ, giving life to the world, carrying this life to all the corners, and there is no single drop of Blood that is more important than any other.

This is the dream that I have for our church; this is the dream that I have for humanity; this is the dream that I have for our world: that this Body of Christ might infuse with his

Blood, with his life and his love the wetlands, the deserts and fertile land alike, the oceans, seas, lakes, rivers, and streams, the mountains and valleys, the suns, moons, stars and all the galaxies of space, together with the entire environment in which they all exist, and thus the whole wide world and all the creatures that do now and will in the future dwell therein. My dream is a dream that fulfills my vision of the purpose of the coming of Christ, which is to let us know that God is not "out there" (in the heavens beyond), but that he is "right here" within each one of us and among us all.

It is up to us to get the message out. Even in retirement, the gospel is our world!

And so I appeal to all of you who read this book to bring the God, the Christ, the Spirit, the Life and the Love to *your* world, and thus be part of my life's dream.

Index